EMPOWERING WOMEN PANCHAYAT MEMBERS

Handbook for Master Trainers Using Participatory Approach

Other books by Rajiv Gandhi Foundation

- Empowering Panchayats: Handbook for Master Trainers (Using Participatory Approach)/ **D. Bandyopadhyay, Amitava Mukherjee & Mitali Sen Gavai**
- पंचायतों का सशक्तिकरण प्रधान प्रशिक्षकों के लिए पुस्तिका (सहभागी उपागम के आधार पर)/ **डी. बन्दोपाध्याय, अमिताभ मुखर्जी, मिताली सेन गवई**
- New Issues in Panchayati Raj/ **D. Bandyopadhyay** and **Amitava Mukherjee**

About the Rajiv Gandhi Foundation

The Rajiv Gandhi Foundation as a registered Trust was set up in 1991 to commemorate Rajiv Gandhi's contributions to the building of a modern India and realise his vision most important being decentralised democracy, literacy, application of science and technology, concern for the deprived and the under-privileged, peace and international cooperation, disarmament and total destruction of nuclear weapons etc. For special emphasis on decentralised governance, the Foundation set up a Task Force on Panchayati Raj in 1993. The handbook is one of the outputs of the Task Force.

About the Authors

D. Bandyopadhyay, IAS (Retd.), was the Secretary, Ministry of Rural Development and Secretary (Revenue), Ministry of Finance, Government of India; Executive Director, Asian Development Bank; and is presently connected in different senior capacities with various States and Central organisations, as also with civil society organisations.

Dr. Amitava Mukherjee is currently Regional Advisor (Poverty Reduction), with the United Nations Economic and Social Council for Asia and Pacific, Bangkok. He was earlier the Executive Director, Development Track, New Delhi, a knowledge company; Professor of Economics and Planning, Lal Bahadur Shastri National Academy of Administration, Mussoorie and Consultant to various UN agencies and international organisations. He has written extensively on decentralisation, poverty and hunger, with over thirty books and numerous papers to his credit.

EMPOWERING WOMEN PANCHAYAT MEMBERS

Handbook for Master Trainers Using Participatory Approach

D. BANDYOPADHYAY
AMITAVA MUKHERJEE

Published for
Task Force on Panchayati Raj
RAJIV GANDHI FOUNDATION
by
CONCEPT PUBLISHING COMPANY, NEW DELHI-110059

Cataloging in Publication Data—DK
Courtesy: D.K. Agencies (P) Ltd. <docinfo@dkagencies.com>

Bandyopadhyay, D.
Empowering women panchayat members : handbook for master trainers using participatory approach / D. Bandyopadhyay, Amitava Mukherjee.
p. cm.
In Indian context.
ISBN 8180693031

1. Women politicians—Training of—India. 2. Women in politics—India. 3. Panchayat—India. I. Bandyopadhyay, D. (Debabrata), 1931-, joint author. II. Title.

DDC 305.433 200 954 22

Views expressed in this volume are solely of the authors and do not in anyway reflect the views of the institutions to which they belong or of the institutions participating in the development of this book.

ISBN : 81-8069-303-1

First Published 2006

Published and Printed by
Ashok Kumar Mittal
Concept Publishing Company
A/15-16, Commercial Block, Mohan Garden
New Delhi-110059 (INDIA)

Phones : 25351460, 25351794
Fax : 091-11-25357103
Email : publishing@conceptpub.com

Preface

The historic 73rd and 74th Constitution amendments, creating the Panchayati Raj Institutions (PRIs) as a third tier of government, are over a decade old now. States have, in keeping with the mandate of the Amendments, enacted conformity Acts. Numerous attempts have been made, both within the governments and outside it, to implement the laws all over the country. Many attempts have been made to dilute the impact of the amendments and the conformity Acts, on economic and political governance. However, the facts that the PRIs have been created and that they have survived, give enough room for optimism that over the years, they would eventually become true instruments of grassroots democracy and units of self-governance, in the true sense of the terms.

This optimism needs to be sustained. One of the many ways, I believe, the optimism can be sustained is to elect men and women of good caliber to the PRIs. However, given the state of our development, the literacy rate (especially of women), the status of women in society[1], social norms, usage and customs, and the overall process of electing functionaries to elected bodies, including the PRIs, it is reasonable to expect that a large number of public spirited people who get elected to these bodies, would require technical backstopping and capacity building. This is particularly true of women elected members for two reasons. One, because many of whom are first timers, attempting very often, though not invariably, to make inroads into an area considered traditionally as men's bastion and two, because many of the elected members of PRIs suffer from the "double jeopardy" of societal exclusion by virtue of being women and from male domination, both within

1. Hark these words of a noted economist, as an example: "A just society provides equal opportunity to all members of society—all religions, all castes, and *both sexes*. India's recode of ill treatment starts before birth—we kill the girl child before it is born. After birth, there is at best benign neglect and later on, especially among the poor families, the girl child is needed to work at home. As she grows up, she becomes an increasing burden, and parents worry about raising dowry for her marriage. And the cycle continues". Surjit Bhalla: "How to eradicate the scourge of poverty from India", *The Indian Express*, 1 January, 2006. [Emphasis added].

the household and outside it. There is, therefore, the need for mechanisms and instruments to technically backstop and provide for capability upgradation of all elected members of PRIs generally and of women elected members specially. This is not only true for reasons of good governance but also for enhancing the capacity of the women in Panchayats to engage in debates and discourses, vital for strengthening grassroots democracy.[2]

Technical backstopping and capacity building of elected members of PRIs should take various forms. Institutional training is one such form. Extension service could be another. A network of progressive and powerful elected members both past and present, also commend itself in this regard. Helpline and resource centres can prove invaluable instruments of providing support.

And the task is gigantic. Providing training and technical backstopping to millions of elected women members can only be carried out by the state. It is hoped that the Governments at the Centre and at the States, would take the necessary steps to provide the warranted support in this respect.

Civil society organizations, especially NGOs and the academia, also have central roles to play. Developing models for training and technical support is at the core of the capacity building role of civil society organizations. The efforts of the Rajiv Gandhi Foundation and its Task Force on Panchayati Raj are to be positioned in that context. This Handbook is an important contribution in that direction. It is the collaborative efforts of a large number of training institutions at the state and national level and leading NGOs. The generic modules presented in the Handbook have been subjected to two expert groups scrutiny. The generic modules as also the state specific modules have also been tested in real life situations in different parts of the country and they have been evaluated. Valuable feedback received from the field-testing of the modules and from the experts. The final product has incorporated all the suggestions received.

I am certain that governmental training institutions, non-governmental organizations, academicians and researchers shall find this Handbook extremely useful. I am more than confident that these institutions and individuals will improve upon, innovate the methodology and disseminate the contents of the Handbook in the years ahead.

D. Bandyopadhyay
Convenor,
Task Force on Panchayati Raj,
Rajiv Gandhi Foundation,
Jawahar Bhawan, New Delhi.

1st January, 2006

---

2. Amartya Sen calls this as "argumentative tradition" in his book *The Argumentative Indian* (London: Allen Lane an imprint of Penguin Books), 2005.

Acknowledgements

The Rajiv Gandhi Foundation is thankful to the following institutions and persons (cited in alphabetical order) who greatly helped in the preparation of this book:

Institutions

1. Directors and Faculty of the following institutions:

   (i) AMR - Andhra Pradesh Academy of Rural Development, Hyderabad, **Andhra Pradesh**
   (ii) Centre for Youth and Social Development (CYSD), Bhubaneswar, **Orissa**
   (iii) Kerala Institute of Local Administration (KILA), Thrissur, **Kerala**
   (iv) Lok Bharti Samaj Sewa Sansthan Pune/Lok Panchayat, Ahmednagar, **Maharashtra**
   (v) Mahatma Gandhi State Institute of Rural Development, Jabalpur, **Madhya Pradesh**
   (vi) Mahila Chetna Manch, Bhopal, **Madhya Pradesh**
   (vii) Mohan Lal Sukhadia University, Udaipur, **Rajasthan**
   (viii) Multiple Action Research Group (MARG), Shahpur Jat, **New Delhi**
   (ix) Rajiv Gandhi Chair for Panchayati Raj Studies, Gandhigram, **Tamil Nadu**
   (x) Rural Litigation & Entitlement Kendra, Dehra Dun, **Uttranchal**
   (xi) Sahbhagi Shikshan Kendra, **Uttar Pradesh**
   (xii) State Institute for Rural Development, Karfector, **South Sikkim**
   (xiii) United Nations Economic & Social Commission for Asia and the Pacific, **Bangkok**
   (xiv) UNNATI, Organisation for Development Education, Ahmedabad, **Gujarat**

Individuals

1. Dept. of Foreign Affairs, Govt. of Ireland, Dublin, for the generous grant which made this project publication and the preparation of other modules possible.
2. Dr. Kim Hak-Su, Under Secretary General, United Nations and Executive Secretary, UNESCAP, Bangkok for extending technical assistance for the implementation of the Project.
3. Task Force Members: Shri L.C. Jain, Shri V. Ramachandran, Dr. C.H. Hanumantha Rao, Dr. M. Shiviah, Dr. V.A. Pai Panandikar, Shri Mani Shankar Aiyar, Prof. B.K. Chandrashekar, Dr. Y.K. Alag, Dr. (Mrs.) Kumud Sharma, Mrs. Nirmala Buch, Prof. M. Aslam, Dr. Ghanshyam Shah, Mrs. Jarjum Ete, Dr. Revathi Narayanan, and Shri C. Narayana Swamy.
4. Participants of various workshops and seminars, particularly the evaluators and participants of Training of Trainers (TOT) Programme and those who tested the state specific training modules.
5. Shri Manmohan Malhoutra, Secretary-General, Rajiv Gandhi Foundation who was instrumental in the formulation of the project proposal and who guided its implementation.
6. Prof. Bibek Debroy, Director, Rajiv Gandhi Institute for Contemporary Studies; Shri O.P. Rehan, Coordinator; Dr. Nupur Tiwary, Fellow, Mrs. Bhavana Nagar, Senior Research Fellow; Mrs. Meetu Jain and Shri Vinod Kumar Verma.

We are also thankful to numerous individuals and institutions who helped us in this endeavour in different ways. We are grateful to all of them. However, lack of space prevents us from thanking them individually. Nevertheless their contribution is thankfully acknowledged.

Contents

List of Figures

Introduction

The historic 73rd Constitutional Amendment Act recognizing the Panchayats as 'institutions of self-governance at the district level and below' has ushered in a process of basic change in the architecture of the Indian polity. It has introduced a third stratum in the governance of the country, creating a multi-layered federal structure in addition to the Union and the States. The Amendment gives constitutional status to Panchayats at the district and sub-district levels and enjoins upon the State Governments to make them effective institutions of self-government. The institution of Panchayati Raj thus moves India towards the goal of democratic decentralization in order to accelerate socio-economic development and bring about *equity and social justice*. It both deepens Indian democracy and broadens its base.

THE PROBLEMATIQUE

However, the process of restoring power to the people in tangible ways faces many roadblocks—political and institutional. The RGF has played a proactive role in promoting Panchayati Raj (local level elected governance) since 1993. It established a Task Force on Panchayati Raj in March 1993 with the primary objective of catalyzing the operationalisation of the 73rd Constitutional Amendment Act. With its help, the Foundation has made a series of endeavours to further the cause of decentralized democratic governance through reorienting attitudes, helping build an institutional infrastructure. Through the 73rd Constitutional Amendment Act, for the first time in the history of the Panchayati Raj system, a high degree of uniformity has been conferred on Panchayats, mainly in terms of structure, position, powers and functions. However, its sustainability and legitimacy depends to a great extent on the availability of the right kind of functionaries, both officials and people's representatives after each election, where at least one-third of the elected members are newly-elected. This requires supportive measures or initiatives like up-gradation of skills, particularly in leadership and planning.

Development training is the key to promoting good Panchayati Raj governance. And the quality of training imparted to the Panchayati Raj Institution's (PRI's) functionaries directly influences the nature of grassroots governance. Training has thus become essential especially for the members of the PRIs. In keeping with the larger vision of the Rajiv Gandhi Foundation (RGF), it seeks to realize this through project interventions in capacity-building, including improving the quality of training through upgrading the software of training institutions dealing with PRIs in different States, holding Training of Trainers (TOT), developing state specific and generic training modules and advocacy workshops and conferences. The Foundation has already published a series of publications in capacity building including an annotated Directory[1] of training institutions for PRIs, and a Handbook for Master Trainers[2] for training of Officials and elected functionaries of PRIs.

During the course of the operation of its functioning over the last several years, the Task Force on Panchayati Raj at the RGF found that capacity building of Officials and elected functionaries of PRIs was important, but the needs of the women elected members of PRIs were different in some very important aspects because, *inter alia*, a majority of them are first-generation entrants into the realm of Panchayat governance, traditionally a male bastion. Given that 33 per cent of the seats in PRIs are reserved for women in the Panchayats, many of whom would not only be "first-timers" but also neo-literates, trying to not only enter a male bastion but also trying to make a dent in a traditional social milieu where the women's rightful place is seen as the home while they suffer from "double jeopardy"[3], as mentioned in the Preface to this book.

Gender training and capability building especially of women elected members of PRIs have, thus, assumed added significance. Additionally, experience has revealed that in keeping with the mandate of the Constitution for securing women's participation in grassroots governance and promoting their rights, more attention must be paid to the *empowerment* of the women PRI functionaries and special affirmative measures and need-

1. Task Force on Panchayati Raj: *Directory of Selected Panchayati Raj Training Institutions in India* (New Delhi: Rajiv Gandhi Foundation) first published in June, 2001 followed by second edition in February, 2005.
2. D. Bandyopadhyay, Amitava Mukherjee and Mitali Sen Gavai: *Empowering Panchayats, Handbook for Master Trainers Using Participatory Approach* (New Delhi: Concept Publishing Company), 2004.
3. Amartya Sen notes in a different context: ".... India has deep inequalities along the lines of gender, class caste and community..." in his pioneering work *The Argumentative Indian* (London: Allen Lane an imprint of Penguin Books), 2005, p. 6.

specific capability building interventions. It is also widely recognized that the absence of appropriate training software and training technology are serious impediments in this regard. Hence the Task force on Panchayati Raj implemented the project on "Strengthening the Role of Women in Grassroots Democracy" one of the output of which is the system of training discussed in this Handbook.

WHAT IS THIS HANDBOOK?

The overall aim of this Handbook is to address the political and social learning needs of women in Panchayati Raj Institutions. It contains both the philosophy and technology of building the capability and empowerment of the elected members of the PRIs, especially the Gram Panchayats. This Handbook thus involves the development and use of thematic gender-focused training modules, on a range of subjects, including social mobilization, use of social capital (natural, physical, financial, human and social) formation for ushering development and changing attitudes and behaviour at the grassroots level and development of a network of women PRIs. It may be added that after developing the philosophy of training strategy the Handbook contains generic modules of training for the master trainers.

A Participatory Action Research approach to capacity building has been adopted in this Handbook, which enables the different stakeholder groups involved to be engaged in *praxis* cycles for deepening and sustaining the impact of the capacity building interventions. By providing for the technology of political and social empowerment of gender as a group, the capacity building suggested in this Handbook will, it is hoped, improve the quality of women's participation in grassroots governance, and in the ultimate analysis help to ensure the right of women to a dignified life.

The women PRI functionaries are targeted in this Handbook, because they are marginalized in society and are inherently "capability poor". Thus, when they galvanize the courage and resources to take a plunge into the area of governance, their "capability poverty" should not in any way stymie their functioning. Additionally, training-ware in this Handbook which attempts to build up a cadre of trainers in at least 10 States is expected to trigger a transition, in the training institutions to which they belong, from traditional to participatory methodologies, which in the last analysis will enhance the capacity building effort of the entire gamut of PRI functionaries. We are not suggesting in this Handbook a straitjacketed manual for regimental training for women members of PRIs. We are all for variety and diversity to take care of the multiplicity of situation prevailing in the country.

This Handbook should be seen as an aid to further develop training of women elected members of PRIs

It needs to be mentioned that though the Handbook, deals with only one set of generic modules, it has been germane to several state specific modules as well. The basic modules were first developed at the RGF and a network of collaborating institutions was established. The institutions of this network adapted the base module and prepared State-specific modules for Andhra Pradesh, Kerala, Rajasthan, Uttaranchal, Orissa, Maharashtra, Gujarat, Punjab, Uttar Pradesh, Madhya Pradesh, Tamil Nadu, and Sikkim.

THE PROCESS

The thirteen participating State training institutes participated not only in the process of preparing but also in validating the State-specific training modules. These modules were given test runs by the responding institutions. Observers from the Foundation were present when the modules were put into operation. These training events were of crucial importance for they validated the training effectiveness of the modules. The State specific modules and their test runs also provided an opportunity for testing their validity with previous TNA exercises and their overall training effectiveness. The test runs suggested important issues for recasting or alterations to be effected in the generic modules.

Since training needs of all evolving institutes are dynamic and PRIs are still evolving, the training interventions cannot be cast in stone. These modules are, therefore, expected to be updated and changed by the users, trainers and training institutes. The methodology adopted will concurrently, it is expected, be changed and improved upon. The Handbook is also expected to trigger new thinking on how to meet the constant challenge of training thousand of *PRI women functionaries*, in the arts of governance, planning and bringing about social justice and gender equality.

Chapter 1

PROFILE OF THE TRAINING PROGRAMME AND GENERAL NOTES TO TRAINERS

I. OBJECTIVES

The training system discussed in this handbook has specific objectives. While broadly the objective is the empower women elected members of Gram Panchayats, there are several specific objective. These are:

- To empower the elected women members of the village Panchayat to realize their true roles and responsibilities and seek their true roles as members of the institution of self-government.
- To empower women elected members to bring about social and economic development, and ensuring gender and social justice.
- To acquaint women elected members with knowledge about the structure of the PRIs in the light of the Constitutional provisions, State Government Acts, Rules and Executive Orders.
- To help them acquire knowledge and the necessary skills in utilising social capital undertaking, social mobilisation and preparing as well as implementing development programmes for gender justice.

Clearly the objectives of the training system in this handbook are focused more on specialised areas, against the backdrop of the Constitutional framework and legal environment in which the Gram Panchayats operate in different states.

II. PARTICIPANTS

Given the specific objectives of the training system, it is best tailored for:

- Women village Panchayat Sarpanchs.
- Women elected members of the village Panchayat.
- Women Chairpersons of Village Panchayat Standing Committees.

However, other PRI functionaries who wish to understand the dynamics of PRI operation will also benefit from the training system.

'RAINER PROFILE

'e shall discuss later, trainers of a certain calibre are critical to deliver training inputs discussed in this handbook. Specifically the following ategory of people are expected to be best suited to deliver the inputs detailed in this handbook.

- Elected members of PRIs/government officers/faculty of state and extension training institutions, especially the women in these categories.
- Well grounded in the subject areas covered in the modules.
- Believes in the participatory training model for adult learning.
- Skilful in using participatory learning and action methods and facilitating learner groups.

IV. CONTENTS

The contents of the training inputs discussed in this handbook have been organised into fourteen sessions as under:

Session I: *General Orientation: Introduction and Icebreaking*
Session II: *General Orientation: Principles of Panchayati Raj Governance*
Session III: *General Orientation: Gender and Social Justice*
Session IV: *Politico-Legal Orientation: Role of Village Panchayat*
Session V: *Politico-Legal Orientation: Panchayati Raj Governance*
Session VI: *Politico-Legal Orientation: Role of Panchayati Raj Institution*
Session VII: *Development Orientation: People Centred Community Development*
Session VIII: *Role Orientation: People Centred Behaviour and Attitudes*
Session IX: *Social Capital: Concepts and Methods of Promoting Social Capital as a Transformative strategy*
Session X: *Social Mobilization: Concept and Methods of Enhancing Social Mobilization*
Session XI: *Networking amongst Women Members of Panchayats: Need and Concept of Networking*
Session XII: *Empowerment of Women Members of Panchayats: Concepts and Tools to Enhance Empowerment of Women Members of Panchayats*
Session XIII: *Participatory Micro-Level Planning for Empowerment of Women: Tools and Methods for Participatory Micro-level Planning as a Transformative Strategy for Empowering Women*
Session XIV: *Group Dynamics and Behaviour.*

Training Methodology

- Participatory Learning and Action Methods
- Lectures restricted to a minimum
- Simulation games
- Field visits/demonstrations
- Case studies
- Experience sharing
- Role play/drama
- Film show

Number of Sessions : 13

Suggested Venue : **Intermix of classroom and village locales**

Seating arrangements

Participants and trainers sit/stand on the ground in a circle for the group work and move around for the games and other activities. If necessary, they can also sit on chairs, in circles.

Number of Trainees: 30 per batch

Duration: Depending on the "mix and match" of the training sessions. Preference is invited to the Note for the Trainers "on Mix and Match".

V. GENERAL NOTES FOR THE TRAINER AND A NOTE ON MIX AND MATCH

The training course suggested in this handbook has 14 sessions as follows:

Session No.	*Sessions*	*Session Theme*	*Time (in minutes)*
1.	General Orientation	Introduction and Icebreaking	80
2.	General Orientation	Principles of Panchayati Raj Governance	190
3.	Politico-Legal Orientation	Role of Village Panchayat	180
4.	Politico-Legal Orientation	Panchayati Raj Governance	90
5.	Politico-Legal Orientation	Role of Panchayati Raj Institutions	150

(*Contd.*)

Session No.	*Sessions*	*Session Theme*	*Time (in minutes)*
6.	General Orientation	Gender and Social Justice	195
7.	Development Orientation	People-centred Community Development	195
8.	Role Orientation	People-centred Behaviours and Attitudes	190
9.	Social Capital	Concept and Methods of Promoting/Enhancing Social Capital	240
10.	Social Mobilization	Concept and Methods of Enhancing Social Mobilization	330
11.	Networking amongst Women Members of Panchayats	Need and Concept of Networking	275
12.	Empowerment of Women Members of Panchayats	Concept and Tools to Enhance Empowerment of Women Members of Panchayats	215
13.	Participatory Micro-Planning for Empowerment of Women	Participatory Planning as a Transformative Strategy for Poverty Reduction	300
14.	Group Dynamics & Behaviour	Widening the understanding of group dynamics and group behaviour	250
Total Duration of Training			**2880**

The intention of the training course suggested in this handbook, taken as a whole, is to provide a comprehensive training to elected women members of the Panchayats, many of whom are first timers and may be neo-literates. The need to build the capacity of such women elected members cannot be over-emphasized.

However, though comprehensiveness has its own value of being thorough, it has some disadvantages as well. First, it is unlikely that women elected members can spare two weeks of time to undergo a comprehensive training programme. Their responsibilities at home and in their new office would place a huge demand on their time. Second, being adults, it is unlikely that the prospective trainees would be able to absorb all the inputs from a very comprehensive training. This will be particularly true of the neo-literate women elected members. Hence, the trainer can "mix and match" the 14 training sessions suggested in this handbook depending upon the training needs of the prospective trainees and the training objectives. There can be numerous permutations and combinations of the "trainees and the training sessions". Some suggestions are provided below.

If the objective of the training programme is to equip the trainees with the nuances of governance of Panchayats, the trainer may design a training course using sessions 1 to 6. These sessions will take the trainees through the entire gamut of principles of Panchayats, role of Panchayati Raj institutions in the democratic fabric of India, Panchayati Raj governance, role of village Panchayats and issues relating to social and gender justice. These sessions will, more or less, equip the elected members of the Panchayats with the basic tools of operating the system.

In several cases, training may be necessary for appropriate development and role orientation of the newly elected women members of Panchayats. For designing such a training course, a combination of sessions 4, 7 and 8 would be fairly appropriate. An understanding of people-centred community development and the appropriate attitudes of behaviour could prove to be assets for elected representatives in bringing the best out of the myriad of development actors whom they would interact and of the constituency whom they represent.

Training would be very critical where the trainer would like to equip the trainees with tools and methods to initiate a process of development. For such a training programme, sessions 9, 10, 11 and 12 would provide a solid basis. The participants of the training course will have a thorough grasp of the role of social capital, social mobilization, networking and empowerment of women members of the Panchayats, in the adventure of development.

It may be necessary in other cases to equip the participants with the nuts and bolts of planning at the local level, as the Panchayats are required to prepare plans for social development under Article 243-ZD of the Constitution of India. In such an eventuality, it is best to run session 13. However, it is important to underscore that for effectively using the tools and techniques of session 13, it will be necessary that the participants are aware of the appropriate "attitudes and behaviours" detailed in session 8. Thus, it is strongly recommended that for a successful training in micro-level planning, session 8 ought to be considered as a prerequisite for session 13.

There can be numerous courses that can be designed by the trainer using the sessions discussed here. The trainer is strongly encouraged to mix and match the training sessions more ingeniously and even adding other sessions as may be required by exigencies of circumstances. For instance, in Panchayats where health hazards are great, the trainer could add a session on managing community health in Panchayats. Where natural calamity is a regular feature, the session on micro-planning (Session 13) could be buttressed with a small session on micro-level planning for disaster preparedness. The possibilities are numerous and they are likely to test the ability of the trainer to be innovative and forward looking.

V.1. How Adults Learn

A trainer has to know how adults learn. Unlike children, adults do not learn on the basis of a "belief system".

Adults learn:

- if they want and need to learn;
- by rechecking their learning messages they receive on the touchstone of their past or present experiences;
- by practising what they have learnt in training sessions;
- with help and guidance from 'outsiders'; and
- where the environment for learning is informal and non-threatening.

These five characteristics of adult learning make training different from teaching. The trainer should always bear in mind this fundamental difference between training and teaching while planning the delivery of training input to elected women members of PRIs.

V.2. Speed/Preferences of the Human Brain

The medium of training also has a strong bearing on adult learning.

Neurologists have in their experiments shown that:

- Generally a participant in a training programme can think on an average at 800 words per minute but the average trainer can only talk approximately at 120 words per minute. So the trainer must give their participants something interesting to do with their spare "mental capacity" (as it were) of 680 words per minute.
- The lecture method does not work very well in a training context as the brain goes into 'auto shut-off' after only 10 minutes of lecturing if it is not given something to stimulate it. Thus trainers, especially in case of training of elected women members of Panchayats, many of whom are neo-literates, must vary the media and give in addition to audio messages, multi-channel messages such as visuals (slides, overheads, power-point presentation, pictures, posters, etc.) and feeling messages (such as smell, touch, etc.).

- It may be mentioned that if a message is given once, the brain remembers only 10 per cent of it, one day later and when the same message is given six times in a year, the brain remembers 90 per cent of it. Hence trainers must repeat, recap and review the training messages several times over. Reference is invited to Figure 1A, which is self-explanatory. A system of training must, therefore, have an in-built mechanism by which training messages are repeated several times over a year (such as handouts, pictures, short refresher courses etc.).
- The trainer must also bear in mind that the brain prefers rounded diagrams and figures to square ones; it prefers "Times" and "Helvetica" type faces and dark letters on light background. Hence all visuals prepared by the trainer should be informed of these features of the brain. This is also one of the reasons why in the seating arrangement for participatory session a circular seating arrangement is strongly recommended.

V.3. Recall: 5 Main Factors

Training imparts skills and knowledge to be applied by the participants in their work situation.

The trainers have to alive of the facts that:

- Participants are more likely to remember the beginning of events or the first in a series of events. People remember, for instance, the first day in school or the birth of their first child, etc.
- The brain's recalls fall rapidly after 24 hours without review (See Figure 1A). Hence recap and review, after regular intervals, of training input are strongly recommended.
- Human beings remember unusual things exceedingly well such as death type experiences, winning a lottery ticket, etc. This is the reason why when a person narrates his "life-history" over a period of time, only major events come to her/his mind. The first day in school, last day in the college, date of marriage, birth of the children, death of a "near and dear" one, first day in employment and such other events are recalled very easily.
- Recall is high for things which are linked by mnemonics or analogy such as "Sen", where "S" stands for somebody "e" for everybody and "n" for nobody.
- We are more likely to remember the end of events or the last in a series of events, just as we remember the beginning of events or the first in the series of events. Examples of such events could be the last day in college or last day in a year.

V.4. How to Activate the Whole Brain

A successful trainer must be able to activate the whole brain of the participants. Where the whole brain is activated both absorption of inputs and contribution to the training programme by the participants improve significantly.

The brain has two parts, the left and the right, as it is called.

Left part of the brain deals with logical aspects of activity of the brain, as under:

- Speaking
- Calculating
- Intellectually analysing
- Reading
- Writing
- Naming
- Ordering
- Sequencing
- Critiquing
- Evaluating
- Logic

The right part of the brain deals with the creative aspects of cerebral activity as under:

- Creativity (new combinations)
- Artistic activity
- Musical ability/rhythm
- Emotions
- Recognition
- Comprehension
- Perception of abstract patterns
- Spatial abilities
- Facial expressions
- Holistic ability
- Intuition
- Images
- Colour

The trainer must, therefore, attempt all the time in the training at stimulating both "parts" of the brain. Professional trainers encourage participants to use both sides of the brain by organising training activity, which induces participants to think logically and at once be creative. The trainer must, however, remember that experiments are said to have demonstrated that:

- Participants, who have been trained traditionally to use only one side of the brain more than the other (accountants, engineers, musicians), find it difficult to 'switch' when necessary. Thus a musician finds it difficult to follow a 'manual' on how to compose a piece. Similarly, chartered accountants find it difficult not to follow the set rules of auditing.
- When the weaker side of the brain is stimulated and encouraged to co-operate with the stronger side of the brain, there is a greater synergy. There will, however, be participants who have both sides of their brains strong and keep them activated.

It is believed that Newton understood the theory of gravity while day dreaming. Thus the trainers should combine analytical exercises with creative, expressive activities during the training sessions, to activate both sides of the brain.

To help participants use both sides of the brain, the trainers should also be cognizant of the fact that information is stored in the brain with Very High Frequency, in VHF form, where 'V' stands for visual, 'H' stands for hearing and 'F' stands for feeling.

(i) Examples of visuals are: pictures, scenes, images, logos, diagrams, graphs, charts, photographs and painting/posters.
(ii) Examples of hearing are: words, music, sounds, accents, conversation/discussions, debates, etc.
(iii) Examples of feeling are: smells, tastes, pain/comfort, pleasure, anger, grief, affection, love, etc.

It is important to reiterate that experiments show that, when tested after 24 hours, participant's 'recall' of a "visual" message leads to 80 per cent correct answers and a "feeling" message leads to 79 per cent correct answers, which is almost twice as good as their recall of a "hearing" message which hovers around 45 per cent correct answers.

Therefore, because participants will store information in the left and the right brain in the form of pictures (V), words (H) or sensations and feelings (F), trainers are well advised to use visuals, words and feelings to provide training inputs, so that multi-channel messages are sent out in training sessions. Thus, lectures, pictures, exercises like mapping and modelling, and actual experience of reality through games and exposure visits have all to be combined for a good training programme. This also means giving colourful visual back up to our verbal messages at the same time as appealing to trainees' emotions and senses. Thus, for example, when the trainer wants to impress upon the participants, the 29 items covered under the Eleventh Schedule of the Constitution, each item while spoken of, is also shown by a picture. That is why posters have been provided with this handbook. The messages when so delivered, by a combination of visual and verbal modes of delivery of training inputs, will be stored simultaneously in several parts of the left and right brain of the participants and, therefore, the chances of recall are greater.

V.5. Seating Arrangements

Seating patterns have a strong impact on both the level of participation of the trainees and their reception. There are basically seven types of seating patterns as under:

(a) 'U' Shaped Seating Arrangement

The advantages of 'U' shaped seating arrangement are:

- It is a business like seating arrangement;
- Trainer can walk into 'U' and contact the trainers;
- Generally such an arrangement provides good participant visibility; and
- It is a standard seating arrangement and is therefore non-threatening for trainees.

But the disadvantages of a 'U' shaped arrangement are also significant:

- It is a somewhat formal arrangement and hence needs ice-breaking;
- Some participants often get masked by audio-visual equipment;
- The participants seated in the front of 'U' have to constantly keep their head at 60-90°, which can cause neck-ache and distract from learning;
- Rear participants are far from screen/flip chart or board and may have difficulty in viewing writings on the board or transparencies or pictures in slides etc. and may, therefore, receive poor visual messages; and
- The eye contact of the participants seated at the corners with those at the front is limited.

Figure 1 A: Learning Theory

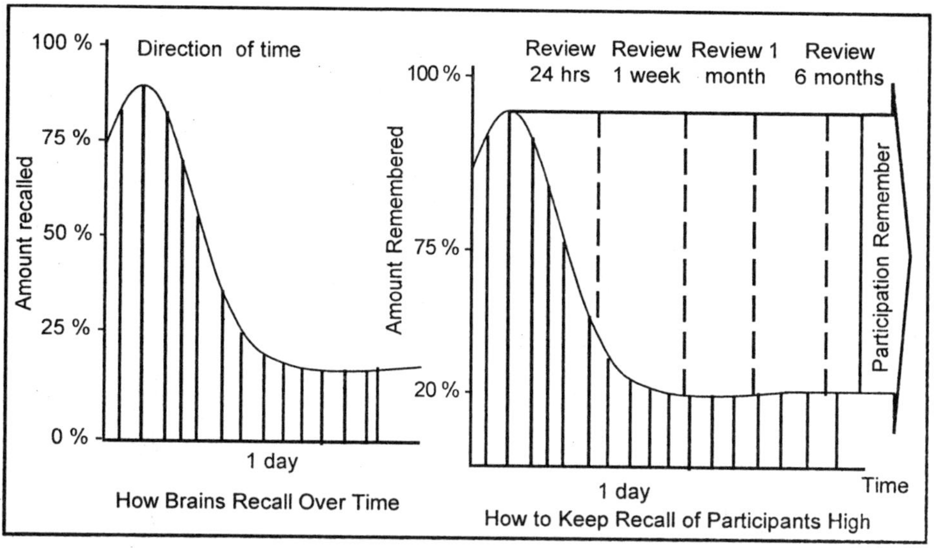

Figure 1 B: Seating Arrangements

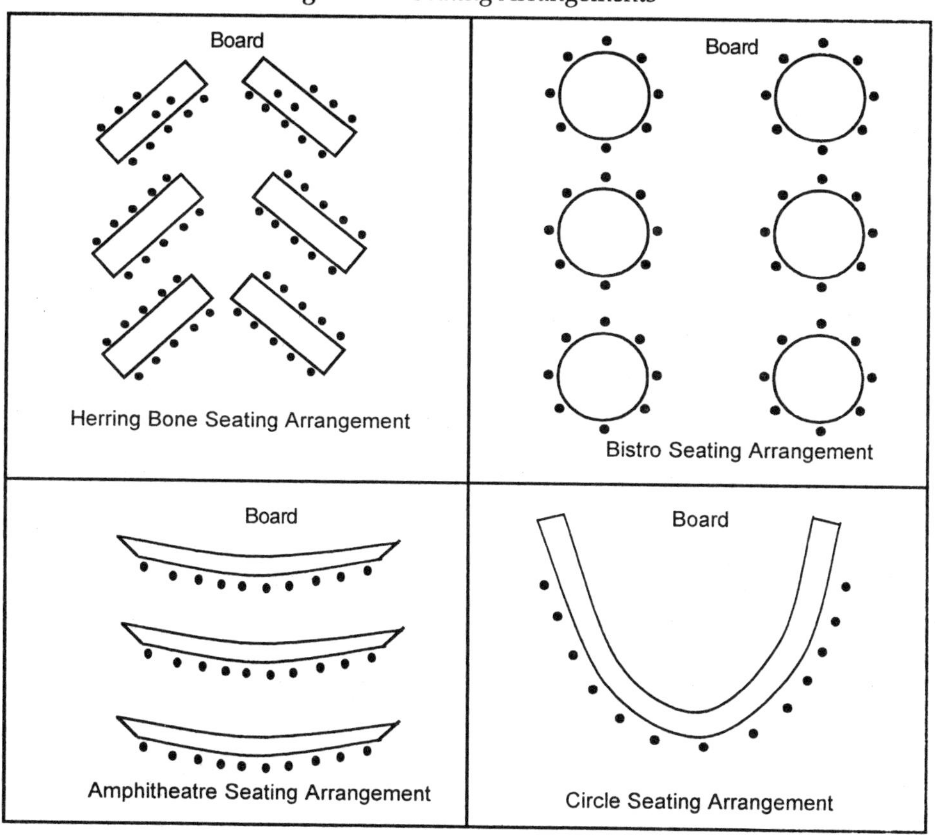

(b) 'V' Shaped Seating Pattern

The advantages of 'V' shaped seating arrangement are:

- It is the best pattern for visibility and problem of neck-ache syndrome is eliminated;
- It usually affords optimum trainer and participant contact and it is easier for the trainer to use his/her "lighthouse"(eye contact); and
- It is a less formal seating arrangement than the 'U' shaped one and hence it is less intimidating than 'U' shaped seating pattern.

However, the disadvantages are:

- Space requirements of a V-shaped seating arrangement are very large;
- It is suited only for small groups. If the number of participants is very large, those seated near the vertex of the 'V' will be too far from the source of visual messages and hence may impair learning a visual message may be poorly received; and
- The eye contact between participants *inter se* on each flank of the 'V' is low, though the eye contact between trainer and the trainees is high.

(c) Herring Bone Seating Arrangement

The advantages of the Herring Bone (See Figure 1B) seating arrangement are as follows:

- Space is used very effectively for large groups of trainees;
- All participants are seated at good angle to screen/flip chart/board, etc. and hence the problems associated with the 'neck-ache' syndrome are eliminated; and
- The trainer can walk down the 'spine' of the seating arrangement and maintain eye contact with the participants very easily.

However, the disadvantages of Herring Bone seating arrangement are:

- Several participants are masked by other participants;
- It is reminiscent of seating arrangement in schools and hence may hinder adult learning;
- It may encourage dysfunctional groupings amongst participants seated on separated tables and hamper learning through absence or lower cross-fertilization of ideas and impairs the overall training environment;

- Participants at the rear rows/tables are far from screen/flip chart/board and hence may be poor recipient of visual messages, which may hinder learning; and
- The participants and trainer contact is relatively poor, especially those seated on the outer-fringes of the tables. Hence the trainer cannot use his "lighthouse" properly.

(d) 'Bistro' Pattern of Seating Arrangement

Bistro pattern has several advantages such as:

- It is ideal for 'teambuilding' sessions and small group workshops/sessions and for small group exercises;
- It is an informal seating pattern and hence encourages maximum trainee participation, identification and bonding;
- It brings out the originality, encourages creativity and open-mindedness amongst the participants; and
- The contact between the participants and the trainer is good because the trainer can 'circulate' between participants and groups.

But the disadvantages are also not insignificant:

- Some participants have poor visibility of the screen, flip charts or boards or may be constantly at an angle to screen/flip chart or board and hence not suitable for plenary work. It also has the problems associated with the 'neck-ache' syndrome;
- The seating arrangement fosters lack of attention and encourages side conversations amongst the small groups (or what may be called, generates "whisperers" and "whisperees"); and
- Encourages splinter group identification, i.e., each group around a table becomes a sub-group and gets isolated from the others. This has consequences similar to formation of dysfunctional groups in Herring Bone seating pattern.

(e) Amphitheatre Seating Arrangement

In Amphitheatre seating arrangement, the participants are seated in rows facing the screen as in a theatre (and hence the name).

The advantages of this arrangement are:

- If room is well designed, excellent visibility of the screen, flip charts and board is ensured and acoustics;
- It is a very space-effective as a large number of participants can be accommodated in a relatively small space; and

- It is suitable for lecture-type presentations and briefing sessions, where the requirement of interaction between the participants *inter se* or between the participants and the trainer is limited.

Disadvantages of Amphitheatre seating pattern are:

- It allows very poor trainer and participant contact and the trainer can hardly use "lighthouse" (eye contact) beyond the second row;
- Difficult to set up an amphitheatre seating arrangement unless the room is designed with a permanent seating system with "steps", otherwise those seated at the back cannot see or even hear what is going on in the front;
- It is a very university-like seating arrangement and hence reminiscent of "school-type" learning which may hinder adult learning; and
- It can encourage formation of dysfunctional groups and/or "whisperers-whisperees" in the back rows.

(f) Circular Seating Arrangement

Here the participants sit in a circle, with a space at one end of the circle for the trainer to enter the circle to interact with the participants.

The advantages of the arrangement are:

- It is ideal for participatory sessions where participants' involvement has to be very high;
- The trainer has excellent contact with the participants and the participants *inter se* have lot of eye contact;
- The participants are focused, have little scope for side conversation, and possibility of formation of dysfunctional groups is eliminated; and
- There is lot of bonding between the participants.

The disadvantages of circular seating are:

- It is not easy to find tables which can be set up in a circular formation. Hence most of the time participants end up seating without tables;
- If the participants are seated without tables, then they may have difficulty in writing/doing individual assignments; and
- Participants when seated in a circle without tables may feel unnecessarily exposed.

All the seating arrangements may be necessary for the training programme. In participatory sessions, the circular seating arrangement is the best, for it allows maximum participation and participant-trainer eye contact. For break away group work, the "Bistro" is the best or alternatively the Herring Bone. For guest speakers or distinguished speakers, the "Amphitheatre" made is recommended. For plenary presentation of group work, 'V' or 'U' shape has been found to be useful. In any training programme, it is best to have one large room for plenary and more than one small room for group work, where different seating arrangements could be made.

In making seating arrangement, the trainer must bear in mind the PSYCHOLOGY of the participants, namely:

- Distance reduces participation-trainees in back rows are less likely to participate than those in front. The trainer should keep social distance between herself/himself and the trainee.
- Any kind of 'row' reduces interaction between the participants *inter se*. Because it is difficult for those seated in the back row to have eye contact with those in the front row(s) and hear contributors from participants seated in the front rows and for those seated in the front row to twist round to interact with participants seated behind them.
- Changes in seating patterns from one session of a training programme to another can be psychologically upsetting for participants but at times such changes may add variety, wake participants out of slumber and break "whisperer-whisperee" combination. Use of best judgment is vital. Hence care has to be taken to manage such disturbance.
- In a long to medium duration training programme, at repetitive sessions in the same room, participants will invariably sit in the same place and form some sub-groups. It is best to rotate people around once in a while both within the room and the rooms themselves.
- Angry or cynical participants will attempt to move away from a group-seating pattern.

V.6. Structure

Recap is very important for retention and recall of training inputs. Hence, a trainer should:

- Review all learning points at the end of each module (or beginning of next); use "VHF" support for better impact.

- Action plan as a follow up is an excellent way to ensure retention of inputs.
- The trainer and the participants should agree on an action plan for the transfer of new skills or knowledge to real life situations and if necessary (and possible) have a written group promise.
- Follow-up action including a refresher course should be worked out.
- The trainer and the participants should agree on any other follow-up action or refresher to increase recall such as periodic handouts or exchanging information.

It is necessary to always finish a session with a succinct and provocative encapsulation of the learning experience of the session.

In structuring the training sessions, the trainer should keep in mind the effectiveness of different methods that are used in training. It is given below:

Ranking of Methods Depending on Teaching Goals (1= high, 8=low)

Method	*Knowledge Acquisition*	*Attitude Change*	*Problem Solving Skills*	*Inter-personal Skills*	*Participant Acceptance*	*Knowledge Retention*
Case Study	4	5	1	5	1	4
Workshop	1	3	4	4	5	2
Lecture	8	7	7	8	7	3
Games	5	4	2	3	2	7
Films	6	6	8	6	4	5
Programmed Instr.	3	8	6	7	8	1
Role-playing	2	2	3	1	3	6

Source: J. Newstrom; "Evaluating Effectiveness of Training Methods"

We have thus suggested a combination of different methods of training in the Handbook, keeping the foregoing table in mind. We encourage the trainers to change the methods as they think best, depending on what they wish to achieve and how the trainees are responding.

V.7. Training Delivery

Training delivery is a critical variable for success of a training. Remember the following points:

(a) Communication is the first golden rule

The trainer must be careful in her/his communication. She/he has to communicate well.

When a trainer gives a spoken message, the participants' understanding and judgment of that message come from three sources: words, paralinguistics and facial expressions.

- Words are only labels and listeners put their interpretation on speakers' words. They convey only seven per cent of the message that a trainer may wish to convey.
- Paralinguistics is the way in which the trainer says something (i.e., accent, tone, inflection, etc.). Paralinguistics is very important to a trainer and trainee for communicating and for understanding respectively of the message being communicated. Paralinguistics communicate 38 per cent of the message.
- Facial expression is what a trainer looks like while delivering a message. Facial expressions affect the participants' understanding most and convey 55 per cent of the message that a trainer may wish to convey.

(b) Trainer's demeanour has a great impact on the participants

The trainer must be enthusiastic about his/her work.

- If the trainer is not enthusiastic about the training, how can the participants be expected to be enthusiastic.
- The trainer should consciously use her/his eyes and eyebrows to communicate enthusiasm.
- The trainer must always keep a sparkle in her/his voice.
- The trainer must fight the boredom of repetitive sessions by introducing new anecdotes, examples, games, ice-breaking, etc., or by changing lesson structure or methods given in the previous session.

(c) Mannerisms of the trainer can make or mar a training session

The trainer must be careful about her/his mannerisms. There are certain tips that come in handy, as under:

- The trainer should not be tempted by or play around with what is called "manual props" such as pens, pencils, pointers, spectacles, key chains, etc., during a training session.

- If the trainer is a male, make sure that he keeps no loose change in his pocket and fiddle around with them during a training session.
- The trainer should be aware of her/his verbal tics and work on eliminating them (i.e. O.K. !-'You know'-'and so forth'-'Now'......)
- The trainer should avoid 'closed' or tense body positions such as clasped hands and crossed arms. She/he should be confident and open. Have open arms.
- The trainer need not worry about pacing, leaning, etc. during the training sessions.
- The trainer should check her/his hair and dress before entering the class/workshop rooms. A neatly dressed trainer is well received just as a neatly organized data is well used.

(d) Dress

In dressing, it is important to be careful. Generally, it helps trainers bear in mind the following:

- It is best if the trainer avoids dressing in black and white and other strongly contrasting colours, for it will distract the attention of the trainees.
- The trainer should wear comfortable, loose-fitting clothes, especially in participatory sessions where body movement is very frequent and essential.
- Where the trainer cannot make up her/his mind, she/he ought to wear something not "loud" so that at least her/his clothes would not detract from the message that she/he would be delivering.
- The trainer should try and dress "one step" above the audience, but should never be in loud or ceremonial dress.

V.8. Ten Tips for Trainers

- The trainer should never be late for his/her session.
- The trainer should never keep his/her eyes on his/her notes.
- She/he must never read out anything except quotations from a text.
- The trainer should exaggerate body movements and verbal emphasis, because paralinguistics and facial expressions convey more than words do.
- The trainer must perform; he should not act.
- The trainer should often pause remembering that silence is much longer for the trainers than for the participants.

- The trainer should use humour in the presentation; "a laugh is worth a thousand frowns".
- The trainer must be enthusiastic about the training. If the trainer is not enthusiastic about the session why should the participants be enthusiastic at all?
- The trainer should not try for technical accuracy to the last detail.
- The trainer should keep the training sessions simple.

Chapter 2

SPECIAL NOTES ON SELECTED SESSIONS FOR TRAINERS

I. INTRODUCTION

In chapter 1, general guidelines and notes to trainers were provided. Trainers are encouraged to read additional material on the subject. In this chapter we should provide special notes to trainers on specific sessions which warrant additional attention. Trainers are encouraged, in this case as well, to consult additional training notes as may be appropriate bearing in mind that these training notes are by no means exhaustive. Trainers are strongly encourage to innovate in both developing the contents and scope of the training notes, and share them with the authors for wider dissemination.

II. PRELUDE

The Sessions are designed to orient the participants with the fundamental concepts related to Panchayati Raj governance. Its contents include the evolution of PRIs, the concept of democratic decentralisation, the shifts in the development paradigm and development approaches and concerns related to gender and social justice. It familiarizes the participants with the two-dimensional role of PRIs as institutions of self-government and agents of community development. The sessions especially focuses upon the neglect of gender interests in the development process and the issues related to social justice and social exclusion. The sessions, therefore, serve to sensitize the participants with their social roles and obligations and generate in them the urge to seek what is their right in the realm of local self-governance. In the process the sessions introduce the participants to the much talked about but scarcely discussed issues pertaining to social capital, networking and social mobilization and their use as transformative strategies. It is for this reason that the notes to trainers for sessions 9 to 14 are more detailed, than the ones relating to sessions 2 to 8.

III. THE SESSION, THEIR TRAINING OBJECTIVES AND EXPECTED LEARNING OUTCOMES

III.1. Session 1: Introductions and Ice-breaking

The introductory part for ice-breaking mixed with the energizing games in the other sessions and the group-work based upon PLA methods serve to promote positive group dynamics among the participants.

The introductory session is in the nature of an ice-breaker, which aims at establishing solidarity among the participants. Any hierarchical lines that usually exist among the trainers and participants and the participants themselves need to be gradually flattened to facilitate group learning. This also supports the subsequent group learning process. An overview of the training goal, design and methodology is done. The trainer explains that the trainer will involve active participation of each participant and also voices an expectation that the participants will join the group work readily. This session sets the overall tenor of training for participatory training.

III.2. Training methodology

The training methodology suggested in this session is predominantly based upon participatory learning and action methods and involves the participants in active group work leading to the construction of social realities in the training sessions. The use of PLA method is best suited to adult learning and generates empathy among the participants. The less motivated and timid participants also learn with less effort through this group learning process.

IV. NOTE TO TRAINERS FOR USING SESSIONS 2, 3, 4 & 5 ON GENERAL ORIENTATION, ROLE OF PANCHAYATS & POLITICO-LEGAL ORIENTATION

IV.1. Introduction

We begin the formal coverage of the subject matter of training from the second session. The use of the Johari's Window emphasises the fact that we value the existing knowledge of the participants about PRIs. This is in keeping with the overall philosophy of participatory training, which believes in the underlying tenet that 'they know'. The participants are first oriented with the basic principles of Panchayati Raj governance and democratic decentralisation. This orientation is achieved through experiential group learning, by relating the village level changes in governance structures as perceived and experienced by the participants to the gradual evolution of the PRIs. In this way, the participants transit from "known to the unknown" in terms of knowledge areas. There is great scope for cross-learning during this session, but its degree essentially rests upon the facilitation skills of the trainer.

Sessions on politico-legal orientation are designed for both the political and legal orientation of the participants. The previous sessions had outlined the evolution of the PRIs and their role in the spheres of both village development and governance. The people-centred development paradigm that gives the overall context for the functioning of the PRIs, different development approaches and programmes were also discussed. The participants were broadly familiarized with the concepts of "democratic decentralization" and "self-government".

These sessions deepen the participants' understanding of both these concepts and serve for furthering the cause of raising the political consciousness of participants. The participants get acquainted with the mandate and features of the Seventy-third Constitutional Amendment Act and the State Conformity Acts which form the legal premise of the Panchayati Raj institution, which in turn is expected to induce in the participants an urge to demand their right to govern at the local level.

IV.2. Training objectives

The Section has the following training objectives:

- To enhance the practical understanding of the participants about the concept of self-government, its institutions, their structures and social mandate;
- To expand the knowledge of the participants about the legal premise of the Panchayati Raj institutions; and
- To conscientise the participants about their rights and duties as members of the Village Panchayat and generate an urge in them to seek their rights.

IV.3. Sessions, their training objectives and expected learning outcomes

There are Several sessions on politico-legal orientation.

The session-wise Training objectives and the expected learning outcomes are given in the following Table:

Session Description	*Training Objective*	*Expected Learning Outcomes*
Principles of Panchayati Raj Institutions	To expand the knowledge of the participants about the legal premise and structure of Panchayati Raj institutions	The participants are increasingly acquainted with the mandate and features of the Seventy-Third Constitutional Amendment Act, the State Conformity Acts for PRIs and structure of PRIs
Role of the Village Panchayat	To conscientise the participants about their rights and duties as members of the Village Panchayat and generate an urge in them to seek their rights	The participants have increased awareness about: • their own rights and duties • the rightful place of the Village Panchayat in grassroots governance • its role, responsibilities and functions • what is necessary for having those rights, responsibilities and functions
Panchayati Raj Governance	To expand the practical understanding of the participants about the concept of self-government and its institutions	The participants have an increased understanding of the principles underlying the concept of self-government, the role and functions of the PRIs as institutions for self government at the grassroots level
Role of Panchayati Raj Institutions	To expand the practical understanding of the participants about the social mandate of the Panchayati Raj institutions	The participants have an enlarged comprehension about: • The social mandate of the PRIs for meeting the ends of gender equity and social justice • The extent of the fulfilment of the social mandate

IV.4. The rights of Panchayati Raj functionaries

One very important feature of these sessions is that their contents have been designed for directly "fictionalizing" the rights conferred upon the PRI functionaries by the Constitutions of India. This is done by conscientising the participants about their right to self-government and political and development participation. There is focus on the role of the Village Panchayat, the institution that is at the very cutting edge of the development process. The Village Panchayat affords a wide range of poor stakeholders with the opportunity of direct political and development participation. In this session, the *de facto* and *de jure* functions of the Village Panchayat are discussed. This makes the participants aware of the powers and functions that are stated in Article 243G read with the Eleventh Schedule of the Constitution of India. The Schedule under reference lists a total of 29 functions that have to be devolved upon the PRIs. It is hoped that the training process will make the participants aware of the rightful powers of the Village Panchayat and their own rights and duties as members of this institution. This awareness should find expression, subsequently, in suitable forums and platforms in raising a demand for a greater devolution of authority (in terms of functions, finances and functionaries) to the PRIs, in keeping with the letter and spirit of the Constitution. The trainers should, therefore, try and link these forums and platforms to networking, social mobilisation and social capital discussed in sessions 11, 10 and 9 respectively.

IV.5. Session: Self-governance

Based upon the concept of "self-government", the session on Role of Panchayati Raj Institutions (Session-5) discusses the consequent implications and the desired agenda of proactive actions for the PRIs. The original mandate of the PRIs during their inception in some states in the sixties and seventies is then discussed. Force field analysis is used to identify how the positive and negative forces acts upon the functioning of the PRIs and the desired direction of future policy interventions.

A game called the Saboteur[1] can be included which is expected to enhance the negotiation skills of the participants thereby helping them to resolve conflicts in analogous Village Panchayat/Gram Sabha scenarios. This session coming at this juncture, gives the trainers an opportunity to deal with how the Seventy-Third Constitution Amendment Act and the State Conformity Acts were mandated to give the desired policy direction to the evolution of self-government in the country. The structures of the three-tiered PRIs and the Gram Sabha are also to be emphasized and discussed in this session.

Session 4 on politico-legal orientation should be used by the trainers to draw the attention of the participants to the 29 statutory development functions of the Village Panchayat. The extent of devolution of functions and funds and the degree of empowerment of the Village Panchayat

---

1. See Pretty *et al.* for games.

are analyzed in this context through participatory exercises. As stated earlier, the underlying training approach relies heavily upon the rights conferred on the PRIs by the Constitution. By conscientising the participants about their roles mandated by the Constitution and hence the rights of the PRIs that are guaranteed to them by statute, it is expected that it may eventually lead to a demand for such rights. Such a demand may lead to policy changes or interventions for devolving functions, functionaries and finances to the PRIs.

IV.6. Session 6: Gender and social justice

The sixth session initiates a discussion about issues related to gender and social justice. The purpose of introducing these issues at a very early stage of training is to emphasise the centrality of the role played by gender in Panchayati Raj governance and development. The discussions in this session would sensitise the participants to the phenomenon of social exclusion whereby certain groups for reasons of gender, caste, ethnicity, age group, lack of control over resources and other factors are excluded from participating in the activities and benefits of development. The trainer should emphasize the obligations of the PRIs in general, and of the elected women members of Gram Panchayats in particular, for promoting social justice including gender equity through their local governance and village development related functions. These are focused upon in the context of the phenomenon of social exclusion in this session.

IV.7. Session: People-centred community development

Session 7 deals with the evolution of the development paradigm in India. It sets the present day development context for the PRIs in the country. It discusses the different development approaches and programmes which the participants assess in terms of consensual criteria determined by playing the 'matching game'.

IV.8. Training methodology

The trainer is encouraged to use with ingenuity the training methodology suggested in these sessions (viz., sessions 2 to 5). It is an inter-mix of Participatory Learning and Action Methods, the lecture method, other visual method using posters and pictures and role/play drama. It has to be remembered that the contents of this section are on the heavier side and, therefore, learner motivation has to be sustained by a greater degree of innovation on the part of the trainer. The trainer will be extensively dealing with hidden knowledge or "what we know and they do not know", namely, Box 3 of the Johari's Window discussed in the previous section.

For this purpose, the trainer is encouraged to use her judgment and introduce short duration energizing games that alleviate learner fatigue. The trainer is referred to several such games that are described in the other sections of the Handbook.

V. NOTE TO TRAINERS FOR USING SESSION 8 ROLE ORIENTATION

V.1. Introduction

Session 8 is entitled "People-Centred Behaviours and Attitudes". This session essentially makes the participants experience a process of sensitisation to the proactive behaviours and attitudes, which are expected of them as members of the institutions of the Village Panchayat. This sensitivity is imperative for enabling them to fulfil their role with a high degree of commitment towards the poor stakeholders in the development process. The participants have to understand that their present day role as people's representatives is not one of being in control and exercising their powers arbitrarily. Their role is that of a facilitator. They have to remember that the development paradigm has shifted from a mechanistic "top-down" approach to an organic people-centred "bottom-up" position. The patterns of normative behaviours and attitudes of the members have to be convergent with the principle of people-centricity, which underpins the development paradigm.

V.2. Training objectives

The training objectives of the section have been articulated as:

- To enable the participants to comprehend the different kinds of people-centred behaviours and attitudes; and
- To arrive at an understanding of what kind of behaviours are most appropriate for ushering people-centred development.

V.3. Expected learning outcomes from the Session

The expected learning outcomes of session 8 that fulfil the stated training objective at the levels of both the individual participants and group can be best described as, *the participants being conscientised about the desired pro-people and pro-poor behaviours and attitudes that are expected of a Village Panchayat member and learn to emulate them.*

Because of the nature of its training content, this section calls for greater communication and facilitation skills on the part of the trainers. Unlike the other sessions, the learning outcomes from this session are not measured in terms of the transfer of knowledge or work-related skills. Instead, the single session involves a portrayal of the normative value systems and behavioural patterns, which the participants as members of the Village Panchayat are expected to emulate. Given the nature of the learning outcomes flowing out, it is expected that they will not be apparent immediately after the session, but will lie embedded in the psyche of the participants.

V.4. The Paradigm of People-centred behaviour

It is important for the trainer to ensure that the participants realize that their role as members of the Village Panchayats consists of facilitating a process of social and economic development. The participants have to be sensitized against adopting a superior stance whereby they regard the poor as beneficiaries and themselves as benefactors. Instead, they have to understand that it is their responsibility to foster the agency of the self and community, so that rural stakeholders can engage in whole-hearted political and development participation.

V.5. Behaviour and attitudes

This session models a variety of people-centred behaviours and portrays many corresponding attitudes. There has to be emphasis on both. Because it is important to remember that most often a person's behavioural patterns are the manifestations of her attitudes.

V.6. Training methodology

The trainer is encouraged to use with ingenuity the training methodology suggested in this session. It uses a mix of Participatory Learning and Action Methods, games and play/drama. The use of slides, cartoons, pictures and video is strongly advocated. However, "role play" could be a very powerful tool to deliver the inputs for this session.

The nature of the training contents renders the task of the trainer doubly difficult. Behaviour modelling on the part of the trainer is crucial in these sessions and in the entire training Module. The trainer has to adopt a learner-centric approach in the classroom. The trainer has to convey herself as a role model who believes in learner participation, even that of the most deprived learners. Only then can the trainer sincerely uphold the analogous philosophy of people-centred development and inclusion of poor stakeholders in the development process.

VI. NOTES TO TRAINERS FOR SESSION 9: SOCIAL CAPITAL

VI.1. Introduction

This session is on "Social Capital", a term widely used but not as well understood. Thus the session on "Social Capital" is to provide an understanding of the meaning of various concepts of social capital amongst the participants and create an awareness that they (the women elected members of Gram Panchayats) can act as a catalyst in creating/enhancing social capital. An understanding of social capital and the related awareness are critical to motivate the participants to act as co-creators of social capital for upliftment of the poor women in particular and of the poor at large.

VI.2. Training objectives

The training objectives of this session are:

- To enable the participants to understand the concept of social capital and its various forms;
- To enable the participants to understand how the different forms of social capital are linked to poverty reduction and empowerment of women elected members of the panchayats in particular and of the poor women in general;
- To enable the participants to learn about the ways and means to promote social capital; and
- To bring about a realization amongst the participants that they can act catalyst in creation of social capital.

VI.3. Expected learning outcomes

The trainers should be careful in facilitating a learning process where expected learning outcomes that fulfil the stated objectives at both the individual level of the participants and at the group level are as under:

(a) The participants are conscientised about the relationship between different forms of social capital and development, especially women's empowerment; and
(b) The participants learn how to be proactive in being co-creators of social capital.

Because of the nature of the training content, this session calls for a clear understanding of social capital on the part of the trainer. The trainer's ability to link social capital to various elements of poverty reduction and empowerment of women, based on experiences of the participants, will be put to test. It is imperative that the trainer has in his/her "training kit" a large number of real life experiences to back-up the inputs of the session.

VI.4. The paradigm of development in relation to Social Capital

The participants must realize that their role as women members of the Panchayats consists of facilitating a process of development embedded in the use of local resources, local knowledge and local technology. The participants have to be sensitized to the fact that social capital is an essential ingredient of local resources and local knowledge. Additionally, the participants must realize that it is their responsibility to catalyze social capital formation, where it does not exist, and to strengthen it where it does exist. Only then will it be possible to include people's institutions, customs, knowledge and technology into the development process.

VI.5. The content flow training methodology

As in the other sessions, the trainer is encouraged to use a mix of Participatory Learning and Action methods, games, slides and lecture. The trainer has to adopt a participant's experience-centric approach in the classroom, to give face to the concept of social capital and its use as a transformative strategy.

The trainer could refer to Appendix-B on the concepts and examples of Social Capital.

VII. NOTE TO TRAINERS FOR USING SESSION 10: SOCIAL MOBILISATION

VII.1. Introduction

Session 10 of the Module is designed to orient the participants with the concept and need related to social mobilization in the context of Panchayati Raj. This session imparts knowledge of social mobilization to the participants to understand and appreciate that social mobilization is necessary for initiating process of development in their areas. The participants have to understand that their presence as women representatives is not only to play their functional role but also to initiate the process of empowerment of women by mobilizing them.

VII.2. Training objectives

The training objectives of the session has been articulated as:

- To enable the women members of Village Panchayats to understand the concept of social mobilization and the possible role they can play; and
- To empower participant to initiate the process of social mobilization for collective action.

VII.3. Social mobilisation and the changing paradigm of development

It has now been recognized all over the world that the people or community, for whom development process is sought, are not the problem but a valuable resource. People must, therefore, be brought at the centrestage of any development process. This critical element in the development process should be clearly understood by women members of PRIs. Having understood the centrality of the role of people in accelerating the process of development, the women members of PRIs must also have a clear idea of the processes by which the people can be brought to centrestage, namely, by community and social mobilization. The trainer should spend adequate time to distinguish community mobilisation from social mobilisation. The distinction is of fundamental importance. The participants should be reminded not to confuse between the two concepts because the results of community mobilization and social mobilization can be very different.

VII.4. Sub-sessions, their training objectives and expected learning outcomes

This session on social mobilisation has eight segments of substantive parts. Their contents have been designed to fulfil the stated training objectives. The introductory sub-session for energizing and the group work based upon PLA methods serve to promote positive group feeling among the participants. For each sub-session, the expected learning outcomes at the end of the sub-session, that would demonstrate the fulfilment of the corresponding training objective, are given in the following chart:

Sr. No.	*Content*	*Training Objective*	*Expected Learning Outcomes*
1.	What is social mobilization? And what is its?	To create the conceptual understanding of the participants about the social mobilization	The participants have increased understanding of the concept of social mobilization. They are made aware of the philosophy of the social mobilization.

(*Contd.*)

Sr. No.	*Content*	*Training Objective*	*Expected Learning Outcomes*
2.	Social mobilization vs community mobilization	To expand the knowledge about the social mobilization and community mobilization.	(a) The participants understand the concepts of community mobilization and social mobilization. (b) They become aware of the main differences between social mobilization and community mobilization
3.	Challenges and probable perspectives	To conscientise the participants that social mobilization is not an easy process. It is a challenging task.	The participants understand the over all perspectives of social mobilization and challenges that may confront any social mobilization process.
4.	Critical steps of social mobilization	To create awareness about the steps of implementation of the processes of social mobilization	(a) The women members of PRIs become aware of the steps of the social mobilization. (b) They understand the whole approach of social mobilization
5.	Presentation of core studies and sharing of experiences in their specific social context	To create awareness amongst the participants on the efforts made in the field on social mobilization in their specific social context	(a) The participants become aware of the fact that social mobilization is possible though difficult. (b) The participants get acquainted with the different approaches of social mobilization from which lesson can be learnt.
6.	Social mobilization with specific emphasis on SC/ST/weaker sections and other disadvantaged groups	To create awareness of the participants about efficacy of social mobilization with specific emphasis on SC/ST/weaker sections and other disadvantaged groups.	The participants become more sensitive about the role that can play social mobilization in context of upliftment of SC/ST/weaker sections and other disadvantaged groups in their Panchayats.

(*Contd.*)

Sr. No.	*Content*	*Training Objective*	*Expected Learning Outcomes*
7.	Role of facilitator/ initiator	To create practical understanding about the role of initiator of social mobilization	The participants understand the role of facilitator to initiate and strengthen the process of social mobilization
8.	How and who will M & E	To impart skills in monitoring and evaluation of social mobilization	The participants are equipped to monitor and evaluate social mobilization process so that they can take corrective measures in time.

Sub-session 1: Energizer

The introductory sub-session is in the form of an energizer. The objective of the game is to energize the group before they begin the sub-session of social mobilization. This also supports the subsequent group learning process.

Sub-session 2: What is Social Mobilization and what is the goal of Social Mobilization?

The Session begins the formal coverage of the subject matter of training from the second sub-session. The use of brainstorming exercise will emphasize the fact that the trainer values the existing knowledge of the participants about social mobilization. The participants are first oriented with the meaning of social mobilization. The concept of social mobilization emerged from the recognition that a genuine participatory approach to development with people at the centre is essential for success and sustainability. Social mobilization processes in development efforts are, therefore, recognized by the communities.

Sub-session 3: Social Mobilization vs. *Community Mobilization*

The third sub-session deals with the sharing of experiences in the context of social mobilization. This sub-session helps the participants understand the differences between social mobilization and community mobilization. The participants assess the differences themselves by brainstorming the ideas. The trainer could use the Case Studies in Chapter 5 to illustrate the two concepts.

Sub-session 4: Challenges and probable perspectives

The forth sub-session initiates a discussion about issues related to challenges that one faces in mobilizing people and have a fair idea of the probable perspective on social mobilization. The purpose of introducing these issues at this stage is to emphasize the strategic approaches of social mobilization. There is great scope for cross-learning during this sub-session, but its degree essentially rests upon the facilitation skills of the trainer and his/her clarity in thinking on the subject.

Sub-session 5: Critical steps of Social Mobilization

The fifth sub-session emphasizes the critical steps of social mobilization. This is a "nuts and bolts" sub-session, as it were. Participants understand the steps of social mobilization. It has to be remembered that the contents of this sub-session are very important for participants to be effective agents of development in the changed context of participatory democracy. To internalise the various nuances of social mobilization, learner motivation has to be sustained by a greater degree of innovation on the part of the trainer. She/he should resort liberally to "VHF" discussed in the introductory Chapter of this Handbook.

Sub-session 6: Presentation of core studies and sharing of experiences in their specific social context

The sixth sub-session deals with the efforts of social mobilization. This sub-session emphasizes the factors affecting social mobilization, which encourage people to work together by sharing common interests for the development of their own community. The participants assess the factors affecting social mobilization by examining the case studies, understanding the problems encountered in the process and how they were overcome.

Sub-session 7: Social Mobilisation with specific emphasis on SC/ST/weaker sections and other disadvantaged groups

The seventh sub-session emphasizes social mobilization with specific emphasis on SC/ST/weaker sections and other disadvantaged groups. The purpose of this sub-session is to sensitize the participants about the criticality of making the process inclusive by ensuring the involvement of weaker sections and other disadvantaged groups in social mobilization, otherwise the voices of these groups may be drowned in the noise of other (more vocal) groups in society.

Sub-session 8: Role of facilitator/initiator of Social Mobilization

The eighth sub-session initiates a discussion about the role of facilitator/ initiator of social mobilization. The operationalisation and creation of a social mobilization process is a big challenge for the facilitator/initiator. This sub-session expands the practical understanding and skills of the participants for the functional management of the social mobilization.

Sub-session 9: How and who will monitor and evaluate

The sub-session imparts the skills in monitoring and evaluation of social mobilization. Monitoring and evaluation play very influential role in the entire process of social mobilization. It is for the tainer to emphasize that an iterative process and each step must be closely monitored/evaluated. Based on such monitoring and evaluation, the participants should be equipped to initiate corrective measures in subsequent steps. It is, therefore, also important to impart skills, attitudes and behaviours appropriate for application of participatory monitoring and evaluation in the process of social mobilization.

VII. 5. Training methodology

The training methodology suggested in this section is predominantly based upon participatory learning and action methods and involves the participants in active small group discussion leading to the construction of social realities in the training sub-session.

The trainer may please refer to Appendix-C for background material on Social Mobilisation. Appendix-D would also be helpful.

VIII. NOTE TO TRAINERS FOR USING SESSION 11: NETWORKING

VIII.1. Introduction

Session 11 of the Module deals with the issue of networking of women elected members of Panchayats. An attempt has been made in this sub-session to consider all managerial functions of the network. It is expected that by now the participants have developed an understanding of the concept and importance of the network as a tool of empowerment. They have thus reached a point where they can obtain and use the functional skills associated with network. Forming of networks, an empowering experience that creates space for effective political action for women elected members of Panchayats to reflect their skills in the functioning of

Panchayat, therefore, it is important to make them aware of the issue of networking.

VIII.2. Training objectives

The sub-session has the following training objectives:

- To enable the participants to understand the concept and importance of networking as a tool of empowerment;
- To enable the participants to understand the different stages of network and its functions, more specifically in relation to building social capital and as an instrument of social mobilisation.
- To orient the participants with the roles of initiator of network; and
- To bring about a realization amongst the participants that they are catalyst in creation of network.

VIII.3. Sub-sessions, their training objectives and expected learning outcomes

There are seven substantive parts in this session and they serially satisfy the sub-session's objectives. The training objective and the expected learning outcomes that fulfil the objective at the levels of both the individual participants and group are given in the following Table:

S. No.	*Content*	*Training objective*	*Expected Learning Outcomes*
1.	What is network?	To create the conceptual understanding of the participants about the concept of a network	The participants have increased understanding of the concept of networking.
2.	Kinds of network – federation, alliance, coalition, partnership, network	To create awareness about the various kinds of network	(a) The women members of PRIs become aware of the different kinds of network. (b) They understand the different approaches of collective action from which they can choose depending on their ground realities and socio-political environment.

(Contd.)

S. No.	*Content*	*Training objective*	*Expected Learning Outcomes*
3.	Stages of network	To conscientise the participants about the stages of network	The participants understand the stages of forming network and are able to identify where they could play a role.
4.	Functions, structure of network secretariat	To expand the knowledge about the networking	The participants understand: • The main function of the network • The structure of network • The fundamentals of managing network.
5.	Role of facilitator (Role of initiator of network)	To create practical understanding about the role of initiator of network	The participants understand the role of facilitator to initiate and strengthen the process of network.
6.	Video case studies	To expand the awareness of process of the network	The participants learn from the process of existing networks.
7.	Critiques of networks	To orient the participants with the critiques of networks	The participants become aware of the possible pitfalls of networks so that they are able to modify their expectations.

VIII.4. The Paradigm of networking of women elected members of Panchayats

The eleventh sub-session introduces the concept and functional role of network as a tool of empowerment of the women elected members. Networks have significant role to strengthen the leadership capacities of women elected members of Panchayats and to contribute to building social capital. It is very important that the participants realize the importance of network to make their role in Panchayat effective and efficient. The participants have to be sensitized to the fact that collective voice is essential for them to create space in the male-dominated mainstream political system.

VIII.5. Sub-session 1: Energizer

The sub-session begins with an energizer. The objective of this sub-session is to energize the group before they begin to get involved in the rather heavy sub-session on networking. This energiser also supports the subsequent group learning process.

VIII.6. Sub-session 2: What is Network?

The second sub-session emphasizes the concept of network. This sub-session equips the participants to understand the idea of network in their context. The trainers should use this sub-session to connect network with social capital and kinds of social capital.

VIII.7. Sub-session 3: Kinds of network – federation, alliance, coalition, partnership, "other " networks

This sub-session draws the attention of the participants to the different kinds of networks. The sub-session also gives information about the practices of different kinds of networks which the communities have adopted. The importance of this sub-session is underscored in the light of the collective experience of all the participants, the fact that any kind of structure (formal/informal) is a necessary (through not sufficient) condition for developing collective strength. The trainers should use the concepts of different kinds of network described in Appendix-A.

VIII.8. Sub-session 4: Stages of networks

This sub-session orients the participants about the stages of network. It is very important or participants to understand that networks cannot be built in one go and that it is a process. The participants should have knowledge of all stages of network for developing a strategy to build any network either of themselves or of the people (poor) themselves in their areas. It has to be remembered that the content of this sub-session is on the heavier side and, therefore, learner motivation has to be sustained by constantly connecting the concepts with real life examples from the experience of the participants and by a greater degree of innovation in the delivery of the inputs on the side of the trainer.

VIII.9. Sub-session 5: Functions and structure of network secretariat

The content matter of this sub-session covers the functions and structure of network secretariat. The purpose of this sub-session is to emphasise the technical issues of building network. There is great scope for cross learning during this sub-session, but it essentially rests upon the facilitation skills and knowledge of the trainer.

VIII.10. Sub-session 6: Role of facilitator (role of initiator of a network)

The sixth sub-session initiates a discussion about the role of facilitator/initiator of network. The operationalisation and creation of a network with elected members is a big challenge for the facilitator/initiator. This sub-session expands the practical understanding and skills of the participants for the functional management of networks.

VIII.11. Sub-session 7: Study of practices in networks of elected women representatives

This sub-session expands the awareness of the participants about the networks and its significant role in strengthening the role of elected women Panchayat members. The trainer should seize the opportunity to link the utility of network in building social capital.

VIII.12. Sub-session 8: Critiques of networks

The sub-session draws the attention of the participants to the critiques of network. It is important for the participants to realize that there are pitfalls in developing networks and there is a need to guard against the same. Avoiding the pitfalls would help avoid complications in using networks in social mobilisation.

VIII.13. Training methodology

The training methodology suggested in this section is predominantly participatory, along with the lecture method, visual method and small group discussion. Amongst the participatory methods experience sharing by the participants ought to be liberally used. Experience has shown that as almost all human beings are members of some networks (either knowingly or unknowingly), relating the concepts of networking to life experience of participants makes the learning enjoyable and durable.

IX. NOTE TO TRAINERS FOR USING SESSION 12: EMPOWERMENT OF WOMEN MEMBERS OF PRIS

IX.1. Introduction

Session 12 of the Module deals with the issue of empowerment of women elected members of Panchayats. Its contents include the concept and need of empowerment, elements of empowerment and strategic direction to strengthen empowerment of women in PRIs. This sub-session especially focuses upon the importance of the role of women elected members in PRIs. The sub-session, therefore, serves to sensitize the participants with their roles as a tool of empowerment of women.

IX.2. Training objectives

The session has the following training objectives:

- To equip the participants about the concept and need of empowerment of women;
- To enable the participants to understand the skills and abilities for empowerment of women PRI members; and
- To bring about a realization amongst the participants that they can act catalysts for empowerment of women.

IX.3. Sub-sessions, their training objectives and expected learning outcomes

There are three sub-sessions in this session which deal with the subject and they serially satisfy the sub-session's objectives. The training objective and the expected learning outcomes that fulfil the objective at the levels of both the individual participants and group are given in the following table:

S. No.	*Content*	*Training Objective*	*Expected Learning Outcomes*
1.	Concept and need (Why?) empowerment	To create the conceptual understanding of the participants about the empowerment	The participants have increased understanding of the concept and need of empowerment
2.	Elements of empowerment (Indicators and tools)	To expand the knowledge and awareness about the elements of women empowerment	The participants understand the elements of empowerment of women
3.	How to strengthen empowerment of women in PRIs	To create practical understanding about the strategy to strengthen empowerment of women elected members	The participants understand the approaches to strengthen empowerment of women elected members

IX.4. The Paradigm of empowerment of women elected members of Panchayats

The session twelve introduces the concept and need of empowerment of women elected members. The development paradigm that now dominates the politico-economic scenario in the country brings people at the centrestage. Additionally, the new paradigm's approach to development is empowerment of the people (poor) as distinct from welfarist approach to development. The 73rd Amendment has significant role to strengthen the leadership capacities of women elected members of Panchayats and empower women. It is very important that the women members of PRIs realize the importance of their role in development and how they can be catalysts in empowering themselves and poor women at large.

IX.5. Sub-session 1: Energizer

The sub-session begins with an energizer. The objective of the sub-session is to energize the group before they begin the sub-session of empowerment of women elected members of Panchayat. This also supports the subsequent group learning process.

IX.6. Sub-session 2: Concept and need (why?) for empowerment?

The second sub-session emphasizes the concept of empowerment. This sub-session equips the participants to understand the idea and need of empowerment. Here the trainer would attempt to tell the particiants more about the operational aspects of empowerment than about the theories underlying the present discourse on empowerment of women.

IX.7. Sub-session 3: Elements of empowerment (indicators and tools)

The content matter of this sub-session covers the elements of empowerment of women elected members. The purpose of this sub-session is to help the participants identify the elements that lead to their empowerment and how these elements can be strengthened to empower women members of PRIs. The trainer will be well-advised to draw the attention of the participants to elements of empowerment in the lives of the participants, such as their election to PRIs. The use of the empowerment circle comes in very handy. The trainer can use the example of Annexure–1 of this session, as an example of how an empowerment circle is contracted and interpreted.

IX.8. Sub-session 4: How to strengthen empowerment of women in PRIs

The fourth sub-session initiates a discussion about the strategic areas to strengthen empowerment of women elected members. It is very important for participants to understand the strategic approaches to empowerment of women in general and of the women members of the Panchayat in particular.

IX.9. Empowerment of women absence of violence

In this session the intention is that the trainer should facilitate a process where the participants reflect on what are the kinds of violence perpetrated on them especially, if any and on women in society generally. Violence against women could be reflected upon in three categories: violence in home; violence in the workplace and violence in larger social environment. Specific legal safe-guards against them and use of social capital and social mobilisation, to counter violence against women, has to be brought into the picture.

IX.10. Training methodology

The training methodology suggested in this section is predominantly based upon Participatory Learning and Action Methods, the lecture method, case study and small group discussions. Role play can also be used depending on the availability of time as role plays take longer than other methods in a training environment.

IX.11. Duration of training

The session requires a day of training. The total duration of the training is estimated to be 215 minutes.

X. NOTES TO TRAINERS FOR USING SESSION 13: MICRO LEVEL PLANNING

X.1. Introduction

This section imparts a set of functional skills to the participants to facilitate micro-level planning that is necessary for initiating community development through *praxis*. The section is a natural sequel to the previous ones, which are designed to sensitize the participants to the philosophy of people-centred development and stakeholder participation in the development process. The seeds of the future involvement of stakeholders are sown at the planning stage. The section thus completes the women *Capability Spectrum* in terms of knowledge, skills and attitudes that the elected members of the Panchayati Raj institutions must necessarily possess for facilitating the process of people-centred development in their communities.

It is classified here that this session is considered important though micro-planning is yet to be initiated in any state on a substantive scale, because the intention here is to equip women will the necessary skills to discharge their responsibilities, including those under Article 243-ZD of the Constitution of India. Judged in that perspective the session is (what we say for want of a better phrase) both "futuristic" and "pre-emptive".

X.2. Training objectives

The training objectives of this session are as follows:

- To enable the participants to comprehend the process of people's participation in planning for empowerment of women for gender equity; and
- To equip the participants with the functional skills required for engaging in planning for gender equity and social justice at the micro-level.

X.3. Sub-sessions, their training objectives and expected learning outcomes

The session has five sub-sessions on Micro-Level Planning. The first five sessions are geared to satisfy the two stated objectives. For each session, the expected learning outcomes at the end of the session that demonstrate the fulfilment of the two training objectives, at the levels of both the individual participants and group have been identified.

The sub-session-wise training objectives and the expected learning outcomes are given in the following Table:

Sub-Session No.	*Sub-Session Description*	*Training Objectives*	*Expected Learning Outcomes*
1	The dream village: **Vision**	(a) To enable the participants to comprehend the process of stakeholder participation in planning for women's development	(a) The participants visualize their dream village and articulate their vision for village development.

(*Contd.*)

Sub-Session No.	*Sub-Session Description*	*Training Objectives*	*Expected Learning Outcomes*
		(b) To equip the participants with the functional skills required for engaging in micro-level planning for gender equity and social justice	(b) They acquire functional skills for using PLA methods in developing a perspective for village development.
2	Context analysis for tactical planning	(a) To help participants learn and understand an analysis of their current status and status of women in general in their villages. (b) To equip the participants with the functional skills required for engaging in analysis of different kinds essential for planning for women's empowerment, gender equity and social justice	(a) The participants are able to contextualize their dream map (vision) to the realities existing at the village level. (b) They acquire functional skills for using PLA methods in analyzing the existing condition of women in general and women elected representatives in particular in their village/Panchayat
3	Problem identification and prioritization	(a) To help participants discover and understand their current problems and problems of women in general in their villages. (b) To equip the participants with the functional skills required for engaging in identification of	(a) The participants acquire functional skills for using PLA methods in identifying the problems contorting for village development. (b) They can adopt a problem-solving approach for prioritizing development problems.

(Contd.)

Sub-Session No.	*Sub-Session Description*	*Training Objectives*	*Expected Learning Outcomes*
		different problems and prioritizing them, vital for women's empowerment, gender equity and social justice	
4	Solution identification and prioritization	(a) To help participants discover and identify solutions to their current problems and problems of women in general in their villages. (b) To equip the participants with the functional skills required for identification of solutions to problems and prioritizing them for women's empowerment, gender equity and social justice	(a) The participants acquire functional skills for using PLA methods in finding solutions to problems identified in the previous session (b) They can adopt a problem-solving approach for prioritizing solutions for development problems
5	Action Planning	(a) To help participants generate an action plan for tackling their current problems and problems of women in general in their villages, from a tactical plan (b) To equip the participants with the functional skills required for developing an action plan for women's empowerment, gender equity and social justice	(a) The participants acquire functional skills for using PLA methods in developing action plans for empowerment of women representatives of PRIs (b) They have a hands-on understanding of how to develop an action plan from a tactical plan.

(*Contd.*)

X. 4. Sub-session 1 of Session 13: Visioning

In this initial sub-session, the participants are encouraged to prepare a map of their dream village as a first step towards micro-level planning. This sub-session seeks to explore and expand the development vision of the participants and help them articulate their perspective of empowering women in PRIs and women in general. It is imperative for women members of Village Panchayats to possess the essential ability to envision their future development in its entirety. They have first to understand what their development is all about, in a state of gender inequity and social injustice? This sub-session, therefore, attempts to develop the participants' vision based upon their own development perspectives in relation to empowerment of women members of PRIs.

X. 5. Sub-session 2 of Session 13: Context analysis

In the second sub-session, participatory methods are used to conduct the context analysis for preparing a development plan to secure gender equity and social justice. This analysis is done based upon village level realities and with reference to four areas:

(a) Analysis of space, which includes analysis of resources available, infrastructure, social condition, etc. by using resource mapping, infrastructure mapping, social mapping etc.
(b) Analysis of time which includes evolution of the village, seasonality of income, food availability, employment, opportunities, credit needs, etc. by using topical seasonality diagrams etc.
(c) Analysis of relationships which includes an analysis of the importance of different institutions and their utility etc. to the community and the inter-relationships between the institutions, with which the community has interface, by using Venn Diagramming etc.
(d) Analysis of preferences and priorities, which includes preferences for crops, trees, food, livelihood, seasons, institutions etc. by using ranking, scoring and matrix ranking etc.

X.6. Sub-session 3 of Session 13: Problem prioritization

This sub-session involves the participants in acquiring the skills required to facilitate the community in identification and prioritization of problems confronting women members of PRIs and their needs which have to be addressed by the planning process. The identification of problems of women and women members of PRIs is done by involving different groups in the process, especially women and other socially excluded groups. It may also be emphasized that there may be a need to carry out the exercise of problem identification with different groups such as aged and old women, girl children, women who are differently-abled etc. The PLA tools used in this sub-session are the same as used in sub-session 2 above.

X.7. Sub-session 4 of Session 13: Solution prioritization

In this sub-session, the skills to help women members of PRIs identify or range of solutions or suitable development activities and match them with the needs voiced in the previous sub-session are imparted. A method/ technique for prioritization of the solution is then applied for arriving at an optimal set of development interventions. Perspectives related to gender and social justice are also explored and included in the set of activities that are listed.

X.8. Sub-session 5 of Session 13: Action planning

In this last sub-session, the *Micro-Level Plan* prepared by the process adopted in the last four sessions is transformed into a *Tactical Plan* by:

(i) Fitting the plan within a definite time frame by specifying the time horizons for the proposed development activities.
(ii) Allocating the activities amongst the major stakeholders: people themselves, PRIs, NGOs, banks, governments, combination of all of these and residual etc.
(iii) Specifying the financial allocations available from different funding sources for each of these activities.

Trainers are also advised to read the discussion on micro planning in D. Bandyopadhyay, Amitava Mukherjee and Mitali Sen Gavai: *Empowering Panchayats, Handbook for Master Trainers*, using *Participatory Approach* (New Delhi: Concept Publishing Co.) 2004.

XI. NOTES TO TRAINERS FOR USING SESSION 14: GROUP DYNAMICS AND GROUP BEHAVIOURS

XI.1. Introduction

This section is designed to widen the understanding of the participants on group dynamics and impart a set of skills to manage group behaviour. This session is considered critical because understanding group-dynamics and managing group behaviour are basic bedrocks on which use of social capital for development, social mobilization and micro-level planning, as transformative strategy is used. Additionally, this session provides the trainer with an opportunity to remind the women members of the Panchayats that they are leaders in their own right and hence managing groups and group behaviour are central to their functioning.

XI.2. Training objectives

The training objectives of this session are as follows:

- To enable the participants to understand the meaning of a group, how groups behave, what are the group processes, how groups make decisions, how conflicts can arise, all common features in Gram Sabhas and Gram Panchayats.
- To equip the participants with skills so that they can resolve conflicts and communicate effectively.
- To impart to the participants some key leadership skills in the context of the Panchayats.

XI.3. Sub-Sessions, and their expected learning outcomes

The session on group dynamics and group behaviours as parts of management orientation of the participants is placed at the end of the training module. This has been done with the deliberate purpose of allowing the trainer to emphasize that the women elected members are leaders in their own areas and relate the role of a leader in different aspects of grass-roots democracy such as networking, social mobilization, social capital formation and micro-level planning. The training objectives and the expected training outcomes are given in the table below:

Sr. No.	*Sub-session contents*	*Training objective*	*Expected training outcomes*
1.	What is a group? Group processes	Impart to the participants an understanding of group processes and relate the same to the functioning of Panchayats with special reference to women	The participants will be equipped to understand the concept of group, what makes a group different from a "set" of individuals and relate the same with their experiences as women elected members of Panchayats, and be able to see how to convert a set of individuals into a group. This is critical for networking, social capital and social mobilization.

(*Contd.*)

Sr. No.	*Sub-session contents*	*Training objective*	*Expected training outcomes*
2.	Participation	To make the participants understand the meaning of participation, a much talked about but less understood term.	The participants will be better placed to understand the different kinds of participation as a fundamental process in a group and their criticality in grassroots democracy.
3.	Decision making in context to Panchayat	The participants are equipped with the knowledge about how decisions are made in a group.	Women elected members become aware of the reasons why decisions are made (or not made) and are equipped to make decisions in different ways.
4.	Conflict resolution	The participants are made aware of the concept of conflicts and the steps necessary for resolving a conflict.	Women elected members have the skills to lead a process of conflict resolution in a situation where conflicts of every description afflict Gram Panchayats almost on a daily basis.
5.	Communication	To make the participants understand that they cannot, not communicate. And appreciate the various modes of communication and barriers to communication.	The participants are able to use different channels of communication better and overcome barriers to communication, so critical in a democratic polity.
6.	Leadership	To make the participants aware of the leadership skills and appreciate the different leadership styles, given that they are all leaders in their own fields.	The participants are able to choose, adopt or develop leadership styles that may be most appropriate for their local level situation.
7.	Synthesis of learning	Summarize the entire Session.	The participants get an integrated view of the different subjects covered and see the inter-relationships.

XI.4. Sub-session on group concept and process

In the initial sub-session of Session-14, the participants are encouraged to think about the concept of group. They reflect on the meaning of a group, organise their thoughts and then articulate their views. Diversity of views should be encouraged by the trainer and then they are synthesized. From the synthesis, the meaning of a group as understood in scientific literature is developed and articulated by the trainer. It is important to bear in mind that adults learn by checking concepts with their experience. Hence reconciling the ideas of a group that participants have with the scientific definition of the term is an essential part of this sub-session.

XI.5. Sub-session 2 of Session XIV: participation

Participation is key to the functioning of the Panchayats as has been repeatedly emphasized in this Handbook. Indeed in the training methodology used in this Handbook and its companion volume, participation is central. Hence clarifying what is meant by participation, the centrality of participation in the functioning of the Panchayats and what are the ways and means through which people participate in a group are so important.

XI.6. Sub-session 3 of Session XIV: Decision making in the context of Panchayats

After having explained and clarified the meaning of group and participation, it becomes necessary to relate these concepts to Panchayats. This sub-session affords the trainer an opportunity to contentualise the concepts of group and participation *vis-à-vis* the Panchayats, in the process of creating an understanding of the process of decision making in the Panchayats. Since people centred development and social capital formation as also social mobilisation are being advocated as a means to uplift the people, their participation in Panchayats needs a special treatment.

XI.7. Sub-session 4 of Session XIV: Conflict Resolution

Conflict is part of our daily lives. Conflicts in Panchayats and in Gram Sabhas are likely to occur. Women members of Panchayats, as local leaders, should be equipped to resolve conflicts both in their communities and in the Panchayats. This sub-session is to impart essential skills in conflict resolution. The focus of sub-session should be more on skill building than on imparting knowledge.

XI.8. Sub-session 5: Communication in group dynamics and group behaviour

Communication in a democracy has multiple roles and there are multiple modes of communication which people use, without often realizing the same. The trainer in this sub-session needs to make the participants aware of the modes of communication and build their capacity to use them effectively. For example, while people are aware of communication through written language or verbal articulation, they do not always realize that their facial expression and their body language communicate more than written or spoken words. The trainer should refer to Chapter 1 for a more detailed discussion on the issue. Similarly the importance of listening (especially for elected representatives) in communication has to be brought out in sharp focus and the art of listening imparted.

XI.9. Sub-session 6: Leadership in group dynamics and group behaviour

Women elected representatives of Panchayats have a leadership role in society, community and the Panchayats. In a men's world providing effective leadership by women elected representatives, is beset with barriers. This sub-session will help participants understand their leadership style and the range of possibilities.

XI.10. Sub-session 7

The trainer has to synthesize the learning. This session deals with an area that forms the basic stepping stone for building the capacity of a woman elected member. Hence the trainer should use the outputs from the sub-sessions to synthesize and summarise the findings.

Chapter 3

TRAINING SESSIONS

SESSION 1 GENERAL ORIENTATION

Session Theme	INTRODUCTIONS AND ICE-BREAKING
Duration	80 minutes
Venue	Classroom without fixed furniture
Seating	Sit and stand on the floor forming a circle; move around the room for the game; sit in circle for the ranking method.
Session Objective	*To create a feeling of comradeship among participants and trainers.*

Expected Learning Outcomes

- The participants and trainers are acquainted with each other and begin to form a sympathetic group.
- The participants understand the training design, purpose and methodology.
- The trainer becomes aware of the expectations of the participants from the training programme.

Content Flow and Training Methodology

Sr. No.	*Content*	*Training Methodology*	*Training Aids*	*Duration (in minutes)*
1.	Welcoming the participants	**Step 1** Talk by the Trainer	As desired by the trainer[1]	10
2.	Game for introductions and ice-breaking	**Step 2** Seed Game	Seeds of various kinds	20

(Contd.)

1. Use as many visual aids as possible.

3.	Overview of training goal, content, methodology and scope	**Step 3** Visual Method	Posters and slides	20
4.	Expectations of participants from the training	**Step 4** Ranking Method	Flash cards, flip charts and marker pens, seeds/ pebbles	30

THE METHODOLOGICAL STEPS FOR SESSION 1

1. The trainer welcomes the participants

This introductory sub-session is crucial for creating the desired ambience for the adult learning process to begin. It also sets the stage for the use of PLA-based training methodology. It creates a feeling of comradeship amongst the participants and the trainers. This solidarity promotes group learning more effectively. The trainer is urged to keep the introductory session informal, open, semi-structured and of good humour. This will serve to induct everybody into a participatory mood and training environment.

In Step 1, it is suggested that heavy, didactic and literary introductory speeches be avoided, since this will not be congruent with the participatory training that follows. The participants should feel that this training is different from any other previous training. It is important to remember that the session has been designed to facilitate the opening up of lines of communication among the participants *inter se* and among the participants and the trainers present in the classroom.

2. Play the Seed Game for making introductions and ice-breaking with the participants

In Step 2, the Seed Game is played for helping the participants know each other and ice-breaking. The objective of the game is to introduce the participants to each other and to begin the training on an informal note that would encourage learner participation in the future. The steps for playing the game are given below:

2.1. This game is suitable for a group of 20-25 participants. Keep four to five kinds of seeds in sufficient numbers on a table. Each participant picks up a number of seeds that is equal to the number of participants. Each participant picks up only one kind of seed and keeps all the seeds in the left hand.

2.2. The participants then go around the room introducing themselves to each other and the trainer. Each time a participant introduces herself to another, she gives away one seed to the person she introduces herself to and gets one seed from that person in return. She keeps the seeds received in this way in her right hand.

2.3. Then at the end of the game, the participant should have no seed in her left hand and as many seeds, but of different varieties collected in her right hand, if she has met all the participants. Each participant thus personally introduces herself to the others. This provides a personal touch to these introductions and also for participant-bonding.

3. *Visual overview of training design, content, methodology and scope*

In step 3, posters and/or flip charts and slides are used for the overview of the training design. This has a greater impact upon the participants, especially on the neo-literates/semi-literates who usually form a major part of such training audiences. The trainer is encouraged to create her own posters, flip charts and slides for introducing the training goal, design and methodology. The trainer must especially inform the participants about the participatory nature of training and express the hope that they will be whole-heartedly involved.

4. *Catalogue and prioritise the expectations of the participants from the training programme*

In Step 4, we use the Ranking Method, the steps for which are described below:

4.1. The participants are provided with flash cards and marker pens with a request to catalogue their expectations and write down one expectation on each flash card. But they can have as many flash cards as they may wish to have. After about five minutes, they are encouraged to place their cards on the floor.

4.2. The expectations are then classified into clusters wherever such classification is possible. For example, expectations of the participants can be to learn negotiation skills, nitty-gritty of Panchayati Raj working, experience sharing, etc. These expectations can be classified under several heads; inter-personal relationships, functional skills, knowledge about structure and role of PRIs, how to conduct the business of the Village Panchayat, information about development programmes and so on.

4.3. The participants are now.encouraged to club together common or similar expectations, if any. Usually, there are several in each cluster. Once the common expectations are clubbed, there will be a single list of expectations under each category.

4.4. The lists are then examined and discussed. It may not be possible to fulfil some of the expectations through training because of resource or other constraints. The situation may be explained to the participants and such expectations may be thereafter discarded by consensus.

4.5. If the number of expectations is too large, there may be a need to prioritise them. For this purpose, scoring may be used. Scoring can be of three kinds: **Free Scoring**[2], **Fixed Scoring**[3] and **Vector Scoring**[4].

4.6. Use any of the Scoring Methods for this exercise by taking up each expectation and asking the participants to give it a score using flexible material like seeds, pebbles, etc. considering its importance.

4.7. Allow participants enough time to reflect. Give them some key questions as pointers to think.

4.8. Once the prioritisaion is over, with the consent of the participants, the top ten expectations may be retained as those that are the most important. This number could vary according to the judgment of the facilitator.

4.9. Cards depicting the chosen expectations are then pasted on flip charts and displayed till the end of training. Recall the relevant expectations whenever they are being fulfilled in the course of the training. The trainer may keep a checklist for self-assessment *vis-à-vis* the list of expectations. The list is also useful for designing future training interventions.

---

2. Scoring is free when the participants score by placing seeds, etc. in ascending or descending quantities, with no upper limit on the number or amount of seeds placed.
3. In Fixed Scoring, scores are given to each item, where the maximum that an item can get will be equal to the number of items.
4. In Vector Scoring places, the scores are allotted on a scale chosen by the participants themselves on say a scale of 0-10 or 0-5 or 1-100 and so on.

SESSION 2 GENERAL ORIENTATION

Session Theme	**PRINCIPLES OF PANCHAYATI RAJ GOVERNANCE**
Duration	190 minutes
Venue	Classroom without fixed furniture
Seating	Sit and stand on the floor forming circles for the group work; move around the room for the games
Session Objective	*To expand the conceptual understanding of the participants about the basic principles of Panchayati Raj governance*

Expected Learning Outcomes

- The participants have an increased understanding of the philosophy of self-government; the concept and principles underlying PRIs; the participants become aware of their rights.

Content Flow and Training Methodology

Sr. No.	*Content*	*Training Methodology*	*Training Aids*	*Duration (in minutes)*
1.	Game for Introductions and Ice-breaking	**Step 1** Name Game	None	15
2.	(a) To emphasise that what the participants know about Panchayati Raj institutions is of value (b) History of the evolution of Panchayati Raj institutions	**Step 2** Johari's Window **Step 3** Timeline to trace the evolution of the PRIs and the underlying motive for setting up the PRI system	Flip charts, flash cards and marker pens	70[5]

(*Contd.*)

5. It is suggested that the duration indicated for the sessions that use PLA based training methods may be factored thus: preparation time: 50 minutes, presentation and Discussion time: 20 minutes, total: 70 minutes. However, this is only a suggested time. The trainer is free to modify these limites using his best judgment.

Sr. No.	*Content*	*Training Methodology*	*Training Aids*	*Duration (in minutes)*
3.	Democratic decentralization (a) Its true meaning; underlying concepts and philosophy (b) Factors that make democratic decentralisation work (c) The fundamental basis of PRIs: self-government with the attendant responsibilities, transparency and accountability	**Step 4** Brainstorming **Step 5** Delphi Technique **Step 6** Listing, Sorting and Matrix Scoring	Cards, marker pens, Flip charts and seeds of different varieties for the scoring/ sorting exercise	45 45
4.	Synthesis of learning points by trainer/participants	**Step 7** Visual Method	Overhead slides, flip charts, cards prepared by the participants	15 minutes

THE METHODOLOGICAL STEPS FOR SESSION 2

1. *Play the Name Game to get to know each other better*

In Step 1, the Name Game[6] has been suggested for which the steps are as follows:

1.1. The objectives of the game are to speed up the process of becoming acquainted and to help everyone learn the names of the other participants.

6. Adapted from Pretty *et al.*, 1995

1.2. Introduce and explain the exercise to the participants. Start the first round in which everybody carefully says his/her name. This is done slowly so that others have time to repeat it and find a way to link the name to that participant. Write the unusual names on the board.
1.3. When this round is completed, then the trainer says, 'My name is ....' Points out another participant (B), says B's name and asks B to look for a person C, giving C's name, and so on. For example, the trainer says: 'My name is Vijaya your name is Meena. Meena will you please find Amrita? The trainer should not look at Amrita herself. Also, ask the rest of the group not to help.
1.4. Continue until everyone has had a turn.
1.5. This is a simple and effective exercise, which works well in new groups. This will also strengthen the introductions already made in the previous session and help facilitate the group dynamics.
1.6. Finally, ask participants to say all the names in the group in the order in which they are seated. The participants may be asked to exchange chairs to crosscheck whether each participants knows the names of the others.

---

2. *Use the Johari's Window to emphasise that the participants know about Panchayati Raj institutions*

Step 2, the Johari's Window provides the starting point for beginning the discussion on the subject of Panchayati Raj institutions in the training programme. The use of the Window will tell the participants that there is a lot to learn from each other. Thus, there is a lot to learn from people. This also helps establish the need for participatory learning, planning, monitoring, evaluation and capacity building. The Window is explained below:

Johari's Windows

	We Know	We do not Know	
They Know	1	2	
They do not Know	3	4	

Please use figure 15 (which is a pictorial depiction of Johari's Window) also to illustrate the concept.

In this exercise, we start from Box 1 of the Window. This box indicates that there is knowledge which is known to both of them (insiders/villager) and us (outsiders). Then we move to Box 2, which indicates that there is knowledge which they know and we do not know. Then in the third stage, we move to Box 3, which indicates that there is some knowledge, which is known to us, but they do not know. Then attention is focused on Box 4, which indicates that some knowledge is unknown to both them and us. Each Box is explored in the context of the evolution of the PRIs. This exercise emphasises the point that people know their knowledge is to be sought and respected.

2.1 The **Johari's Window**[7] is further illustrated below:

Box 1: Open Knowledge What we know and what they know	*Box 2: Hidden Knowledge* What they know and we do not know
Box 3: Blindness What we know and they do not know	***Box 4: Knowledge that will be revealed*** What we do not know and they do not know

3. Trace the evolution of the Panchayati Raj institutions by drawing a Timeline

In step 3, the participants draw a Timeline that traces the evolution of the PRIs. The Timeline traces the evolution of the Panchayati Raj Institutions and visualises the gradual changes that have occurred in village level power structures. It initiates a process of group learning. An example of a Timeline of a PRIs in India prepared in a different context, is given in Figure 2. The steps in doing the Timeline are described below:

3.1. Identify a group of persons and request them to talk about the history of their village. Initiate a discussion about the history of their Village Panchayat. Alternatively, an elderly person of village may be engaged in this activity.

3.2. Some suggested key Village Panchayat established?

- When was the village panchayat established?
- What are the important events in the history of the village panchayat?
- What major changes took place?
- How have these changes affected the community?
- What are the reasons for these changes?

7. Adapted from Pretty *et al.*, 1995

Figure 2: Time-Line: Decentralisation and Local Governance in India

Year	*Major Events*
1952	Community Development and Sahakari Samaj
1957	Balwantrai Mehta Committee
1958-1959	State Government enacting Panchayat Acts
1959	Jawaharlal Nehru inaugurating the first generation Panchayats in Rajasthan (Nagaur)
1962	ZP Act of UP
1964-1977	Decline of First Generation of PR
1966-1967	Ministry of Community Development became a department under Ministry of Food & Agriculture
1977	Tribal sub-plan in Tribal Area commenced
1977	Asoka Mehta Committee
1978	Asoka Mehta Committee Report Submitted
1978	West Bengal Panchayat elections on political party lines. The beginning of second generation PR
1978	Zinabhai Darj Committee on Social Justice/Orient elections
1983	Karnataka Government following West Bengal Panchayat Act, ushers in PR
1985	Andhra Pradesh followed suit
1980's	Idea of district government especially the writings of Nirmal Mukharji came to be recognized
1988	Parliament Consultative Committee under P.K. Thungan made its recommendations
1989 May 15	63th Constitutional Amendment Bill introduced in Parliament
1989 Oct. 15	The 63th Constitutional Amendment Bill was defeated in Rajya Sabha
1990 Sep. 7	64th Constitutional Amendment Bill introduced in Parliament
1990	Panchayats were brought under Administrators in Karnataka
1991 Sep.	72nd (Panchayats) and 73rd (Nagarpalika) Amendments introduced in Parliament, Referred to Joint Select Committee of Parliament
1992 Dec. 22	Lok Sabha passed the Bills (as 73rd and 74th Amendments) on Panchayats and Nagarpalikas
1992 Dec. 23	Rajya Sabha passed the Bills
1993 April 24	The 73rd Amendment Act was brought into force
May 30	The 74th Amendment Act was brought in force
1994 May 30	Madhya Pradesh was the first state to hold the Panchayat elections under the new dispensation
1996 Dec.	The 73rd Amendment was extended to Scheduled Areas
1996	Kerala launched People's Plan Campaign a unique experiment under the new Panchayati Raj lauded nationally and internationally
2001	Bihar was the last state to hold the first election (after 23 years) under the new system

3.3. Ask one of the participants to note downs the major events briefly on cards in bold letters. If the participants are unable to do so, one of the facilitators can help.
3.4. Once the participants feel the list of events is more or less complete, ask them to keep the cards in a chronological order—the earlier events on the top and the later events lower down. Request them to read out the events and ask them whether they are happy with the order or if they would like to modify it.
3.5. Add years to the left side of the events. Failure of memory and not using their system of calendar may come as a big block for the participants in getting the exact years. Use the best judgment to arrive at the years.
3.6. Now initiate a discussion on the Timeline to help the participants analyze and reflect on it. Interview the Timeline by asking open-ended questions to clarify doubts or to get an in-depth understanding about the evolution of the Village Panchayat.
3.7. The trainer may fill in any gaps as and when required, but record what gaps the trainer is filling.
3.8. Then request them to relate these events to years. If years cannot be recalled, ask them to associate the events to major happenings such as a war, flood, drought, death of a national figure and so on. Then locate the year of occurrence, according to the major happenings.

4. Brainstorm to catalogue the concepts and philosophy of Panchayati Raj governance

In Step 4, use Brainstorm, for which the process is described below:

4.1. The objective of the Brainstorm exercise is to catalogue the concepts and philosophy of Panchayati Raj governance. This provides a valuable starting point for discussing about the fundamentals of the PRI system. The list of the concepts developed through this exercise is based upon the collective insights of the participant-group. It forms the basis for further discussion, grouping, sorting, prioritization and problem solving.
4.2. Ask the participants to nominate a facilitator who will not participate, but merely record the ideas.
4.3. Ask the group to think of the concepts and philosophy of PRIs based upon their own experience.
4.4. Encourage all the participants to think adventurously. Emphasize the number rather than the quality of ideas.

4.5. Let the ideas flow freely without any comments or evaluation being made.
4.6. The facilitator writes each idea on a flash card. All the flash cards are laid on the floor of the classroom in one column or row.
4.7. Evaluate the list after the Brainstorm if over.

---

5. Next cluster the brainstorm ideas by the Delphi Technique

In Step 5, use the Delphi Technique for which the steps are described below:

5.1. The Brainstorm exercise would have generated a list of the underlying concepts and philosophy of Panchayati Raj governance and each idea/concept would have been recorded on a card (only one idea per card).
5.2. The cards are then grouped according to the concept areas such as "units of self governance", "power to the people", and so on. One, some or all the participants can do this exercise. Exact duplicated are removed.
5.3. Each concept cluster denotes a particular theme area which is then discussed with the participants.

---

6. Do Matrix Scoring to examine the functioning of the Village Panchayat

---

In Step 6, Listing, Scoring and Matrix Scoring are done by the participants on the responsibilities of the Village Panchayat. This exercise helps the participants:

- Facilitate so that the participants catalogue their responsibilities as members of the Village Panchayat.
- Facilitate so that the participants reflect on the concept of self-government.

The steps to be followed in this exercise are given below:

6.1. Explain clearly the purpose of the exercise to the participants, namely, that it will help to bring out their responsibilities as Village Panchayat functionaries.
6.2. Initiate a discussion about the responsibilities of the Village Panchayat. Let the participants list down the various responsibilities that are discussed, one on each flash cards. Place the flash cards as one column.

6.3. Ask the participants to score or rank their responsibilities, scoring can be done by either the free, fixed or vector scoring method.

6.4. Now ask the participants the criteria against which they have ranked/scored their responsibilities. Place these as the first row.

6.5. Now facilitate so that the participants score each responsibility against the criteria.

6.6. Ensure that the criteria are all positive and precise. Use of positive and negative criteria in the same exercise can be confusing.

6.7. Help the participants draw up a matrix with the responsibilities top to bottom and criteria left to right. The participants can do it the other way round also. However, keep in mind that the comparisons are made by the participants criterion-wise and not responsibility-wise. It means that the participants take up a criterion and then do scoring for all the responsibilities. Once one criterion is over, they move to the next, do the scoring for all the responsibilities and record them until all criteria are covered for each of the items.

6.8. Now ask the participants to score/rank each responsibility against *"accountability"* and *"transparency"*.

6.9. (Note: There will be two matrices scored, one with the criteria against responsibility suggested by the participants, and the other with the criteria of *"accountability"* and *"transparency"* against the responsibilities).

6.10. Now initiate discussion. See if they perceive that the more important responsibilities (according to the first Matrix mentioned above) are also the responsibilities that they carry out with transparency and accountability. If not, explore these questions:

- What are the reasons?
- What needs to be done?
- What are the inhibiting and facilitating factors? etc.

6.11. Figure 3 gives an example of using the Matrix Scoring Method for the institutions that the Village Panchayat has to network with. The same method can be used for analyzing the functioning of the Village Panchayat as described above.

7. Visual method for synthesizing what we have learnt from this Session

In Step 7, the trainer fills in any knowledge gaps that may remain and then concludes the session by synthesizing the learning points. The trainer should point out that she is now trying to fill in Box 3 of Johari's Window. This may be done by using a set of overhead transparencies stating the points in very simple language. The flip charts or the cards prepared by the participants can be used. Alternatively, one of the participants can be requested to do the synthesis.

Figure 3: Example of Matrix Scoring for Institutional Analysis[8]

Criteria *Institutions*	*Sensitivity to the Problems of the Village Panchayat*	*Willingness to work in villages*	*Enforcement/ compliance with rules*	*Honesty*	*Local problem solving ability*	*Overall rank*
Police Station	●●	●●●●● ●●●●● ●●●●	●●●●● ●●●●	●	●●●●● ●●●●● ●●●●	3
Health Centre	●●●●● ●●●●●	●●●●●● ●●●●●●	●●●●● ●●●●● ●●●●	●●●●●	●●●●● ●●●●●	2
School	●●●●● ●●●●●	●●●●●● ●●●●●●	●●●●● ●●●●●	●●●●● ●●●●● ●●●●	●●●●● ●●●●● ●●●●	1
Patwari's Office	●●●●● ●●	●●●●●● ●●●	●●●●	●	●●●●● ●●●●● ●●●●	5
Block Office	●●	●●●●●● ●●●●	●●●●● ●●●	●	●●●●● ●●	8
Collector's Office	●●	●●●●●●	●●●●● ●●●●● ●●●●	●●●●	●●●●●	6
DRDA	●●●●●	●●●●●	●●●●● ●●●●● ●●●●	●●●●	●●●● ●●●●● ●	4
Election Commission	●	●●	●●●●● ●●●●●	●●●●● ●●●●● ●●●●	●●●	7
State Government	●●	●●	●●●●● ●●●●●	●●●●●	●●	9

Note:

1. **Free Scoring** has been used. The ranking has been done vertically for each criterion. The next step is to analyse the **Matrix Scoring** by highlighting the emerging issues and drawing relevant action points. For instance, from the above **Matrix Scoring** exercise, the following points emerge:

---

8. *Source*: Training of Trainers Workshop at HIPA, Gurgaon; Participants: Rajeshwari, Ramakanthan, Rita Singh, Pokhriyal and others; Facilitated by Amitava Mukherjee and Mitali Sen Gavai.

2. Very few of the institutions are sensitive to the problems of the Village Panchayat.
3. All the institutions are very keen to implement and enforce rules and are bureaucratic.
4. A majority of the institutions get low scores for the criterion of "*Honesty*".
5. The institutions outside the village do not score well for the criterion "Willingness to work in villages".
6. This exercise, therefore, conscientises the participants about these institutions. They can consider the following course of action for their Village Panchayats:
   - The participants, especially the elected Village Panchayat members, can demand that these institutions become more sensitive to their needs and helped effectively in solving local level problems. They can demand better quality service from them.
   - After exploring as to why these institutions are not rated very high on "honesty", the participants can seek greater transparency, accountability and social audit.

SESSION 3 ROLE OF VILLAGE PANCHAYATS

Session Theme	ROLE OF VILLAGE PANCHAYAT
Duration	180 minutes
Venue	Classroom without any fixed furnitures
Seating	Sit/stand on the ground forming a circle
Session Objectives	*To conscientise the participants about their rights and duties as members of the Village Panchayat and generate an urge in them to seek their rights*

Expected Learning Outcomes

Increased awareness about:

- Their own rights and duties,
- The rightful place of the Village Panchayat in grassroots governance,
- Its role, responsibilities and functions; and
- What is necessary for having those rights, responsibilities and functions?

Content Flow and Training Methodology

Sr. No.	*Content*	*Training Methodology*	*Training Aids*	*Duration (in minutes)*
1.	*De jure* Functions of the Village Panchayat	**Step 1** Brainstorming **Step 2** Delphi Method	Flip charts, flash cards, marker pens	15 45
2.	*De facto* functions of the Village Panchayat	**Step 3** Brainstorming **Step 4** Delphi Method	Flip charts, flash cards, marker pens	15 45

(*Contd.*)

Sr. No.	*Content*	*Training Methodology*	*Training Aids*	*Duration (in minutes)*
3.	How empowered is the Village Panchayat?	**Step 5** Empowerment Circle	Large sheets of paper, flip charts, several coloured marker pens, flash cards, seeds, Post-It stickers, bindis	45
4.	Synthesis of learning points by trainer/ participant (s)	**Step 6** Visual Method	Overhead slides, Flip Charts	15

THE METHODOLOGICAL STEPS FOR SESSION 3

1. Brainstorm the de jure functions of the Village Panchayat

In Step 1, use Brainstorming to determine the de jure functions of the Village Panchayat, i.e., those functions which the Village Panchayat is required to perform according to the rules or statute. The attention of the participants should be drawn to the 29 development functions that are listed in the Eleventh Schedule of the Indian Constitution. These may be discussed with particular reference to the following areas:

- The raising of resources in the Village Panchayat;
- The powers of taxation and borrowing of the Village Panchayat;
- Planning for social development at the Village Panchayat level;
- Affirmative action for gender and social justice;
- Management of programmes for social and economic development at the Village Panchayat level; and
- Public service delivery by the Village Panchayat based upon the principles of equity, responsiveness, transparency, accountability, etc.

2. Use the Delphi Method to make the concept clusters of the de jure functions

2.1. Request volunteers to write each function on a card/paper (only one function per card/paper).

Figure 4: Empowerment Circle

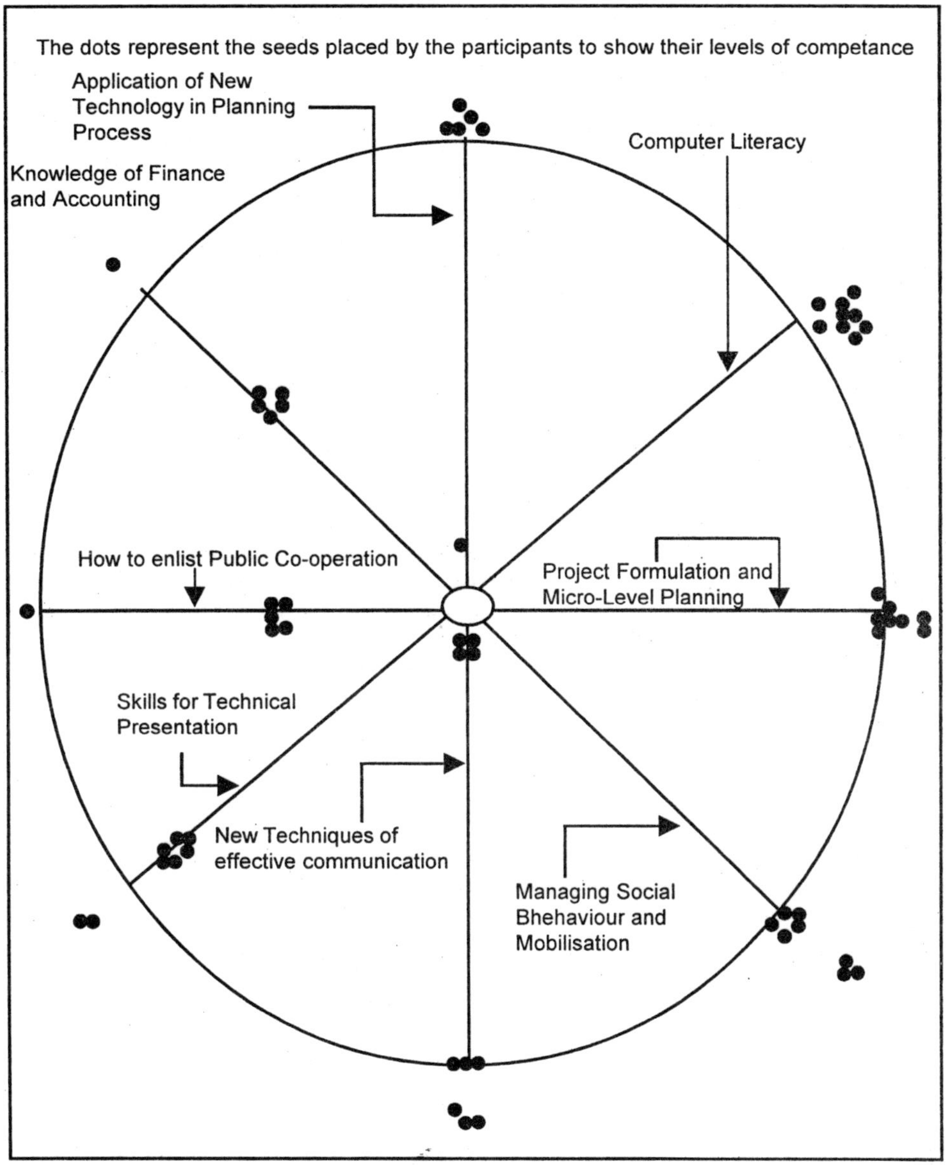

2.2. The cards/papers are then placed upon the ground or pinned or pasted on the wall and grouped according to their concept areas. One, some or all the participants can do this exercise. Exact duplicates are removed.
2.3. The participants must agree on the criteria for grouping or clustering, since these provide the theme areas.
2.4. Now discuss each theme with the participants.

3. *Next Brainstorm the de facto functions of the Village Panchayat*

In Step 3, again use brainstorming to generate the de facto functions, i.e., those functions, which the Village Panchayat performs, but is not required, repeat not required to perform according to the rules or statute.

4. *Use the Delphi Method to make the concept clusters of the de facto functions*

In Step 4, use the Delphi Method to form the concept clusters of the de facto functions of the Village Panchayat.

5. *How empowered is the Village Panchayat? Draw the Empowerment Circle to explore to what extent it performs its de jure functions*

In Step 5, first discuss and compare the de jure and de facto functions of the Village Panchayat. Discuss the various gaps and what needs to be done to close the gaps. That is, reduce the de facto functions which do not add value to the work of the Village Panchayat and increase the de jure functions which will make the Village Panchayats the true units of self-government.

5.1. Next, use the Empowerment Circle[9] for focusing attention on the extent to which the Village Panchayat is empowered. Since the de jure functions are guaranteed by statute, and if functions, functionaries and finances have been transferred to the Village Panchayat, these could be used as a measure of its degree of empowerment. An example is given in Figure 4. The steps for drawing the circle are as follow:
5.2. Ask the participants to define the concept of "empowerment "and identify its elements. List the elements thus if there are seven elements that constitute empowerment, there will be seven radii.
5.3. Ask the participants to draw a large circle on a sheet of paper or

9. Adapted from the field notes of Mukherjee, 2002.

on the floor with as many radii originating from the centre of the circle, as there are elements that make the Village Panchayat feel that it is empowered. Write one element along one radius.

5.4. Now explain that the centre of the circle from where the radii originate indicates the position that the Village Panchayat feels it is 100 per cent empowered in respect of the respective element. Therefore, if the Village Panchayat is at the centre of the circle on any radius, then in respect of the element represented by that radius, the Panchayat is fully empowered.

5.5. The position halfway on any radius indicates that the Village Panchayat feels that on the element of empowerment represented by that radius, it is empowered to the extent of 50 per cent. Thus the distance from the centre of the circle along any radius measures the extent to which the Village Panchayat feels it is empowered.

5.6. Any point on the circumference or outside the circle indicates the zero position, that is, the Panchayat in respect of the element shown by the radius is fully disempowered.

5.7. Now discuss each concept of the elements that constitute empowerment and facilitate the participants to decide to what extent the Village Panchayat is empowered with respect to that element. Facilitate so that the participants stick either bindis or post-it stickers along the radius for each cluster at an appropriate distance to indicate the extent to which the Village Panchayat is empowered.

5.8. If most of the stickers or bindis are at the centre of the circle, Panchayats are empowered. If most of the stickers or *bindis* are at the middle of the radii, the Panchayats are moderately empowered. If most of the stickers or bindis are on the circumference and beyond, the Panchayats are disempowered. If the stickers or bindis depict no pattern, then there is confusion about the empowerment of the Panchayat.

5.9. Discuss the Empowerment Circle with the participants and the ways and means of empowering the Village Panchayat. What are the factors that restrain the empowerment process? Who are the principal individuals/institutions responsible for the impediments? What are the policy measures suggested for improving this situation?

6. Visual Method for synthesizing what we have learnt from this Session

In Step 6, the trainer synthesizes the session learnings as done in the earlier sessions. She can invite one or more of the participants to help in doing this. In particular, focus during the synthesis should be on the **Empowerment Circle.**

SESSION 4 POLITICO-LEGAL ORIENTATION

Session Theme PANCHAYATI RAJ GOVERNANCE
Duration 90 minutes
Venue Classroom without fixed furniture.
Seating Sit and/or stand on the floor forming a circle move around the room for the game and picture/poster sessions. The participants are free to sit on the chairs should they wish to.
Session Objective *To expand the practical understanding of the participants about the concept of self-government and its institutions.*

Expected Learning Outcomes

- Increased understanding of the principles underlying the concept of self-government, the role and functions of PRIs as institutions for self-government at the grassroots level.

Content Flow and Training Methodology

Sr. No.	*Content*	*Training Methodology*	*Training Aids*	*Duration (in minutes)*
1.	Game for experience sharing among the participants about Village Panchayat governance	**Step 1** Stepping Stones	None	30
2.	Self-government and the Panchayati Raj institutions : concept and status	**Step 2** Poster and picture based discussions and lecture method	Posters/pictures and any other aids as desired by the trainer	45
3.	Synthesis of learning points by trainer/ participants	**Step 3** Visual method	Overhead slides, flip charts	15

THE METHODOLOGICAL STEPS FOR SESSION 4

1. *Play the game of Stepping Stones for experience sharing about Village Panchayat governance*

In step 1, the Stepping Stones game is played by the participants. See the following steps:

1.1. The objective of this game[10] is to share the experiences of the participants about Village Panchayat governance and discuss about what they think is important to them in this context. This helps the participants comprehend the subsequent training sessions in the light of their own experiences.

1.2. First discuss and decide with the participants some important events (or what are called 'stepping stones') in their experience of Village Panchayat governance that have significantly influenced them. Some suggested questions for eliciting the stepping stones are:
   - How have the actions/inactions of the local Village Panchayat affected them in the past?
   - What are the key events that made them elected members of the Village Panchayat?
   - What are their main experiences since they became members in terms of realizations, meetings, training experience, social attitudes, barriers to political/development participation, interaction with extension staff, self-esteem, satisfaction, frustrations, access to development information, etc.?

1.3. The trainer can start the game by giving an example of one of her own stepping-stones.

1.4. Ask the participants to work in pairs, interviewing each other. Each pair may interview about 3-4 stepping-stones from the list.

1.5. The participants then present the findings of the interviews very briefly to the group. This can be done either by presenting directly to the group by paired introductions or visually by displaying the stepping-stone for group viewing. The last method is recommended since this session relies heavily on the Visual Method as a training methodology for discussing the other training contents.

---

10. Adapted from Pretty *et al.*, 1995.

1.6. This game may take sometime, especially in large groups of 20 or more. The trainer will have to remind the participants to keep to only 3-4 stepping-stones and be brief.

1.7. The game is an experience sharing exercise and helps in placing the subsequent discussions in the session in the context of the participants' experiences about Village Panchayat governance. It also unlocks any reserve that the participants may still have about participating in the discussions.

2. *Hold poster and picture based discussions about self-government and PRIs*

In Step 2, extensively use the Visual Method involving discussions based upon posters and pictures, followed by a lecture. Paste the posters on the walls all over the classroom before the participants arrive. A sample of poster/picture is provided with this Handbook. The posters should relate to the Parliament, the State Legislature and the Panchayati Raj Institutions as also their functions. Lead the discussions from the posters and pictures in the following way:

2.1. On one table have cards on which the key concept areas and status of PRIs are written down, one on each card. For instance "The PRIs were created by the 73rd Constitutional Amendment Act" is written on one card. "One-third of the PRI members have to be women" is written on another card. A third card can have "The PRIs are the institutions of local self-government". And so on. Now ask the participants to paste the cards at the foot of the corresponding pictures with which they are connected. For example, the first card with the comment "The PRIs were created by the 73rd Constitutional Amendment Act" could be pasted below the picture of the Parliament. The card with "One-third of the PRI members have to be women" could be pasted below the picture of institutions of local self-government".

2.2. Check with the participants if all the caption cards and posters/pictures have been correctly paired. If not, ask the participants to make amends. In case, they are unable to do so, the trainer should help the participants make the corrections.

2.3. Now provide the participants with bindis or post-it stickers or any removable sticker. Ask them to place the stickers on these pictures about which they do not know or want to get more information about.

2.4. The trainer then provides the information sought by the participants through a brief lecture, pictures, drawings, video screening or whatever, followed by discussions among the participants.

---

3. *Visual Method for synthesizing what we have learnt from this Session*

In step 3, the trainer synthesizes the session learnings as done in the earlier sessions. She can invite one or more of the participants to help in doing this.

SESSION 5 ROLE OF PRIs

Session Theme	ROLE OF PANCHAYATI RAJ INSTITUTIONS
Duration	150 minutes
Venue	Classroom without fixed furnitures
Seating	Sit/stand on the ground forming a circle; move around the room for the Force Field analysis and picture based discussions
Session Objective	*To expand the practical understanding of the participants about the mandate of the Panchayati Raj Institutions*

Expected Learning Outcomes

Enlarged comprehension of the participants about:

- The mandate of the PRIs for meeting the ends of gender equity and social justice; and
- The extent of the fulfilment of the mandate.

Content Flow and Training Methodology

Sr. No.	*Content*	*Training Methodology*	*Training Aids*	*Duration (in minutes)*
1.	Self-government and PRIs: Implications and frame of action for economic development, gender equity and social justice	**Step 1** Visual Method using a cartoon show and picture based discussions	Cartoons and pictures	45[11]
2.	What were the original intentions of legislation and protagonists for the movement for self-government?	**Step 2** Lecture Method	Flash cards/ slides/ trans- parencies	30

(Contd.)

11. It is suggested that the duration indicated for the sessions may be factored thus: Cartoon Show and Display of Pictured: 30; Discussion Time: 15; Total: 45

Sr. No.	*Content*	*Training Methodology*	*Training Aids*	*Duration (in minutes)*
3.	What happened to the original ideas and justifications for the PRIs?	**Step 3** Force Field Analysis **Step 4** Brainstorming	Different coloured cards, flip charts, marker pens	60 minutes
4.	Synthesis of learning points	**Step 5** Visual Method	As desired by trainer	15

THE METHODOLOGICAL STEPS FOR SESSION 5

1. *Use cartoons and pictures to illustrate the frame of action for PRIs*

Step 1 uses the Visual Method with a cartoon show and/or picture based discussions to illustrate the frame of action for economic development, gender equity and social justice that the PRIs as institutions of self-government are expected to adopt.

2. *Use a brief lecture to discuss the original intentions of legislation and protagonists for the self-government movement*

In step 2, the trainer uses the Lecture Method, and since this knowledge area is mostly situated in Box 3 of the Johari's Window (see Figure 15) the trainer is required to use flash cards/transparencies/slides giving the original intentions of legislation and the protagonists. Discuss with the participants in order to identify which of them have been fulfilled. Write down the gaps on flip charts and paste them on the walls of the classroom. The context of this discussion is threefold:

- How is it possible to bring about village level economic development?
- What are the remedies for gender injustices as discussed in Session 3?
- How to remove/lessen social exclusion in the development process?

3. *Do the Force Field Analysis to determine the positive and negative forces that influence the gap between the original intentions and actual functioning of the PRIs*

Step 3: For analyzing the forces that have caused the gap between the original ideas and justifications for the PRIs and what is happening in practice, a Force Field Analysis (FFA) is done. The steps for doing the FFA are described below:

3.1. Explain the objectives of the exercise to the participants.
3.2. Please clarify that force is an energy that can cause or tend to cause a change. This is different from a problem or an advantage. Also, distinguish between positive and negative forces.
3.3. Keep a sheet of paper with the problem written or depicted on it, in front of the participants and ask them to concentrate on the problem. Ask them to visualize the problem situation in a state of temporary equilibrium by two sets of opposing force, one favouring changes (positive forces) towards closing the gap and the other thwarting them (negative forces), that is, preventing the gap from being closed. Ask them to list one set of forces followed by the other.
3.4. Ask the participants to write down or depict the forces identified on flash cards in bold letters. Write one force on one card. Clarify that if a force seems to be made of multiple elements, each component should be listed separately as a force. Different colour cards can be used for positive and negative forces.
3.5. Keep the sheet of paper with the problem written on it in the centre and draw a line across it. This line represents the present state of the PRIs. Ask the participants to spread the cards with negative forces below the line and those with positive forces above the line.
3.6. Ask them to take a look at the cards and see if they would like to make any changes.
3.7. Next ask the participants to assign weights to each of the forces by requesting them to keep each card force with the name of the force written on it, at varying distance from the present status line in such a way that the distance denotes the strength of the force. Greater the distance, the stronger is the perceived effect of the force on the problem. Arrows pointing downwards may be used to indicate negative forces. Arrows pointing upwards may be used to indicate positive forces.
3.8. Check with the participants whether they are satisfied with the diagram and relative strength of the forces as depicted or would they like to make any modifications.
3.9. Once they are satisfied with the diagram, ask them to discuss on how they can bring changes in the situation. Which of the positive forces can be reinforced and which negative forces can be diminished?
3.10. An example of a Force Field Analysis is at Figure 5.

Figure 5: Example of a Force Field Analysis[10]

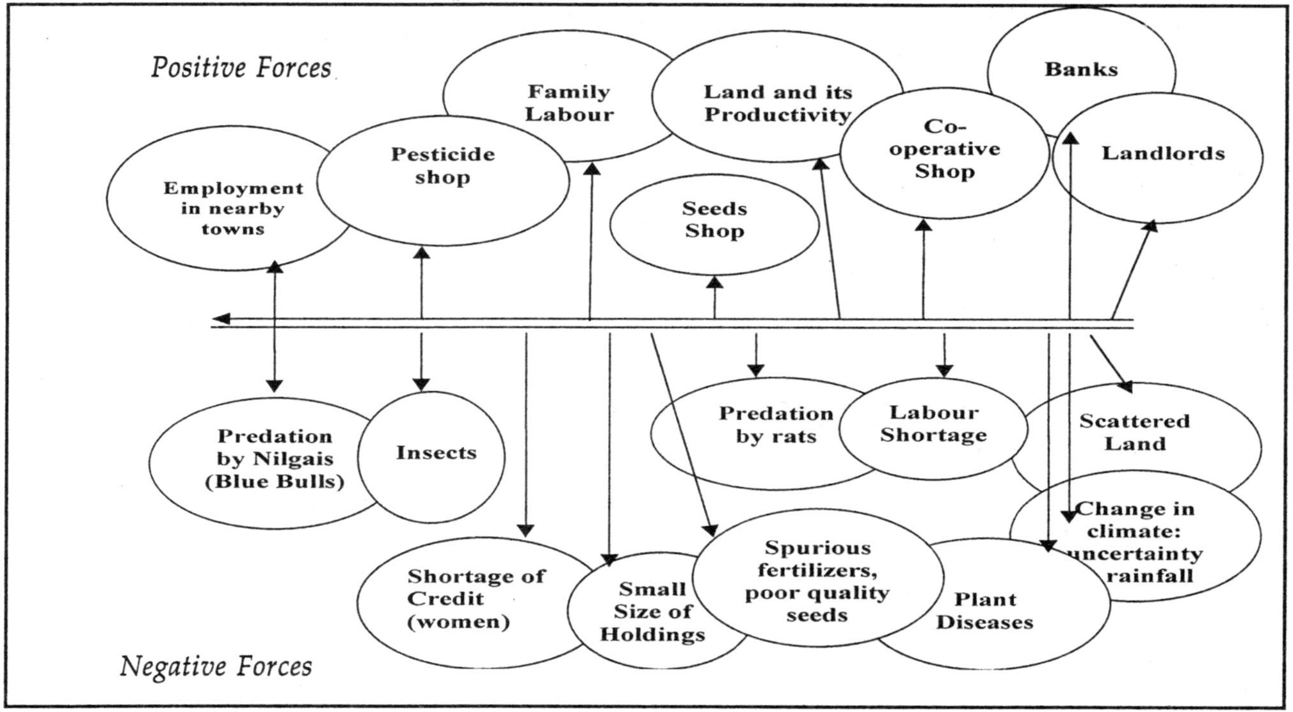

(1) The central line denotes the present status of hunger.
(2) The villagers of Tikri, Varanasi participated in the FFA.

Source: Mukherjee, Amitava: '*Hunger: Theory, Perspectives and Reality—Analysis Through Participatory Methods*', Aldershot: Ashgate Publishing Ltd. and Concept Publishing Company, New Delhi, 2002, p. 292.

4. Brainstorm about how to strengthen positive forces and reduce negative ones

Use the Brainstorming technique for detailed analysis and in-depth probing by the participants. Smaller cards, preferably of different colours, can be used to write down possible interventions for each of the positive or negative forces to increase or reduce its magnitude. Each of the possible interventions can be further weighed in the light of various factors, e.g., resources available, time, ideology of the organization, etc. The idea is generally to capitalize on those that would bring the greatest change.

5. Visual Method for synthesizing what we have learnt from this Session

In Step 5, the trainer synthesizes the session learnings as done in the earlier sessions. She can invite one or more of the participants to help in doing this.

Session 6 GENERAL ORIENTATION

Session Theme	GENDER AND SOCIAL JUSTICE
Duration	165 minutes
Venue	Classroom without fixed furniture
Seating	Sit/stand on the ground forming a circle for the group work, move around the room for the games
Session Objective	*To conscientise the participants about the social concerns related to gender, social justice and social exclusion.*

Expected Learning Outcomes

- The participants understand the issues related to gender and social exclusion that are prevalent in village-level society.
- They become aware of the duty of the Village Panchayat for promoting social justice through both its governance and development related functions.

Content Flow and Training Methodology

Sr. No.	*Content*	*Training Methodology*	*Training Aids*	*Duration (in minutes)*
1.	Energising game	Step 1 Who are we?	None	15
2.	Concept of gender, Differences between sexuality and gender	Step 2 Gender analysis through pictures	Flip charts and marker pens	45[13]
3.	Neglect of gender and social justice	Step 3 Gendered resource mapping	Flip charts and marker pens	45

(Contd.)

13. It is suggested that the duration be factored thus: preparation time: 30 minutes, presentation and discussion time: 15 minutes, total: 45 minutes. However, the trainer is free to vary these according to the needs of the trainees.

Sr. No.	*Content*	*Training Methodology*	*Training Aids*	*Duration (in minutes)*
4.	Explore ways and means to rectify the situation	Step 4 Access social mapping Step 5 Solution tree	Flip charts and marker pens	45
5.	Synthesis of learning points by trainer/ participant (s)	Step 6 Visual method	Overhead slides/maps, pictures	15

THE METHODOLOGICAL STEPS FOR SESSION 6

1. Know each other better by playing who are we?

In Step 1, an energizing game, who are we?[14] has been suggested, the steps for which are given below:

1.1. The objective of the game is to familiarize the participants with each other even further and promote group bonding.
1.2. Ask participants to raise their hands in response to some questions, like:
- Who is a Sarpanch/Upsarpanch?
- Who is a Village Panchayat member for the first time?
- Who is a Village Panchayat member for a second term?
- Who has been a Village Panchayat member more than twice?
- Whose Village Panchayat has a problem related to drinking water?
- Who has been trained before?

1.3. Use as many questions as possible. Briefly discuss after each such question. Most of the participants are interested in knowing more about the others. This exercise raises mutual awareness among them about each other.

2. Use pictures to understand the concept of gender

In Step 2, for the Gender Analysis, follow these steps:

14. Adapted from Pretty *et al.*, 1995.

2.1. Ask the participants to draw two pictures, one of a man and the other of a woman showing what each one does. The trainer analyses the pictures with them. Usually in most cases, the participants draw the eyes, ears, etc. in both the pictures and add bindis and ornaments on the picture of the woman.

2.2. Initiate the gender related discussions based upon these pictures. The trainer should use Appendix-A as background material. The trainer should encourage the participants to talk about the differences. The trainer points out that many of the differences between a man and a woman are biological. This is not gender. They relate to the sexuality of man and woman. Gender is different. Gender relates to the social construction of the roles of man and woman and the power relationship between them. To help introduce the concept of gender, the trainer can facilitate the participants to analyze the pictures based upon questions, like:
- What are the tasks done by men and women?
- Who decides what the women will do?
- Who decides when the women will do what?
- Who decides when the woman will work?
- Who decides why the woman will work the way she does?

---

3. Do Gendered Resource Mapping to understand deprivation due to gender discrimination

---

In Step 3, the Gendered Resource Mapping will help the participants explore the gendered dimensions of social justice. An example of the Gendered Resource Mapping is given in Figure 6 and Figure 6A. The steps for the Gendered Resource Mapping are described below:

3.1. The participants draw a map of the available resources in one of their villages. The map can be drawn on the floor of a building, on the ground or on paper.

3.2. Then ask the participants to choose symbols for showing the following:
- control over the natural resource, say 'C'
- providing labour and inputs for using the natural resource, say 'L'
- Having enduse of the products of the resource, say 'U'

3.3. Participants then choose symbols to show a man and woman, for example ♀ can show a man and ♂ depict a woman.

Figure 6: Resource Map from Ghusel, VDC, Lalitpur District, Nepal

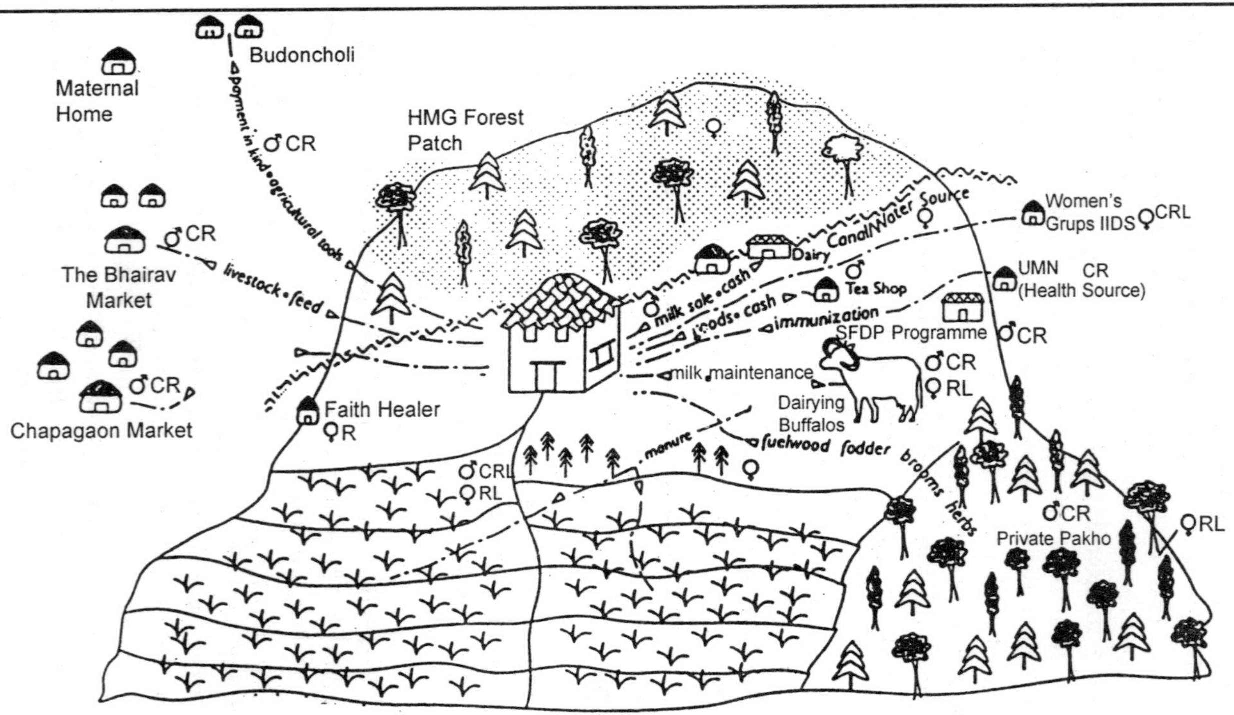

Pakho: Informal management system in which village households plant species suitable for fuelwood and fodder on government 'wasteland' (once forested, now barren), thereby converting that land to private property. Access to Pakho land varies widely by class, caste, and ethnicity.

UMN : United Mission to Nepal
SFDP : Small Farmer Development Programme
HMG : His Majesty's Government

C = Control of site/plants/products/relationship
R = Responsibility to provide products from the site
L = Labour input on site/actual use

Source: *Power, Process and Participation* (London: Intermediate Technology Press) 1996.

Figure 6 A: Gendered Household and Community Resources in Panano, Dominican Republic

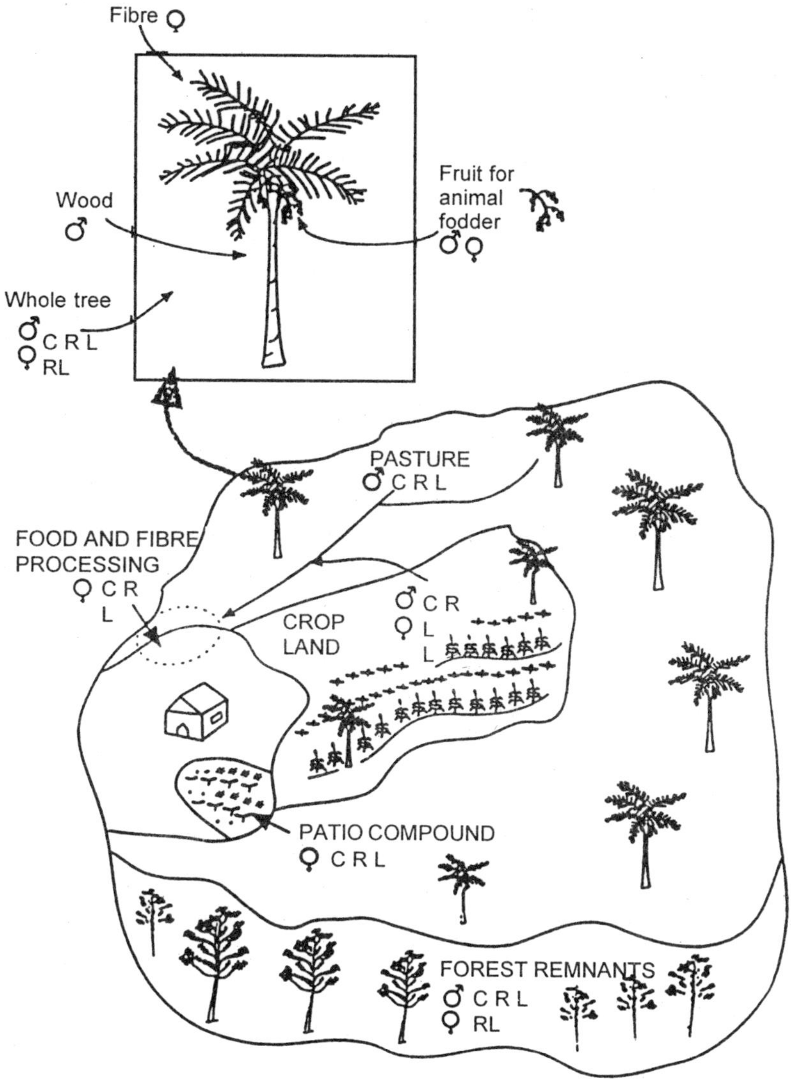

Multi-purpose use of land and trees in Pananao (La Sierra, Dominican Republic), Both men and women are present in this household, R = responsibility to provide a product thereof to the household, L = labour for the establishment, maintenance or harvest, and C = control of resource or process.

3.4. Next, ask the participants to combine the two of symbols for control, labour, inputs and man and woman and show who controls, who provides labour and inputs and who uses the resources. Thus, for example, against coconut trees show that the man controls them and also uses the income from the trees. Similarly, ♂ shows that women put in labour to grow/maintain the tree and also use the income from it. And so on.

3.5. This exercise should be done for every resource shown on the map.

3.6. From this exercise, the participants would understand the following issues, namely:

- How much labour does both men and women contribute in generating different resources used in pursuing rural livelihoods?
- Who controls the resources required for the livelihoods?
- Who puts in the labour? And in which resources?
- Who controls the production of the resources?

3.7. Then discuss with the participants:

- Is there equity in providing labour?
- Is there equity in the use of the benefits of the resources?
- Is the control fair? Is the control of the resources commensurate with the labour and inputs provided by women and men?
- Ask other questions which you may consider appropriate.

3.8. Once the participants have drawn the Gendered Resource Map, it is displayed on the wall. In order to bring out the gender justice dimension with respect to the control over resources, the participants are again asked to identify the following resources:

- For which resource they provide labour, but have no control over the produce.
- For which resource they provide labour and share control over the produce with the men.
- For which resource they provide labour and have full control over the produce.
- Is the control over produce equitable?
- What can be done to remedy the situation?

---

4. *Do Access Social Mapping to understand deprivation from access to social development services/public utilities due to gender discrimination*

In Step 4, the Access Social Mapping will help the participants understand the phenomenon of social exclusion whereby certain groups like gender,

Figure 6B: Access Social Maping

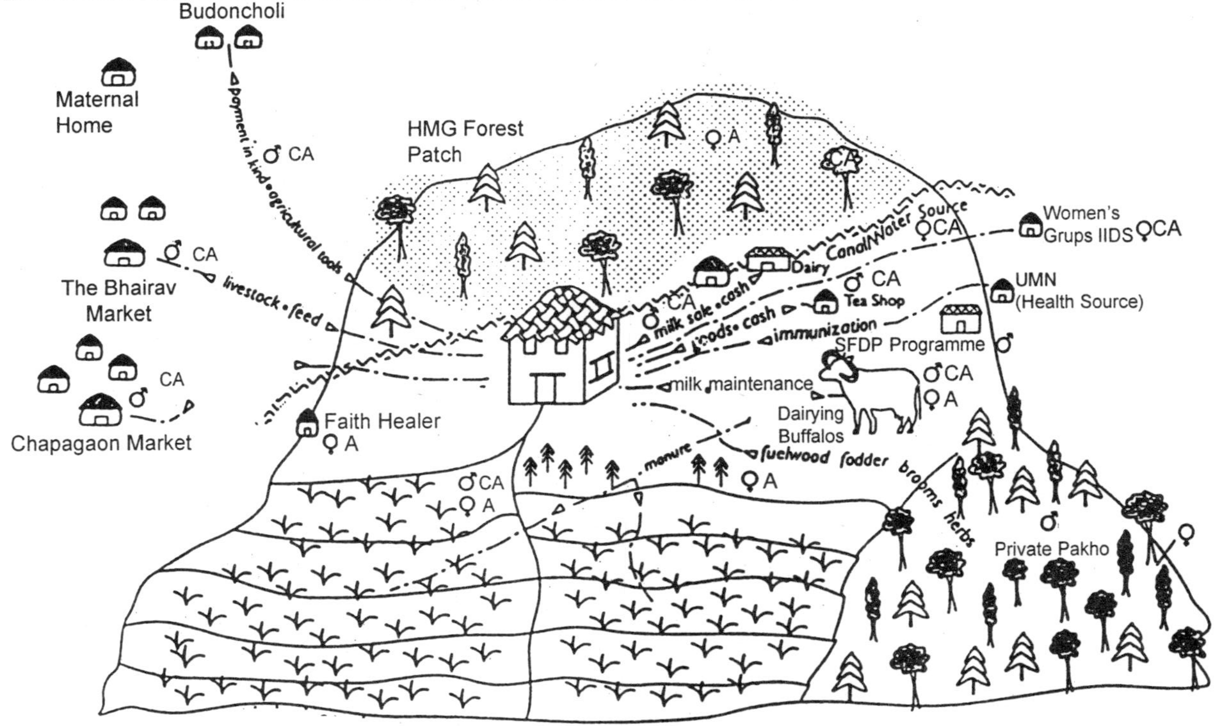

Pakho: Informal management system in which village households plant species suitable for fuelwood and fodder on government 'wasteland' (once forested, now barren), thereby converting that land to private property. Access to Pakho land varies widely by class, caste, and ethnicity.

UMN : United Mission to Nepal
SFDP : Small Farmer Development Programme
HMG : His Majesty's Government
C : Control
A : Access

Source: Modification from *Power, Process and Participation* (London: Intermediate Technology Press) 1996.

scheduled castes, scheduled tribes and others have limited or no access to public utilities, development resources and services. This will help the participants to identify injustices and explore ways of rectifying them. Figure 6B is an example of Access Social Mapping. The steps for the **Access Social Mapping** are given below:

4.1. The participants draw a Social Map of a village showing the social infrastructure like anganwadis[15], primary schools, community health centres, etc. The process of Social Mapping is described below.

4.2. Explain the purpose of the exercise to the participants. Request them to start with drawing the prominent physical features of their village. One way to start is to request the participants to mark the roads in the village or the temple or the village pond etc. Leave it to them to use whatever materials they choose local as well as other materials as creatively as possible.

4.3. Keep a track of which participants are actively involved and which sections of the society they belong to and who are left out. Take proactive steps to involve those participants who are not involved in the mapping process.

4.4. The trainer's role is that of mere facilitator. Intervene when strictly necessary, especially when the participants are in a rough patch.

4.5. If the trainer has something to add or clarify, she would wait for the right moment and not disrupt the process.

4.6. After the mapping is over, ask the participants to devise separate symbols to show full, partial and nil access, e.g. a shaded circle can show full access; a partially shaded circle show can partial access and a blank circle can show no access.

4.7. The participants then choose symbols to show a man and a woman, as done earlier in case of Gendered Resource Mapping.

4.8. Then mark each social institution drawn on the map by combining the two sets of symbols for access and man and woman to show what kind of access is available. For example, if only men have access to the temple, mark ♀ beside the temple; if women have no access to the temple, mark ♂ beside the temple; and if both have access then mark ♀ ♂.

4.9. A similar exercise may be done for the scheduled castes, scheduled tribes and other socially excluded groups, as may be necessary.

4.10. Once the **Access Social Maps** are prepared, the participants are required to paste them on the walls and make a brief presentation.

---

15. Village child-care centre providing services under the Integrated Child Development Services Programme.

4.11. Ask the participants whether the Access Social Map shows that women have less access than the men to the social infrastructure, development services, etc., existing in the village or not. In this context, the trainer should now draw the attention of the participants to the concerns related to gender in equality and social justice for the socially excluded groups like women, scheduled castes, scheduled tribes etc. and lead a discussion.

4.12. Draw the attention of the participants to the social injustices/ inequalities, which may emerge from the mapping exercise. Discuss the obligations of the Village Panchayat for promoting social justice through their local governance and village development related functions. These discussions should increase the participants' sensitivity to the phenomenon of social exclusion whereby certain groups because of reasons of gender, caste, ethnicity, age group, lack of control over resources, etc. are excluded from participating in the activities and benefits of the social infrastructure and development services.

4.13. Seek solutions from the participants. Request the participants to write down on separate cards the problems that may emerge from the mapping exercises and the discussions that follow.

5. Solution Tree Format for visualizing problems and their solutions

In Step 5, ask the participants to write down the solutions to the problems discussed in the previous step, in a Solution Tree Format. In this exercise the problems are thought of as the roots of a tree and the corresponding solutions as the branches of the tree. An example of a Solution Tree is given in Figure 7.

6. Visual Method for synthesizing what we have learnt from this Session

Step 6, the session ends with the trainer synthesizing the learnings that have flowed. The trainer may like to invite one or more of the participants to help in the synthesis.

Figure 7: Solution Tree: Equitable and Sustainable Development

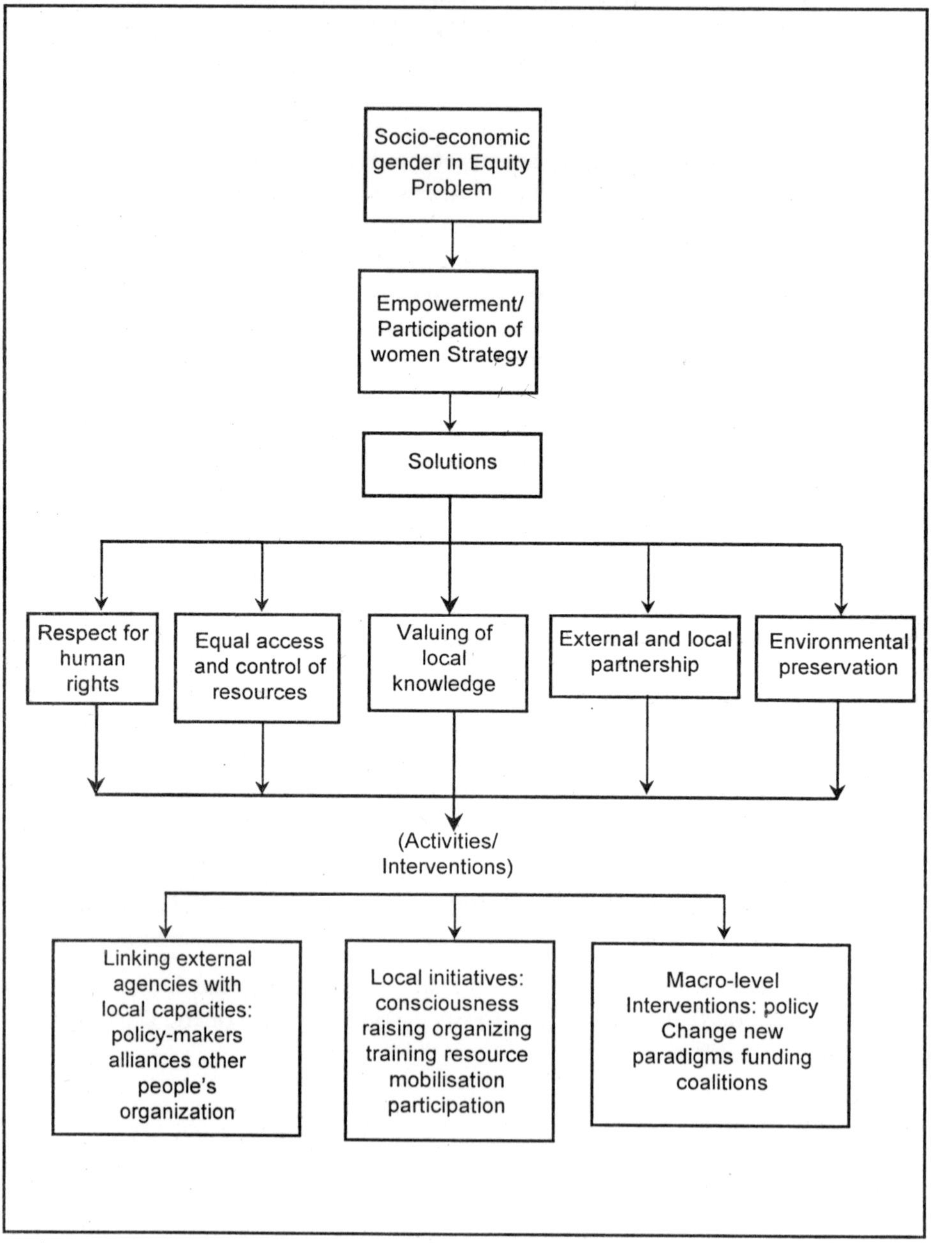

Session 7 PEOPLE-CENTRED COMMUNITY DEVELOPMENT

Session Theme	PEOPLE-CENTRED COMMUNITY DEVELOPMENT
Duration	195 minutes
Venue	Classroom without fixed furnitures
Seating	Sit or stand on the floor forming a circle for group work; move around the room for the game and picture/poster sessions
Session Objective	*To impart to the participants a conceptual understanding of people-centred community development.*

Expected Learning Outcomes

- The participants get acquainted with the different approaches and programmes for village development; and
- They are able to appreciate the centrality of people-centred community development.

Content Flow and Training Methodology

Sr. No.	*Content*	*Training Methodology*	*Training Aids*	*Duration (in minutes)*
1.	(a) Changes in the development paradigm (b) The consistency of the status of decentralisation in India with the changing development paradigm	**Step 1** Historical Transect **Step 2** Lecture Method	Flip charts, marker pens, overhead slides, cards	45
2.	Different approaches to development and the approach most appropriate for village level development	**Step 3** Matching Game	Cards, marker pens, seeds or pebbles	30

(*Contd.*)

Sr. No.	*Content*	*Training Methodology*	*Training Aids*	*Duration (in minutes)*
3.	(a) Status of village development in India in the context of the different development approaches (b) Status of gender equity and social justice in this context	Step 4 Pictures	Slides, drawings of cartoons	30
4.	Ways and means to improve the status of village development in India	Step 5 Ranking and Scoring	Cards, marker pens, seeds or pebbles	45
5.	Development programmes as well as ways and means to improve their efficiency	Step 6 Pie Charts Step 7 Ranking and Scoring	Flip Charts, marker pens, cards, coins of different denominations adding to a rupee, seeds or pebbles	45
6.	Synthesis of learning points by trainer/ participant (s)	Step 8 Visual Method	Overhead slides/ flip charts prepared by the participants	15

THE METHODOLOGICAL STEPS FOR SESSION 7

1. Draw a Historical Transect to trace the shifts in the development paradigm

In Step 1, a Historical Transect is drawn to trace the important stages in the changes/shifts in the development paradigm. The trainer may need some outside help. It may be likely that the trainer will have to start from Box 3 of the Johari's Window: We know and they do not know and then move to Box 2 that is they know and we do not know. Examples of Historical Transect are given in Figures 8 and 8A.

Figure 8: Historical Transect of the Development Paradigm

Decade	*Development Paradigm*	*Programmes Initiated*	*Reasons for Success/Failure*
1950-60	• First phase of Panchayati Raj • Socialistic pattern of society • Plan emphasis on industry	• Establishment of Community Development Blocks • Role of the public sector emphasised	• Public sector expanded • Agriculture neglected
1960-70	• Panchayati Raj established in many States like Maharashtra and Gujarat • Emphasis on agriculture and planned development • Trickle Down Theory	• Green Revolution (use of HYV seeds, fertilisers, irrigation) introduced.	• States did not want to devolve power to PRIs • Trickle Down theory did not deliver according to expectations
1970-80	• Food sufficiency achieved • Programmes for agricultural development given priority • Slogan of "Garibi Hatao"[16] • Launching of the Integrated Rural Development Programme and Integrated Child Development Services Programme with involvement of Panchayats in several states • First ever survey of Below Poverty Line families	• Poverty alleviation programmes like IRDP and TRYSEM were initiated • Gender needs in development were being recognized • Maternal and child health received attention	• Emphasis on decreasing income poverty with no linkages for enhancing human capabilities • Social sector programmes were sectoral with little or no integration • Top-down development approach

(Contd.)

16. Slogan which literally means "Remove Poverty"

Figure 8 (*Contd.*)

1980-90	• Institutional reforms to reorganise the PRIs was done in Andhra Pradesh and Karnataka • IRDP continued but new programmes like Jawahar Rozgar Yojana, Jeevandhara Wells Programme, Indira Awas Yojana for ensuring wage employment on public works, land development and housing for the BPL were begun • Greater emphasis on the creation of social infrastructure	• Panchayats were given development funds under the new schemes • Involvement of poor stakeholders in development initiatives was emphasized • Village development plans prepared. ICDS Programme started	• Two-fold emphasis, viz. creation of self and wage employment and creation of rural social infrastructure • Village Panchayats were actively involved in development programmes
1990-2000	• Major shift in the development paradigm, viz. empowerment of PRIs through the 73rd and 74th Constitutional Amendment Acts • Micro-credit model initiated through Save and Thrift groups and later Self Help Groups • Social mobilization of poor stakeholders emphasised	• 73rd Constitution Amendment enacted • Many states passed new Panchayati Raj Acts or modified existing legislation • Capacity building of PRI functionaries commenced. • Revamping of IRDP • Micro-credit model based poverty alleviation programme launched. Revamped PDS started	• Social mobilisation seen as the vehicle for promoting social change • Poverty recognized as multidimensional and not limited to income poverty

Figure 8A: Historical Transects of Ardanarypura Village

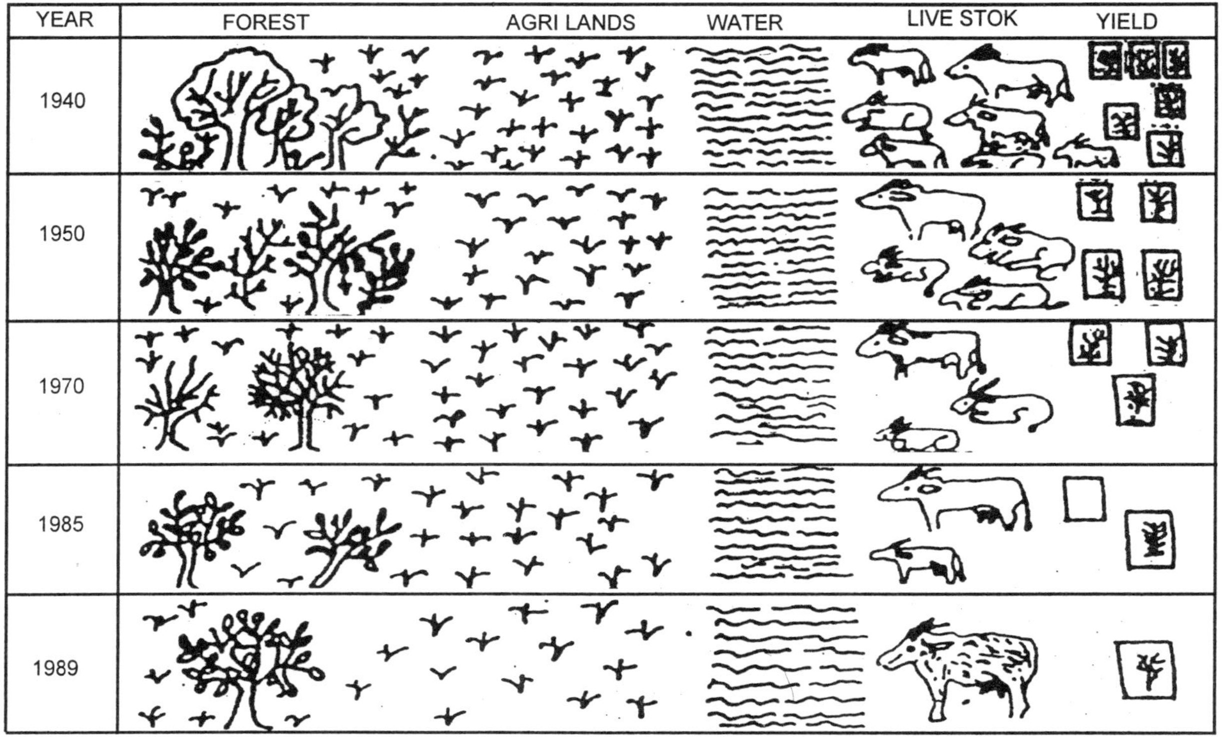

MYRADA STAFF
1. CHAKRA PAKI 2. KIRAN 3. VINSENT 4. SHEELA

PARTICIPANTS
1. SHUNDA DAMMA 2. MADAMMA 3. MARE 4. SODE MADAMMA 5. SHIDDAMMA

Source: Forest, Trees and People Newsletter No. 15/16.

2. Give a brief lecture about the status of decentralization in India

In Step 2, by means of a brief lecture, discuss the consistency of the status of decentralization in India compared to the changing development paradigm. For this purpose, the trainer is urged to use transparencies worded in simple language. The seating arrangement suggested for this purpose is that the trainer should be seated on the floor with the participants behind her, all of them facing the slide projector that is kept at a higher level.

3. Play the Matching Game to explore the different development approaches

In Step 3, for the Matching Game, follow this sequence:

3.1. Brainstorm the different development approaches with the participants. The trainer is requested to refer to Figure 10 for details about development approaches.
3.2. Encourage the participants to write down each approach on a single card.
3.3. Facilitate so that the participants arrange the cards in one column.
3.4. Initiate discussions amongst the participants about the merits and demerits of each approach.
3.5. Let the participants write a merit/demerit of an approach on a single card.
3.6. Place these cards alongside the card for the concerned approach.
3.7. Use free scoring to explore the participants' views about which approach is the most appropriate for village-level development.
3.8. Discuss with the participants. Try and arrive at a conclusion about the approach that is best suited to the modern times.

4. Use cartoons to discuss the state of village development in India

In Step 4, pictures can be used in the form of cartoons. Have a cartoon show with slides, transparencies or drawings. The cartoons of R.K. Laxman have been published in several volumes. They have excellent material to make this show. Many of his cartoons deal with development problems and approaches. Ask the participants whether they can relate their situation to the pictures and lead a discussion. Separate the pictures with which they can relate and discuss further. Use the learnings from the previous session to discuss the status of gender equity and social justice in this context. A set of cartoons showing the different kinds of development problems is at Figures 9 to 13.

5. *Rank and Score to determine ways to improve the status of village development in India*

In Step 5, for the Ranking and Scoring exercise, use the learnings from the cartoon show and ask the participants to write down the ways and means for improving the status of village development they have depicted by the cartoons. The participants are encouraged to write each suggestion on a separate card. Sort the cards and arrange them in a column. Ask the participants to rank them.
Now after the Scoring/Ranking, use the Seven Helpers to interview the Ranking done by the participants:

- Who can improve the status of village development in India?
- Why is the status so?
- When can it be done?
- How can it be done?
- Where can it be done?
- By whom will it be done?
- For whom will it be done?

6. *Draw Pie Charts for determining the relative importance of development programmes*

In Step 6, ask the participants to draw Pie Charts to depict the relative relevance/importance of development programme for the well-being of village communities. Follow these steps:

6.1. First ask the participants to list the development programmes which are being implemented at the village level.
6.2. Give the participants coins of different denominations adding unto a rupee.
6.3. Then ask them to decide on the relative importance of the programmes by giving weights to each in terms of the coins provided. The weights are expressed in terms of a certain proportion of the Rupee, say 50 paisa, 5 paise and so on, noting that the total cannot exceed Re. one.

Figure 9: The Government's View of the Poor and the Poor's View of Themselves, Concerning Money

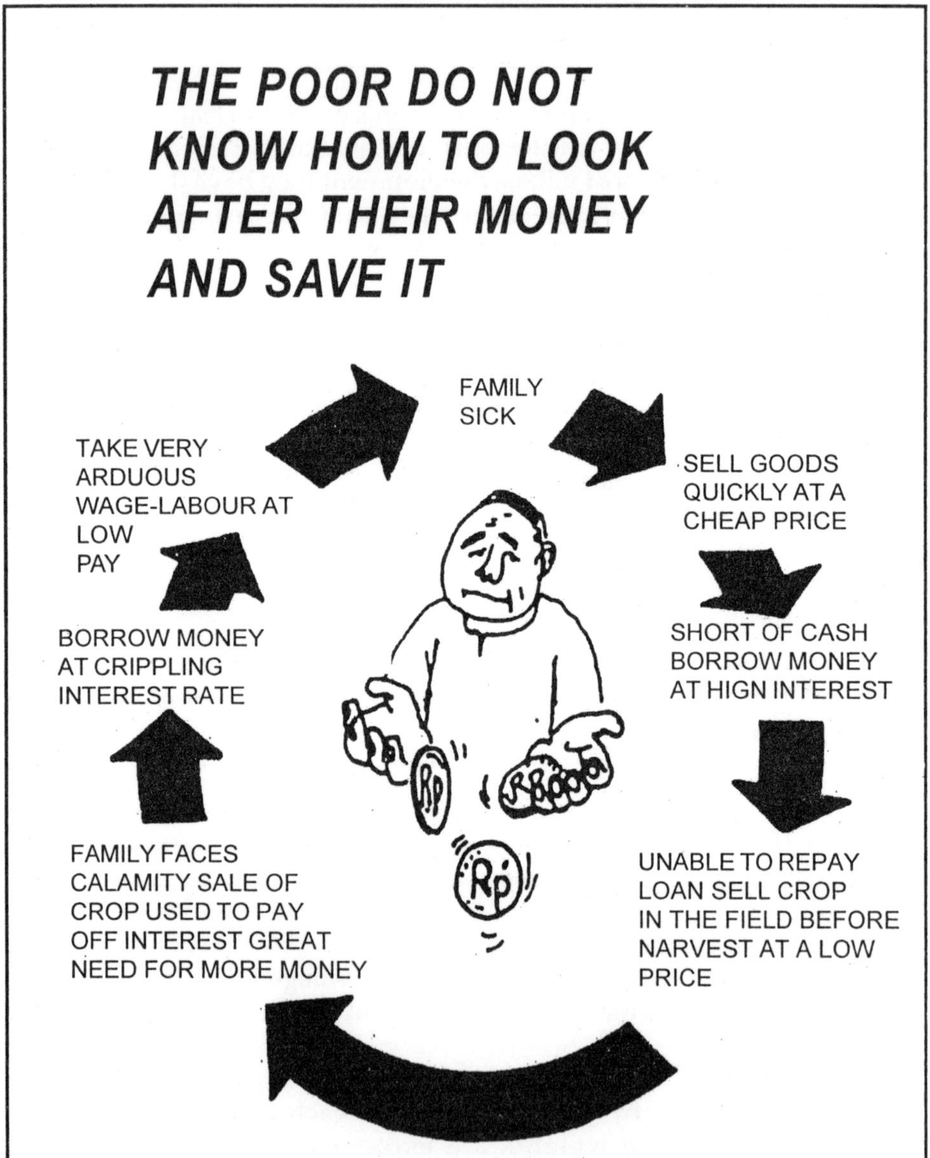

Source: Richard Holloway and David Watson (eds), *Changing Focus-involving the Rural Poor in Development Planning* (Oxford and IBH Publishing Co., New Delhi, 1989).

Figure 10: Blockages in the System

Source: *Bulletin Nelayan*, a publication of the All Indonesia Fishermen's Association, out of print (1980).

Figure 11: "Leakages" and the Resultant Weakening of Government Policies

"You might just as well stay there—there's just not enough water to go round".

Source: Cartoon by Richard Wilson, reproduced by kind permission of *Development Forum*, a magazine published by the UN Division for Economic and Social Information, and the United Nations University: New York.

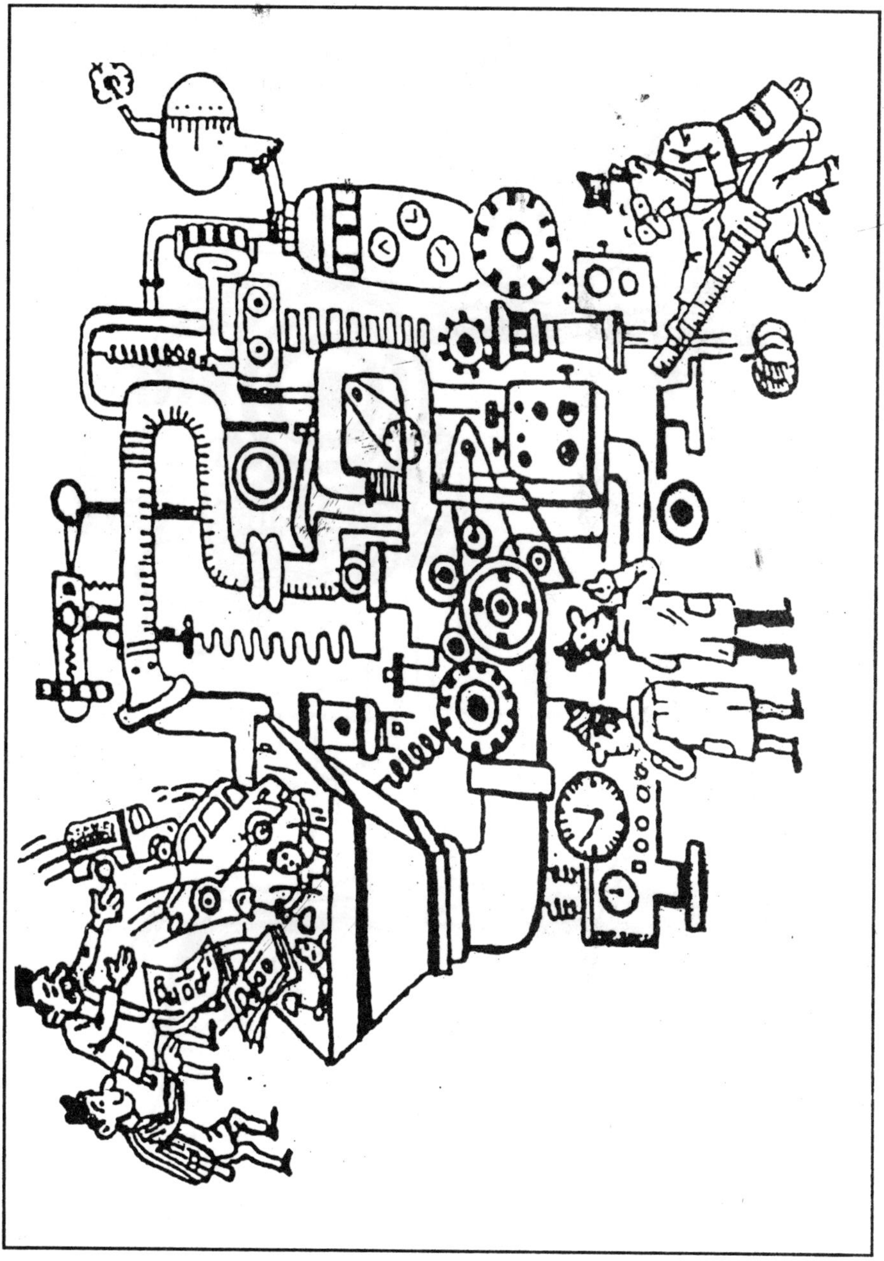

Figure 12: Disharmony Between Inputs, Complicate Process Output and Monitoring Quantitative Target

Figure 13: Target Adjustment all the Time and Missing all the Time

6.4. Then represent this analysis visually by asking the participants to draw a pie diagram where the entire circle is equivalent to a rupee and different portions or quadrants to the proportionate weights assigned to them. Example of a Pie Chart is given at Figure 14.

6.5. Discuss about the different weights assigned to various development programmes.

Figure 14: Example of a Pie Chart[17]

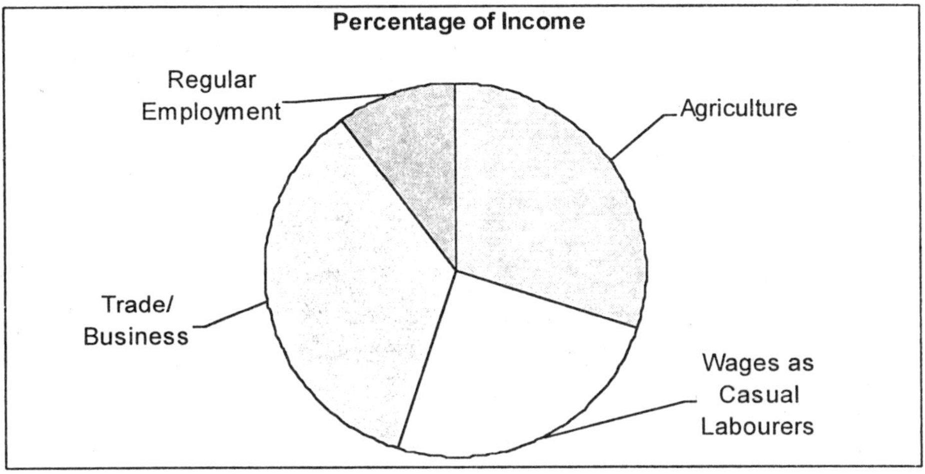

---

7. Rank and Score to determine ways to improve the status of development programmes

---

In Step 7, for the second ranking and scoring exercise, ask the participants to repeat the process as in Step 5 above. Participants will first list the ways and means for improving each development programme and proceed to analyze this information using the Seven Helpers that were discussed in Step 5 above.

---

8. Visual Method for synthesizing what we have learnt from this Session

---

Step 8: The session ends with the trainer synthesizing the learnings that have flowed. It is suggested that the trainer invites one or more of the participants to help in the synthesis.

17. *Source*: Amitava Mukherjee: *Hunger, Theory, Perspectives and Reality—Analysis Through Participatory Methods* (Aldershot: Ashgate Publishing Ltd. and New Delhi: Concept Publishing Company) 2002 pp. 147.

SESSION 8 ROLE ORIENTATION

Session Theme PEOPLE-CENTRED BEHAVIOURS AND ATTITUDES

Duration 190 minutes

Venue Classroom without fixed furniture

Seating Sit/stand on the floor forming a circle; move around the room for the role-play and group work. Participants may also sit on chairs if they like to.

Session Objective *To enable the participants to comprehend the different kinds of people-centred behaviours and attitudes.*

Expected Learning Outcomes

The participants are conscientised about the desired pro-people and pro-poor behaviours and attitudes that are expected of a Village Panchayat member and learn to emulate them.

Content Flow and Training Methodology

Sr. No.	*Content*	*Training Methodology*	*Training Aids*	*Duration (in minutes)*
1	(a) How does a Village Panchayat member/ development functionary usually behave?	**Step 1** Game "As a Village Panchayat member, I mainly..."[18]	Flash cards, marker pens, flip charts, slides, transparencies	30
	(b) What are the appropriate behaviours for a member/functionary?	**Step 2** Brainstorming		30
2	Non-verbal behaviour	**Step 3** Game: Non-Verbal Circles	Chairs, sticks to improvise	25

(*Contd.*)

18. Adopted from Chambers 2002.

Sr. No.	*Content*	*Training Methodology*	*Training Aids*	*Duration (in minutes)*
3	Role of a Village Panchayat Member	**Step 4** Role Play/ Drama	As may be necessary	30
4	Game for enhancing group dynamics	**Step 5** Chairs	Chairs	30
5	Modelling of people-centred attitudes	**Step 6** Johari's Window **Step 7** Slide Show	Slides, sketches	30
6	Synthesis of learning points	**Step 8** Visual Method	Flip charts, marker pens	15

1. Game: "As a Village Panchayat Member, I mainly"

In Step 1, play the game as a Village Panchayat member, I mainly.... This is a game for reflecting on one's own behaviour and how we are seen by others. Follow these steps:

1.1. Facilitate a brainstorming exercise to complete the sentence 'As a Village Panchayat member, mainly. 'Make a short list of behaviours like listen, think, argue, lecture, dominate, lead. Facilitate, and of roles, listener, thinker, debater, leader, facilitator, etc. Ask participants to record each idea or similar ideas on a flash card.

1.2. The next step is to join others who are similar. Post the words in different parts of the room and ask the participants to move quickly to the word each thinks represents her best. Encourage the participants to move fast at this stage of the game. If any participant cannot choose a word, they can form their own group.

1.3. The groups formed under each word, then discuss their role or behaviours and decide:

- What is helpful about it?
- What is unhelpful about it?
- How do others see me?
- Do I want to make any changes?
- How does it affect my role as a Village Panchayat member or development functionary?

- Does it meet the needs of people-centred development? If not, why?
- Any other reflections.

1.4. The groups discuss their insights with the other groups. These discussions can help the participants recognize the value of all kinds of behaviours and roles and identify which of these are congruent with the philosophy of people-centred development.

2. Brainstorming for the appropriate behaviours of a member or functionary

In Step 2, based upon the previous discussions, brainstorm with the participants about the appropriate bahaviours for a member or functionary. Use slides and transparencies of pictures, wherever possible. Some behaviours are suggested below:

- Avoid Dominance. Dominance behaviour is characterized by the inability to listen to others and appreciate the fact "that they know", the tendency to ignore/override the development interests of others, impose one's own views and beliefs upon others, etc.

- Avoid biases. There are eight kinds of biases to be avoided:
  - (a) Gender bias—ignoring men or women.
  - (b) People bias—talking to vocal people, clean people, people with clean clothes, etc.
  - (c) Road side bias—visiting places nearer the road.
  - (d) Project bias—look at pet projects where nothing has gone wrong.
  - (e) Professional bias—looking at development problems and solutions from the narrow perspective of one profession.
  - (f) Seasonal bias—carrying out fieldwork, important sessions etc. when it is most inconvenient for the people.
  - (g) Time bias—carrying out fieldwork, important meetings (like a Gram Sabha) etc. when it is not convenient for the people.
  - (h) Diplomacy bias—not expressing opinions or views in order not to offend other or when people say what they think "outsiders" want to hear.

- Eschew arrogance like not listening to others' views; acting as "Mr/Mrs know-A;" being disrespectful towards the views of socially excluded sections; being very conscious of one's own status as a Village Panchayat member, etc.
- Do not lecture since this is against the principle of participation. They know their problems and solutions.

- Do not seek 'blueprint' since development interventions have to be specific to community/stakeholder needs and hence cannot conform to one fixed pattern.
- Seek and respect diversity since there are diverse perspectives and needs of development stakeholders and "their reality" counts.
- Be self-critical and be self-aware. Do not be judgmental. Encourage others to express themselves freely and listen to them. Be self-introspective and realize your strengths and weaknesses.
- Be culturally sensitive by recognizing the tradition, usage, dress, culture, language, religion, customs, etc. of the different sections of society and communities and respecting them. Respect others and their points of view by listening to others and encouraging debates.
- 'Deal with people', do not avoid them or cut them out if they are 'difficult' or if they do not agree with you. Difficult people are dominant people, "Mr./Mrs. Know-All, the trappers, the arrogant people, the destroyers, the thin skinned and bored people, the shy people, people with limited vocabulary and the procrastinators." Such people may include some government functionaries who do not wish to share information and power or community members who ask many questions in the Gram Sabha to disturb the proceedings only.

---

3. Game to sensitize the participants to non-verbal behaviour

---

In Step 3, Non-Verbal Circles, an energizing game has been suggested with the objective of sensitizing the participants to how non-verbal behaviour can indicate dominance, submissiveness and friendliness. Follow the steps given below:

3.1. Form two sub-groups of the participants. The two sub-groups sit in two circles, facing inwards.
3.2. One person in each sub-group is elected scorer, who also takes part in the game.
3.3. The first competition for each sub-group is to show and perform non-verbal actions that demonstrate dominance. One person does the action, and then all other members repeat it for it to count in the score.
3.4. Continue until one of the two groups runs out of ideas.
3.5. Quickly ask the scores, and invite each sub-group to choose its best non-verbal action.
3.6. Repeat for submissiveness.

3.7. Repeat for being 'nice to people'.
3.8. Repeat for different kinds of behaviours which have been identified in the previous steps.
3.9. Now discuss about the importance of non-verbal bahaviour. Analyze how much we communicate with our words and how much through non-verbal behaviour, especially in exhibiting the behaviours which have been either recommended or discouraged in the previous step.
3.10. Discuss the importance of paralinguistic and facial expression. Indicate that current thinking on the subject maintains that we communicate only 7 per cent of what we communicate by words, 38 per cent by paralinguistic (tone, voice inflexion, etc.) and 55 per cent by facial expression.

4. Role Play or Drama to illustrate the role of a Village Panchayat member

In Step 4, highlight the role of a Village Panchayat member using Role Play/Drama staged jointly by the participants and trainers. The script can narrate Case Studies if so desired. Several role models may be portrayed by the script like:

- Facilitator of participatory development and governance at the grassroots.
- Promoters of gender and social justice at the grassroots with special reference to the management of conflict and conflict resolution.
- Facilitator of the process of social and economic change.
- Proactive agent of community development.
- Regulator of the units of self-government at the village level.
- Custodian of public property at the village level.

5. Game for Enhancing Group Dynamics

In Step 5, the participants play a game of Chairs[19] for enhancing their group dynamics, even further. The steps to be followed are given below:

5.1. Prepare three kinds of instructions on slips of paper, an example of which is given below:
- A: Put all the chairs in a circle within 15 minutes.

19. Adopted from Pretty *et al.*, 1995.

- B: Put all the chairs near the door within 15 minutes.
- C: Put all the chairs near the window within 15 minutes.

5.2. Explain to the participants the objectives of the game which are:
- To illustrate how to manage conflict by turning it into co-operation.
- To help them focus on the possible differences in the interpretation of instructions.
- To make the participants aware of the cultural and gender differences in handling conflicts.

5.3. Give each participant one kind of instruction (either A, B or C), distributing equal numbers of the three instructions. Ask them to keep the instruction given to them a secret.

5.4. Tell the participants to start the game following the instructions they have been given.

5.5. The focus of the exercise is on cooperation and conflict resolution by non-aggression. The three sub-groups cannot carry out their given tasks unless they cooperate. Several mutual solutions are possible, like:
- Putting all the chairs in a circle between the door and the window.
- Putting first all the chairs in a circle, then near the door and next near the window.
- Putting one-third chairs in a circle, one-third near the door and one-third near the window.

5.6. The groups will be seen to be using force and carrying their chairs desperately away or sitting on them near the door or window to avoid the chairs being displaced. Some participants will be seen trying to find a co-operative solution, while others will continue collecting and defending their chairs. The latter will frustrate the good intentions of the former who then join the argument.

5.7. Analyze the experience with the participants exploring how they felt about their chairs, the others who tried to take their chairs away and about the participants who were trying to co-operate. Ask them whether they would play the game differently a second time. Also explore how they related the game to real-life situations; say the dynamics they experienced in a Gram Sabha or a meeting of the Village Panchayat.

---

6. Use Johari's Window to Model People-centred Attitudes

In Step 6, use the Johari's Window (See Figure 15) to focus attention on the

Figure 15: Johari's Window

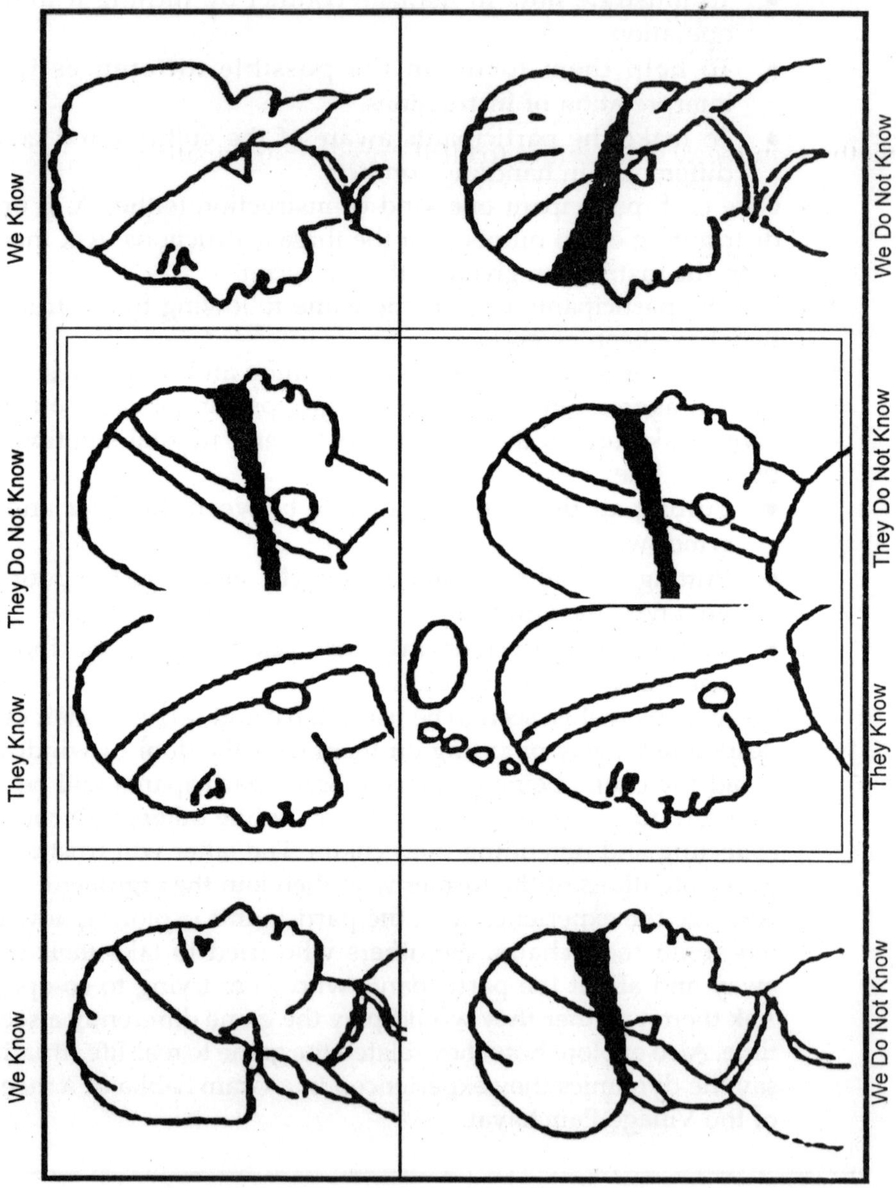

fact that it is important to believe that people know their problems and are capable of suggesting solutions. Also, that the realities of the poor people count. People's analysis, people's criteria, people's monitoring, people's evaluation, people's view and people's knowledge count and not ours. Discuss how these principles have underpinned the entire training programme where the trainer has given more emphasis to the realities and knowledge of the participants than her own. The whole training process itself has been one of both behaviour and attitude modelling by the trainer. The trainer should discuss how the participants could use the training methods in their communities to elicit popular participation.

7. Use Slides to Model People-Centred Attitudes

In Step 7, use slides with pictures/sketches to model a spectrum of people-centred attitudes with a particular reference to the following attitudes:

- "They know". It is important for a Village Panchayat member to appreciate the knowledge of the people since this is the first step towards facilitating their development through participation and understand that their knowledge, their technology, their priorities, their preferences, their planning, their monitoring and their evaluation count.
- Embrace error since this ability denotes humility and non-dominant behaviour and leads to efficient development choices and decisions. This helps to inculcate the attitude of learning from mistakes and moving ahead.
- "Fail forward", i.e. learn through your mistakes and move forward but do not either repeat mistakes or get demoralized by failure. Positive Person: "Yes I have an Idea." It indicates that the leader has enthusiasm. This is the essential quality of a leader as someone who has a vision and motivates others. If the leader is not enthusiastic, how can the people be expected to be?
- "I will not talk the talk, unless I walk the talk." The Village Panchayat member has to be a role model for her community and must exhibit the behaviours which she expects others to emulate. Practise what you preach.
- Improvise, Innovate and Adapt. The quality of village development depends upon the creativity and flexibility of the Village Panchayat member. The Village Panchayat members must, therefore, constantly improvise, innovate and adapt existing ways of doing things.

- Listening, Observing for Learning. This attitude is significant because unless the Village Panchayat member is prepared to listen to people, she cannot learn and if she is not in a state of continuous learning, she cannot innovate and adapt for the development needs of her community. Also, learning from the people is important for making informed development decisions which conform to people's priorities, their needs and their preferences. To learn, it is imperative to listen, observe and learn.
- Communicate well, so that others can understand and participate. Communication is critical to make the process of development interactive.
- We are Facilitators: They do it. People are the real actors; not us. We are there to facilitate the process so that people can analyze, plan, implement, act, monitor and evaluate. This attitude underlies non-dominant behaviour and is important for initiating stakeholder participation in development.

8. Visual Method for synthesizing what we have learnt from this Session

In Step 8, the synthesis of the learning points is done by the trainer with help from the participants. To introduce good humour, do the synthesis by asking the participants to act out some of the desired and undesired bahaviours and attitudes for a Village Panchayat member.

SESSION 9 SOCIAL CAPITAL

Session Name	SOCIAL CAPITAL
Duration	240 minutes
Seating	Sit on the floor or on chairs in groups of 5 or so.
Session objective	*For conscientisation of women members of Village Panchayats about Social Capital.*

Expected Learning Outcome

- The participants will understand the concept of social capital and its role in empowerment of women/women PRI functionaries; and
- They become aware of ways and means to promote social capital.

Content Flow and Training Methodology

Sr. No.	*Content*	*Training Methodology*	*Training Aids*	*Duration and in Minutes*
1.	Energizer	**Step 1** Changing places	None	10
2.	Concepts of Social Capital	**Step 2** Lecture	OHP, poster and pictures	20
3.	Relating to experiences: Social capital as a transformative strategy	**Step 3** Group work, brainstorming	Flip charts, marker pens, OHP	40
4.	Identification of relationship/social capital to development	**Step 4** Group work, discussion and presentation	Flip charts, marker pens and pin boards	40
5.	Positive and negative efforts of social capital. How Panchayat leaders can make use of social capital for empowerment of women ?	**Step 5** Group discussion, lecture	Flash cards, flip charts	40

(*Contd.*)

Sr. No.	*Content*	*Training Methodology*	*Training Aids*	*Duration and in Minutes*
6.	Mobilizing social capital as transformative strategy	**Step 6** Brainstorming, circulation of copies of successful reports/stories.	Flash cards, boards, pens	30
7.	Using social capital as a transformative strategy	**Step 7** Group work and Delphi	Flash cards, flip charts, pens, etc.	30
8.	Summary	**Step 8** Lecture	Overhead projector	30

THE TRAINING METHODOLOGY

1. Play the game: Changing Places

In step 1, play the game "changing places". This is a game for bringing about a realization of how even within a small ambit and group, social capital is formed and how it is disturbed. Follow the following steps:

1.1. Ask participants to sit in groups of people with whom they are most comfortable or in their usual groups.
1.2. Facilitate a brainstorming exercise to think what have they gained from each other as members of the group, what have been their relationships and what have been their learnings.
1.3. Ask the groups to write these on charts/flash cards.
1.4. Now reshuffle the groups by playing the Fruit Salad Game.
1.5. Repeat step 1.2.
1.6. Repeat step 1.3.
1.7. Compare the two outputs (from steps 1.3 and 1.6).
1.8. Points to note will be that in the latter groups, some of the positive features of the earlier group will be missing (such as friendship, trust, bonding etc.).
1.9. Indicate to the participants that this "changing of places" has diminished their friendship, bonding, trust, etc. That is, changing of the composition of the groups has lessened the social capital of the group.

2. *Lecture on concept of Social Capital*

In step 2, the concept of Social Capital is introduced. The attached teaching notes at Annexure-I to Session 9 can be used. The trainer can use slides and transparencies. The trainers should ensure that the participants understand:

(a) The difference between "social capital", "linking social capital", "bonding social capital" and "bridging social capital"; and
(b) The relationship between bonding, bridging and linking social capital, to the processes of development/poverty reduction and empowerment of women.

The trainer could link the concepts of social capital to issues like friendship, bonding, etc., which emerged from the 'changing places' game played earlier.

3. *Relating to experiences: Social Capital*

In **Step 3,** the following process is followed:

3.1. Ask the participants to break out into 4 groups.
3.2. Each group should be required to discuss and identify elements from one of the four issues of: "social capital", "bonding social capital", "bridging social capital" and "linking social capital" available to women elected members of the panchayats, based on their experiences.
3.3. The groups should be encouraged to write their outputs on flip charts or flash cards.
3.4. The "output" from the groups should be pasted on the walls/pin boards and presented to the plenary. Other groups would be free to seek clarification, add, amend or request deletion of items included into each of the four categories of "social capital".
3.5. Trainer to sum up the discussion. She/he can use the contents of Annexure-1 to this session.

4. *Identification of missing links and understanding the relationship of Social Capital to development*

In **step 4,** the links between various forms of social capital to essential elements of poverty reduction should be discussed. A suggested sequence is as under:

4.1. Reshuffle the groups but form 3 or 4 groups.

4.2. Each group should take with them "one output" from the previous exercise. Thus one group will have the outputs on "social capital", one group will have outputs on "bonding social capital", one group will have outputs on "bridging social capital" and one group will have outputs on "linking social capital".

4.3. Each group will now link their respective outputs to elements of poverty eradication. The trainer could provide the following hints either on flip charts or through transparencies, after the groups had some discussion on the subject:

(a) "Bonding social capital" plays critical role in protecting basic needs of the poor and in mediating risks.

(b) "Bridging social capital" is critical for information sharing and knowledge management, building solidarity and mobilizing public opinion.

(c) "Linking social capital" helps in procuring new economic opportunities, higher wages, better jobs, etc.

The trainer can, as stated earlier, use the material provided in Annexure-1 to Session-9.

4.4. The groups will now be requested to present their group work in the plenary and the process detailed in Step 3.4 be repeated.

5. The positive and negative effects of Social Capital

While social capital was seen in Step 3 as being a force that helps development, there is also a need to make the participants aware that under certain circumstances, social capital formation may have negative consequences. This is what is explored in step 5.

5.1. Divide the participants into two groups.

5.2. The two groups may be required to brainstorm both on the positive side of social capital and on the negative side of social capital. The groups may be requested to write down the key points on flash cards.

5.3. The flash cards on the positive and negative sides of social capital produced by both the groups may then be laid on the floor and using the Delphi Method one set of negative and one set of positive aspects of social capital may be formed.

This will give participants a chance to reflect on social capital and its effects.

5.4. The trainer to sum up the discussion.

---

6. Mobilizing Social Capital as a transformative strategy

In step 6, the participants will explore for themselves how social capital formation and/or strengthening social capital can lead to transformation of the status of women and hence usher in socio-economic development.

6.1. Break the participants into four groups.

6.2. Request each of the first three groups to explore ways of building social capital and/or strengthening existing social capital. The fourth group may be asked to find out ways and means to circumvent the negative effects of social capital identified in step 6.

6.3. The groups may be encouraged to share their experiences and discuss the various possibilities.

6.4. Then groups may only write down on flip charts the "doables" to build or strengthen social capital. The fourth group will jot down the "doables" in circumventing the negative aspects of social capital.

6.5. The groups will present their outputs at the plenary.

6.6. The participants may then be encouraged to reflect on whether the ways and means enumerated by the groups are actually happening in the panchayats.

6.7. Trainer may summarize the discussion by drawing up a "Mock Action Plan" on how to increase the positive impact of social capital and how to eliminate the negative impact of social capital.

---

7. Using Social Capital as a transformative strategy

Step 7 is a prelude to planning step. In this step the participants can reflect on what they could do to use social capital for development of their respective areas.

7.1. Break the participants into three groups.

7.2. One group will be assigned to deal with issues relating to social capital for social justice. The second group will deal with issues of social capital for meeting basic needs. The third group will deal with issues relating to social capital for livelihoods.

7.3. The three groups will write down on flash cards/flip charts how they can use their existing social capital to ensure greater social justice, improved access to basic needs and better livelihoods, based on the "Mock Action Plan" developed at the end of Step 6.

7.4. The groups will then make a presentation at the plenary.

---

8. Summary

The trainer should now summarize the learnings from the session. The highlights should be:

(a) What is social capital?
(b) What are the kinds of social capital?
(c) How are the various kinds of social capital related to meeting basic needs, information/experience sharing and obtaining economic opportunities etc.?
(d) What social capital exists in the Panchayats?
(e) What can the participants do to enhance the various kinds of social capital?
(f) How can the participants use social capital for various purposes?

SESSION 10 SOCIAL MOBILISATION

Session Name	SOCIAL MOBILISATION
Duration	330 minutes
Seating	Classroom without fixed furniture
Session Objective	*To conscientise the participants about the social mobilization*

Expected Learning Outcome

- The participants will understand the concept of social mobilization;
- They become aware of the need for social mobilization and the role of social capital in it;
- The participants have knowledge of the steps unvalued in social mobilization; and
- The participants learn how to monitor and evaluate social mobilization.

Content Flow and Training Methodology

Sr. No.	*Content*	*Training Methodology*	*Training Aids*	*Duration Minutes*
1.	Energizer	**Step 1** Catch the Leader	None	10
2.	What is social mobilization? What is the goal of social mobilization?	**Step 2** Small group discussion and lecture	Flash cards	30
3.	Social mobilization vs community mobilization	**Step 3** Lecture and brainstorming	Chart, flash cards and markers	30
4.	Challenges and probable perspectives	**Step 4** Brainstorming followed by lecture	Projector, charts, OHP	45
5.	Critical steps of social mobilization	**Step 5** Lecture	Projector, charts, OHP	30

(*Contd.*)

Sr. No.	*Content*	*Training Methodology*	*Training Aids*	*Duration Minutes*
6.	Presentation of case studies and sharing of experiences in their specific social context	**Step 6** Lecture and case studies	Flip charts	45
7.	Social mobilization with specific emphasis on SC/ST/weaker sections and other disadvantaged groups	**Step 7** PRA-relation matrixes	White board, markers, OHP	50
8.	Role of facilitator/initiator of social mobilization	**Step 8** Small group discussion and lecture	Flash cards, board	45
9.	How and who will M & E	**Step 9** Small group discussion and lecture		30
10.	Synthesis of learning points by trainer/participants	**Step 10** Visual method	Chart, marker	15

THE METHODOLOGICAL STEPS FOR SESSION 10

1. Play the energizing game catch the leader

In step 1, the energizing game has been suggested for which the steps are as follows:

1.1. The objective of the game is to energize the groups before they begin the next phase of sub-session.
1.2. Ask the participants to form a circle in the room.
1.3. Ask the participants to select one "volunteer" amongst them. Request that person to go out from the room.

1.4. Ask the participants to select a leader. Facilitator explains that all the participants will follow leader's actions. Ask the leader to do simple movements (such as scratching her/his hair, slow clapping, shaking her/his head etc.), which will be repeated by the other participants. Indicate to the participants that they should not look at the leader. Ask the leader to change her/his movement once in a while making sure the "volunteer" does not notice this. Ask the "volunteer" to come in and identify the leader. If she identifies the leader then leader goes out from the room and same round will start again. If the volunteer fails to identify the leader, she/he has to go out again and repeat the exercise.
1.5. Continue until four-five participants can get a chance to become a leader.
1.6. This will result in a lot of laughing and energizing. This provides a brief and energizing break for the participants in the training.
1.7. The moral of the game is that a good leader does not show-off and it is difficult to locate a good leader.

---

2. *Small group discussion and lecture to catalogue the concept and goal of social mobilization*

In step 2, use small group discussion and lecture, for which the process is described below:

2.1. Objective of the small group discussion exercise is to catalogue the meaning of social mobilization. This provides a valuable starting point for discussing about the fundamentals of the social mobilization. The list of the meaning developed through this exercise is based upon the collective insights of the participant-groups. It forms the meaning of the social mobilization.
2.2. Divide the participants in the small groups of 4-5 participants.
2.3. Ask the participants to nominate a recorder, who will write the points of the group discussion on flash cards/flip charts.
2.4. Ask the group to think of the meaning of social mobilization based upon their own experiences.
2.5. Give 5-7 minutes time for discussion.
2.6. Encourage all participants to think adventurously. Emphasize the participation of each member in the discussion.
2.7. Let the ideas flow freely without any comments or evaluation being made.
2.8. The recorder writes each idea on a flash card. All the flash cards are put on the board.

2.9. Evaluate the list after the group discussion is over. The trainer then explains the definition of social mobilization. For this purpose, the trainer is urged to use transparencies. Following is the definition of the social mobilization:

" Social mobilization is an approach and a tool that enables people to organize for collective action, by pooling resources and building solidarity required to resolve common problems and work towards community advancement."

---

3. ***Use of lecture and brainstorming to explain the difference between social mobilization and community mobilization***

In step 3, first use the lecture method to explain the differences between social mobilization and community mobilization. (See Appendix C and Appendices D and E). Social mobilization seems to cover mostly social movements initiated from the top in which persuasion and/or "manipulation" techniques are used to reach the objectives on a massive and rapid scale (it is a facilitated process). Community mobilization is spontaneous movements initiated from grassroots, which take the form of self-help and small-scale projects (it is an autonomous process). The basic difference between community mobilisation and social mobilisation can be seen in the figure below.

3.1. After explaining the differences, use brainstorming method to evolve a list of examples of social mobilization and community mobilization.
3.2. Divide the participants in small groups.
3.3. Ask the participants to nominate a recorder, who will write the points of the group discussion on flash cards/flip charts.

3.4. Ask the group to think of the meaning of social mobilization based upon their own experiences.
3.5. Give 5-7 minutes time for discussion.
3.6. The brainstorming would have generated a list of examples and each example would have been recorded on a card (only one example per card).
3.7. The cards are then grouped according to the examples of social mobilization and community mobilization.
3.8. The facilitator analyzes the two lists and points out which of the classification needs changes.

---

4. Lecture method to catalogue the challenges and probable perspectives

---

In step 4, the lecture method is used by the trainer to outline the challenges and probable perspectives of social mobilization.

4.1. Now ask participants whether they have ever undertaken any form of social mobilization.
4.2. Ask them to write on flash cards the challenges they faced.
4.3. Compare these challenges with the challenges outlined by the trainer.
4.4. If none of the participants had seen or undertaken any form of social mobilization, request them to reflect on the trainer's presentation on the probable challenges.
4.5. The participants then write the challenges they expect to face in social mobilization on the basis of their experience, group realities and politico-social motive of their Panchayats.
4.6. The trainer to quickly summarize the sub-session's learning.

---

5. Give a lecture about the critical steps of social mobilization

---

In step 5, it is suggested that the trainer uses the lecture method with the suitable aids for presenting the steps. Trainers are encouraged to use the attached material in Annexure-1 of this sub-session.

5.1. Now ask participants whether they have ever undertaken any form of social mobilization.
5.2. Ask them to write on flash cards the steps they adopted.
5.3. Compare these steps with the steps outlined by the trainer.
5.4. If none of the participants had seen or undertaken any form of social mobilization, request them to reflect on the trainer's presentation on the steps of social mobilization.

5.5. The participants then write the steps they expect in social mobilization on the basis of their experience, group realities and politico-social motive of their Panchayats.
5.6. The trainer to quickly summarize the sub-session's learning.

6. Case studies on the experiences of social mobilization

In step 6, use the case studies of social mobilization to make them aware of the processes of social mobilization. The trainer intersperses the discussion, wherever necessary with brief lecture.

6.1. Divide the participants into 2 or 3 groups.
6.2. Distribute 2 or 3 case studies to the groups. Allow them 15-20 minutes to study the case studies.
6.3. Now ask the groups to analyze the case studies and answer the following questions:
   (a) What was the problem(s) sought to be solved in the social mobilization case studies?
   (b) What were the steps taken in social mobilization?
   (c) What were the challenges faced? How were they overcome?
6.4. Discuss the outcomes of each case study and explain if the analyses are correct.

Note: The trainer should have read the case studies in advance. Comparison of the two analyses should be to provide different perspectives and not criticize the group work.

7. Draw a Relational Matrix of the issue regarding social mobilization with specific emphasis on weaker sections and other disadvantaged groups

In step 7, the participants draw the Relational Matrices for the social mobilization with specific emphasis on weaker sections and other disadvantaged groups of the society.

7.1. Ask the participants to write the types of disadvantaged groups on flash cards and place them as items in the first column of a Matrix.
7.2. Ask the participants to write the elements of social mobilization in the first row.
7.3. Now encourage the participants to ask whether there is a direct or an indirect connection between the type of disadvantage group number 1 and element number 1.
7.4. If there is a direct connection between the two writes ✔ in the square common to them; if there is an indirect connection, put a cross.

7.5. Repeat the process for all types of groups in relation to element number 1.
7.6. Repeat the process for all types of groups in relation to element number 2.
7.7. Repeat the process till the types of groups have been pitted against all the elements of social mobilization.
7.8. Remember to always ask the question whether element has a direct relationship with the type of disadvantaged group. Never do it the other way around.
7.9. Now ask the participants to count the number of direct and indirect connections.
7.10. Ask the participants to record each count at the bottom of each column.
7.11. If the elements address the tick mark, then the element would meet the requirement of the relevant group.
7.12. In case the participants of a marginalized group are not addressed by the element of social mobilization, then the element would not meet requirement of the relevant group.

An example of Relational Matrix of elements of social mobilization and the target groups

The Marginalized groups	*Elements of social mobilization*			
	Organizational development (1)	*Capital Formation (2)*	*Capacity building (3)*	*Socio-economic development (4)*
SC/ST	✔	✔	✔	✔
OBC	×	×	✔	✔
General	×	×	×	✔
Women	✔	✔	✔	✔
Disabled	✔	✔	✔	✔
Scavengers	✔	✔	✔	✔

Note: The tick mark indicates that there is a direct benefit of the elements of social mobilization to the relevant group. A cross mark indicates non-relevance of the elements to the relevant group.

---

8. Small group discussion and lecture for role of facilitator/initiator of social mobilization

---

In step 8, use small group discussion and lecture, for which the process is described below:

8.1. Divide the participants in the small groups of 5-6 participants.
8.2. Ask the groups to discuss the role of facilitator/initiator of social mobilization.
8.3. Ask the groups to note the points of group discussion.
8.4. Give the 10-15 minutes for the discussion.
8.5. Ask the groups to present their points of discussion.
8.6. Evaluate the points after the group discussion is over. The trainer then explains the role of facilitator/initiator of the social mobilization. The trainer is encouraged to draw upon the material in Appendices C & D.

---

9. *Use small group discussion to explain the monitoring and evaluation process of social mobilization*

In step 9, based upon the previous discussions, brainstorm with the participants about how and who will monitor and evaluate the process of social mobilization. The participants understand the methods and responsibilities of monitoring and evaluation of social mobilization after the brainstorming exercise.

9.1. Divide the participants in the small groups.
9.2. Ask the participants to nominate a recorder, who will write the points of the group discussion on flip charts.
9.3. Ask the groups to think of the monitoring and evaluation processes of social mobilization.
9.4. Give 10-15 minutes time for discussion.
9.5. Ask each group to present the findings of group discussion.
9.6. Evaluate the findings after the group presentation is over. The trainer then explains the monitoring and evaluation processes of social mobilization.

The trainer is encouraged to use the material at Annexure–3 of this session.

---

10. *Visual Method for synthesizing what we have learnt from the sub-session*

In step 10, synthesize the important learning from the sub-session by asking each participant to list at least one important lesson.

SESSION 11 NETWORKING

Session Name	**Networking for Empowerment of Women Members of PRIs**
Duration	275 minutes
Venue	Classroom with furniture
Seating	Sit on the floor or on chairs
Session objective	*To equip the participants about the need and technology of networking*

Expected Learning Outcome

- The participants will understand the need for networking and its "concepts"; and
- They would know the steps in developing and nurturing networks.

Content flow and training methodology

Sr. No.	*Content*	*Training Methodology*	*Training Aids*	*Duration in Minutes*
1.	Energizer	Step 1 Dragon	None	15
2.	What is network	Step 2 Small group discussion and lecture	Flash cards, board, markers	20
3.	Kinds of network – federation, alliance, coalition, partnership, network	Step 3 Brainstorming and lecture	OHP	30
4.	Stages of network	Step 4 Lecture	Board, markers	45
5.	Functions, structure of network secretariat	Step 5 Fish bowl, debate, lecture	Board, markers	45
6.	Role of facilitator (Role of initiator of network)	Step 6 Small group discussion and lecture	Flash cards, board	45

(*Contd.*)

Sr. No.	*Content*	*Training Methodology*	*Training Aids*	*Duration in Minutes*
7.	Study of practices in networks of elected women representatives	Step 7 Visual case studies, lecture	TV, VCR	40
8.	Critiques of networks	Step 8 Lecture	Flash cards	20
9.	Synthesis of learning points by trainer/participants	Step 9 Visual Method	Chart, marker	15

THE METHODOLOGICAL STEPS FOR SUB-SESSION 11

1. Play an energizing game Dragon

In step 1, the participants play "Dragon", an active game as follows:

1.1. The objective of the game is to energize the group before they begin the next phase of sub-session.
1.2. Find an open space outside and invite everyone to stand there.
1.3. Ask the participants to form a line or a dragon and ask them to run. And concurrently ask the front of the line to catch its tail. Then stop the dragon, turn the participants to face the other direction, and have the tail then catch the head.
1.4. This will result in a lot of smiling and laughing. Then the participants to select a leader. This provides only a brief and energizing break for the participants. This fact should be told to the participants, otherwise, they would be expecting a moral theme from the game.

2. Small group discussion and lecture to catalogue the concept of network

In step 2, use mall group discussion and lecture, for which the process is described below:

2.1. Objective of the brainstorming exercise is to catalogue the meaning of network. This provides a valuable starting point for discussing about the network. The list of the meaning developed through this exercise is based upon the collective insights of the participant-groups. It forms the meaning of the network.
2.2. Divide the participants in the small groups of 4-5 participants.

2.3. Ask the participants to nominate a recorder, who will write the points of the group discussion
2.4. Ask the group to think of the meaning of network based upon their own experiences.
2.5. Give 5-7 minutes time for discussion.
2.6. The recorder writes each idea on a flash card. All the flash cards are put on the board.
2.7. Evaluate the list after the group discussion is over, trainer explains the definition of network. For this purpose, the trainer is urged to use transparencies. The trainer should indicate that network is also a group.

---

3. Use brainstorming and lecture to explain the kinds of network – federation, alliance, coalition, partnership, network

---

In step 3, use brainstorming and lecture, for which the process is described below:

3.1. Trainer to explain the differences between federation, alliance, partnership and network.
3.2. The objective of the brainstorming exercise is to catalogue the different kinds of networks. The list of the kinds of networks developed through this exercise is based upon the experience of the participants in the group in being parts of different groups, alliances, coalition, partnership, network, etc.
3.3. Ask the participants to nominate a facilitator who will not participate, but merely record the ideas.
3.4. Ask the group to think of the kinds of network based upon their experience.
3.5. Emphasize the quality of idea is more important than numbers.
3.6. The group facilitator writes each idea on a flash card. All the flash cards are laid on the floor of the classroom in one column or row.
3.7. Evaluate the list after the brainstorming is over.
3.8. Use the boxes at the end of this session for a description of the types of Network and the material in Appendix-A.

---

4. Lecture method to catalogue the stages of network

In step 4, the lecture method is used by the trainer to reinforce the stages of network. The stages of forming, norming, storming and adjourning should be spelt out. Activities in each stage that any group (such as a network) engages in should be explained. The trainer could use the teaching aid given at Annexure-1 of this session.

5. *Use the "fish bowl debate" and lecture to explain functions, structure of network secretariat*

In step 5, it is suggested that the trainer uses the lecture method with the suitable aids for presenting the steps in developing a network. The sub-session also gives the strategic input which will promote the level of transparency, responsiveness, participation and accountability in the each stage of network.

5.1. Divide the participants in the two groups: Groups A and B.
5.2. Make one participant from each group to sit in the middle facing each other.
5.3. One person from group-A asks a question to the representative of group-B about function/structure etc. of network. The person at the middle will have 3 seconds to answer. If the answer is correct, group B gets 1 point. If the answer is wrong or there is no answer in three seconds or there is a "pass", the representative from group-A gets a chance to answer. If the answer is correct, group A gets 1 point.
5.4. Now reverse the process with members from group-B asking the question and representative from group-A at the middle answers.
5.5. Continue the process till all the functions/structures etc. of the network/network secretariat are brought out.
5.6. The trainer should have the correct answers recorded on flip charts/boards and displayed for all participants to see and absorb.
5.7. At the beginning, the trainer should also appoint a score who keeps the scorecard.
5.8. The trainer to supplement the answers in case the fish-bowl debate does not bring out all the essential elements.
5.9. It is very important that the trainer prepares well in advance and all the questions ready for the two groups to begin with.

6. *Small group discussion and lecture for role of facilitator/initiator of network*

In step 6, use small group discussion and lecture, for which the process is described below:

6.1. Divide the participants in small groups of 5-6 participants.
6.2. Ask the groups to discuss the role of facilitator/initiator of network.
6.3. Ask the groups to note the points of group discussion.
6.4. Give 10-15 minutes for the discussion.

6.5. Ask the groups to present their points of discussion.
6.6. Evaluate the points after the group discussion is over. The trainer then explains the role of facilitator/initiator of the network. The trainer is encouraged to draw upon the material in Appendix-D.

---

7. *Use video case studies to show practices in networks of elected women representatives*

In step 7, use the video case studies to illustrate the practices in network of elected women Panchayat members. This is a very effective medium for learning.

7.1. Ask the participants to note down the learning points from the video.
7.2. Explain the back group information about the cases, if necessary.
7.3. Show the video case studies of network of elected women PRI members.
7.4. Ask the learning points from each participant after the video show is over.

---

8. *Use the lecture method to explain critiques of networks*

In step 8, use the lecture method to illustrate critiques of networks.

8.1. Ask the participants whether they have ever undertaken any form of network.
8.2. Ask them to write on flash cards the critique they observed.
8.3. Compare these critiques with the critiques outlined by the trainer.
4.4. If none of the participants not seen or undertaken any form of network, request them to reflect on the trainer presentation on the probable critiques.
4.5. The participants then write the critique they expect in network on the basis of their experience.
4.6. The trainer to summarize the sub-session's learning using visuals like transparencies, flip charts or power point presentation.

---

9. *Visual method for synthesizing what we have learnt from the sub-session*

In step 9, synthesize the important learning from the sub-session.

9.1. Each participant to list at least one important lesson. The participants should be encouraged to write on flash cards the lessons they have learnt.
9.2. Place the flash cards on the floor.
9.3. Club together cards which indicate the same or similar lessons learnt.
9.4. Compile one list of lessons learnt.
9.5. If there is any important lesson learnt is missing, in the opinion of the trainer, she/he should add the missing lesson(s) learnt.

Types of Network

Informal Support Networks

It is particularly valuable in the early days of trying to mainstream gender *within* an organisation, policy development process or project for staff trying to promote attention to gender to from an informal support network of *like-minded people.* People attend as individuals, not as organisational representatives. The key issue is that members choose to attend and have a reasonable relationship of trust from the outset. These informal network provide much needed personal support in what can be a very stressful and marginalised role. They provide a stressful and marginalised role. They provide a supportive environment to brainstorm ideas, reflect on experiences and recover from disasters!

Formal Internal Networks and Working Parties

These are networks recognised and legitimised by the organisation or organisations involved, with people attending in their professional capacity and reporting back They include gender working parties, gender focal point networks, and donor gender networks.

Gender Working Parties

A network formed when there is some degree of recognisation within an organisation that gender is an issue that needs to be addressed. The aim is to involve a range of staff in developing strategies that will be effective and relevant to all aspect of the organisation's work. Tasks might include co-ordinating the developing of a gender mainstreaming policy, with individual members representing the interests of different departments; developing an appropriate gender training strategy, with individual an appropriate gender training strategy, with individual members responsible for assessing training needs in their different departments; and co-ordinating the implementation and monitoring of a gender policy.

(*Contd.*)

(*Contd.*)

Focal Point Networks

Government ministries, in particular, frequently appoint/nominate "gender focal staff" to promote attention to gender in their own sector/department, in pursuance of policy commitments to gender mainstreaming. It is particularly beneficial to form focal staff networks, usually under the co-ordination of the national women's machinery, to link together staff trying to promote attention to gender in different ministries and departments. These are a forum for developing strategies, building capacity and providing personal and professional support.

Donor Gender Networks

These bring together staff within donor organisations responsible for mainstreaming gender within their own organisations on programmes, as well as supporting women-specific initiatives. They are important to co-ordinate the work of different donor and avoid duplication; share experiences on and approaches to mainstreaming gender; share approaches to supporting the local women's movement; and share information about local organisation and consultants.

Advocacy Networks

Gender advocates lobbying development organisations either from the inside or outside to promote attention to gender equality in legislation, policies and programmes are far more effective when efforts are co-ordinated. In the context of national policy frameworks, individual staff and organisations, including donors, have limited power on their own to influence the agenda. It is essential for gender advocates within donor organisations to co-ordinate with gender focal staff within government and with civil society groups to co-ordinate activities, develop strategies and take advantage of opportunities.

Internal advocates linking with external networks.

An important part of effective advocacy is for focal staff within government and development organisations to communicate with and gain the confidence and support of support of constituents outside the organisation. Links between gender focal staff and women's organisations, gender equality advocates and research centres enrich the resources, knowledge and expertise available internally, broaden the input and influence of outside organisations, provide moral support to internal advocates and can increase their leverage.

(*Contd.*)

(*Contd.*)

External pressure groups

It has been "seen time and time again that effective mainstreaming requires sustained pressure, over a long period, on governments, bilateral and multilateral agencies, the private sector, the media and other actors by women, women's movements and their allies. Without an empowered group of women advocating for and guiding gender sensitive policies and practice, the work of mainstreaming is prey to the particular skills and interests of a changing cast of governmental, bilateral, and multilateral personnel who may or may not have a commitment to or understanding of gender mainstreaming and equality.

Electronic Networks

There are a number of gender and development email networks. These can be a useful opportunity to share information, ideas and experiences, although clearly access is restricted to those who have the necessary hardware, infrastructure and resources.

SESSION 12 EMPOWERMENT OF WOMEN MEMBERS OF PRIs

Session Name	EMPOWERMENT OF WOMEN MEMBERS OF PRIs
Duration	215 minutes
Venue	Classroom with furniture
Seating	Sit on the floor or on chairs
Session objective	*To equip the participants about the concept and need of empowerment of women and skills and abilities for empowerment of women*

Expected Learning Outcomes

- The participants understand the concept and need of empowerment of women; and
- They are equipped with skills to enhance skills and abilities for empowerment of women in general and of the women members of PRIs in particular.

Content flow and training methodology

Sr. No.	*Content*	*Training Methodology*	*Training Aids*	*Duration in Minutes*
1.	Energizer game	Step 1 Dragon	None	15
2.	Concept and need (Why?) empowerment	Step 2 Small group discussion and lecture (roles/responsibi-lities) Participatory discussion on disempowering/ empowering factors -Self -Family -Community -State	Flash cards	30

(*Contd.*)

Sr. No.	*Content*	*Training Methodology*	*Training Aids*	*Duration Minutes*
3.	Elements of empowerment (Indicators and tools)	Step 3 Empowerment circle	Flash cards, flip charts, markers and *bindis*	110
4.	How to strengthen empowerment of women in PRIs	Step 4 Experience sharing	Flash cards	45
5.	Violence against women and women members of Panchayats	Experience sharing, sorting, reflection and lecture	Flash cards, pens, flip charts, white-board and white-board markers	90
6.	Synthesis of learning points by trainer/participants	Step 5 Visual method	Chart, marker	15

THE METHODOLOGICAL STEPS FOR SUB-SESSION 12

1. Play an energizing game Dragon

In step 1, the participants play "Dragon", an active game as follows:

1.1. The objective of the game is to energize the group before they begin the next phase of sub-session.

1.2. Find an open space outside and invite everyone to stand there.

1.3. Ask the participants to form a line or a dragon and ask them to run. And concurrently ask the front of the line to catch its tail. Then stop the dragon, turn the participants to face the other direction, and have the tail then catch the head.

1.4. This will result in a lot of smiling and laughing. This provides only a brief and energizing break for the participants. This fact should be told to the participants, otherwise, they would be expecting a moral theme from the game.

2. *Use Small group discussion and lecture to explain the concept and need of empowerment*

In step 2, there is a need to first explain the concept of empowerment. Follow these steps:

2.1. Form small groups of 4-5 participants depending upon the number of participants.

2.2. Ask the participants to discuss among them empowering factors in their life and factors which facilitate their work as representatives of the people in PRIs.

2.3. Ask the participants to organize and categorise these factors into following four categorise:

- Self
- Family
- Community
- State

Flash cards of different colours can be used for separate categories.

2.4. Repeat the process for disempowering factors.

2.5. Paste the cards from different groups on big sheets category-wise and ask the participants to have a good look at them. Participants can also be asked to read out cards.

2.6. Evaluate the list after the group presentation is over. The trainer then explains the concept and need of women empowerment.

---

3. *Use empowerment circle exercise to explain elements of empowerment of women Panchayat members*

In step 3, use empowerment circle exercise to explain the elements of empowerment. The example of empowerment circle is attached in teaching notes at Annexure-1 of this sub-session.

3.1. Ask the participants to identify various elements of empowerments. This can be done by asking them to identify traits of our empowered women PRI members.

3.2. Draw a "huge circle" either on the ground or on several flip charts joined together.

3.3. Write each of these elements on separate cards and keep them on the radius of a big circle.

3.4. Draw different radii from each of the elements to the centre of the circle. Each radius represents one skill/ability/traits.

3.5. Ask the participants to place themselves according to their understanding on each radius. The point at the centre of the circle for a particular radius indicates the status that the skill/ability/traits represented by the radius is zero for the participants. As against this, the point where the relative radius meets the circumference of the circle, participants indicate the presence of 100 per cent of the relative skill/ability/traits represented by the radius. Explain this to all the participants.

3.6. Give each of the participants "bindis" or seeds or post-it slips, with the advice to place one bindi/seed/slip along one radius indicating the level of availability of skills/abilities in the women members/ functionaries of PRIs in the states they represent (on a "zero to hundred" scale explained above).

3.7. The participants have the option of not indicating the skill/ability if they are not sure or ambivalent about the position they should indicate for their state.

3.8. The trainer then explains the findings of exercise. If on a particular radius most of the bindis are towards the centre, then the particular skill/ability/trait is low in the state. If on the other hand, most of the bindis on a radius are nearer to the circumference then the availability of the skill/ability/trait represented by the radius is high in the state.

3.9. The trainer should then be able to integrate the findings of all the radius together. If, for instance, most of the bindis on most of the radii are towards the circumference, then the state of empowerment of the women members of PRIs is good. If, on the contrary, most of the bindis on most of the radii are near the centre, then the status of empowerment of women members of PRIs is poor.

3.10. The trainer should also indicate that similar exercises could be done for a particular state or for a particular Panchayat or even for individual women members of Panchayats.

---

4. *Use experience-sharing exercise to explain strategic areas to strengthen empowerment of women elected members*

In step 4, it is suggested that the trainer uses discussion and experience sharing method with the suitable aids for explaining the strategic areas to strengthen empowerment of women elected members.

4.1. Ask each participant to think of one incidence during their tenure as representatives where they were able to get a particular job/ work done or put things assertively and have gone success through that.

4.2. While the participant is telling her story, put important factors behind the success, as coming up from the story, on a chart. Questions could be: 'What do you think made the work it possible?' 'What (according to you) was the reason that was responsible for the success?' can be asked in between for facilitation.

4.3. Similar processes can be repeated asking participants to recite an incident when they felt constrained due to lack of a particular skill/ understanding and other reason.

4.4. At the end, the trainer will have a list of areas/abilities/traits responsible for success and failures coming out from experiences of the participants.
4.5. At the end, the facilitator can consolidate and explain the emerging points on empowerment to the participants.

5. *Combating Violence Against Women*

5.1. The trainer should first explain the concept of violence and its various forms: physical and psychological.
5.2. The participants should then be divided into three groups, each group being asked to think about violence against women in the household, violence in the workplace and violence against women in society, respectively. The groups should write the outcome of their reflection on flip-charts.
5.3. The participants from each group is then requested to present their reflection to the plenary.
5.4. The trainer then gives a brief presentation on the legal safeguards available against each type of violence.
5.5. The participants are again asked to return to their respective groups and reflect on what could be done through building social capital and through social mobilisation to combat the kind of violence against women they had discussed earlier. The participants should write these measures on "Flash Cards", which are used to prepare posters.
5.6. The participants then present their findings as posters: one poster on measures to combat domestic violence against women, one on measures to combat violence against women in the work place and the third on measures to combat violence against women in society.
5.7. The groups should then view each others, posters and seek clarifications, of any and suggest additional measures as required.
5.8. The trainer should then synthesise the leanings using either flip charts or transparencies.

6. *Visual method for synthesizing what we have learnt from the sub-session*

In step 5, the trainer fills in any knowledge gaps that remain and then concludes the session by synthesizing the learning points. The flip charts or cards prepared by the participants can be used. Alternatively, one of the participants can be requested to do the synthesis.

In the synthesis, the trainer can also analyze the skills/abilities/traits of an empowered woman, known to the participants.

Annexure-1 of Session-12

EXAMPLE OF EMPOWERMENT CIRCLE EXERCISE[20]

Once the participants (women Panchayat members) identified the problems, challenges and opportunities facing women members/functionaries of PRIs, the issue of empowerment of women members of Panchayats was taken up for examination. During the course of the workshop, women representatives repeatedly mentioned one specific area for improving the effectiveness of women Panchayat leaders and that was *self-empowerment*. The participants themselves identified the skills and abilities as in Box 1 that need to be developed in the women leaders, to call them "empowered".

Box 1: Skills and Abilities for Empowerment

(i) Self-confidence
(ii) Ability to understand the public
(iii) Ability to view public equally without discrimination
(iv) Ability to march forward
(v) Ability to take decision
(vi) Ability to ensure public participation
(vii) Ability to provide total literacy
(viii) Financial independence

Having identified the skills and abilities that are critical for empowerment of women members of PRIs, the participants were taken through participatory process of assessing the level of empowerment of women members/functionaries in the different states, namely, preparing and analyzing the empowerment circle. The process followed was somewhat like the following:

A circle was drawn with eight radii. Each radius represented one skill/ability along which the relative skill/ability was written. The point at the centre of the circle for a particular radius indicated the position that the skill/ability represented by the radius as zero. As against this, the point

---

20. Extracted from Workshop Report on Training Needs Assessment of Women PRIs Members held at New Delhi from 10th-12th January, 2004, Organized by Rajiv Gandhi Foundation, New Delhi.

where the relative radius met the circumference of the circle indicated the presence of 100 per cent of the relative skill/ability represented by the radius. This was explained to all the participants.

Each of the participants were then given eight "bindis" with the advice to place one bindi along one radius indicating the level of availability of skills/abilities in the women members/functionaries of PRIs in the states they represented (on a "zero to hundred" scale explained above). The participants had the option of not indicating the skill/ability if they were not sure or ambivalent about the position she should indicate.

EMPOWERMENT CIRCLE EXERCISE

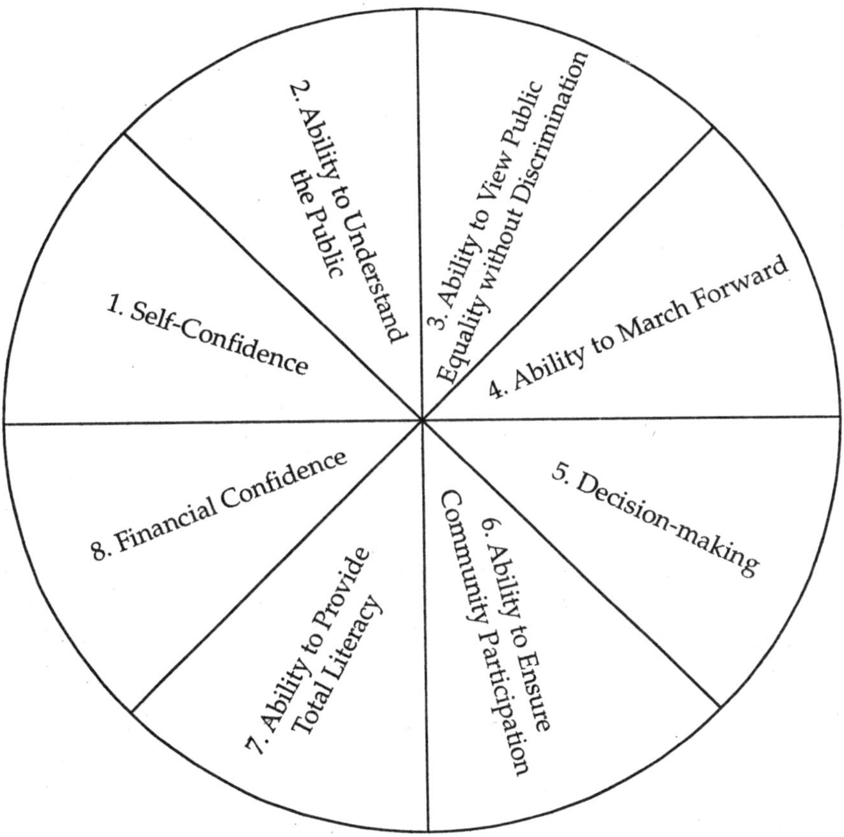

Skills and abilities for empowerment of women functionaries in PRIs

An analysis of the empowerment circle is as below.

Skills and abilities for empowerment of women functionaries in PRIs

S. No.	*Percentage→ Skills and Abilities for Empowerment ↓*	*Total no. of responses*	*0-25*	*26-50*	*51-75*	*76-100*
1.	Self-confidence	23	-	-	13.04	86.95
2.	Ability to understand the public	21	14.28	33.33	52.38	-
3.	Ability to view public equally without discrimination	20	5	40	55	-
4.	Ability to march forward	24	-	16.66	41.66	41.66
5.	Ability to take decisions	20	-	-	30	70
6.	Ability to ensure public participation	22	-	18.18	40.90	40.90
7.	Ability to provide total literacy (educate)	22	4.54	9.09	27.27	59.09
8.	Financial independence	22	-	13.63	31.81	54.54

The empowerment circle indicates fairly clearly that women functionaries of PRIs have fairly high levels of skills and abilities to feel that they are empowered. However, about 40-60 per cent of them still fall short of the "optimum levels" of ability to march forward, ability to ensure public participation and educate their constituencies impartially. Thus, the picture that the empowerment circle and its analysis present is a mixed one. While most of the elements of empowerment were present in the women functionaries, it was somewhat surprising that many of them had the characteristics of empowerment at levels, just above the 50 per cent mark and only a few saw themselves as fully empowered. Thus while women functionaries/members in PRIs are in the decision making process, there is something that is left to be desired on many of the elements. The message was clear: much more work on empowerment of women in PRIs is urgently called for.

SESSION 13 MICRO PLANNING FOR PANCHAYATS

Session Name PARTICIPATORY PLANNING FOR PANCHAYAT PLANNING

Duration 300 minutes

Venue Classroom with furniture those are movable

Seating Sit on the floor or on chairs

Session objective *To equip the participants about the concept and need of participatory planning and skills and abilities to develop village plan for gender equity and social justice*

Expected Learning Outcomes

- To enable the participants to comprehend the process of people's participation in planning for empowerment of women for gender equity; and
- To equip the participants with the functional skills required for engaging in planning for gender equity and social justice at the micro-level.

Content flow and training methodology

Sr. No.	*Content*	*Training Methodology*	*Training Aids*	*Duration and Minutes*
1.	The dream village: vision	**Step 1** The participants visualize and prepare a map of their dream village and articulate their vision for their village with gender equity and empowered women	Flip charts, flash cards and markers	60

(*Contd.*)

Sr. No.	*Content*	*Training Methodology*	*Training Aids*	*Duration and Minutes*
2.	Problem identification of problems encountered by women functionaries regarding space, time, priorities, relationships and institutions in guaranteeing gender equity and empowerment of women members of PRIs and their prioritization	**Step 2** PLA: Listing, oral history, time lines, transects and historical transects, seasonality analysis, force field analysis and scoring/ranking can be selectively used.	Flip charts, flash cards and markers	60
3.	Context analysis for tactical planning: Analysis of space, time, priorities, relationships and institutions in guaranteeing gender equity and empowerment of women members of PRIs	**Step 3** PLA: Gendered Maps (Literacy Maps, Health Maps, Access Maps etc.), Gendered Venn Diagramming, Relational Diagramming; Gendered Social Interface Diagramming etc. can be selectively used.	Flip charts, flash cards, chart papers, flip charts, pencils, scissors, gums/pastes and markers	60

(*Contd.*)

Sr. No.	*Content*	*Training Methodology*	*Training Aids*	*Duration and Minutes*
4.	Solutions of problems of space, time, priorities, relationships and institutions in guaranteeing gender equity and empowerment of women members of PRIs and prioritization	**Step 4** PLA: Listing, Relational Matrices, genealogical charts, group discussion and scoring/ranking can be selectively used.	Flip charts, flash cards and markers	60
5.	Action planning	**Step 5** PLA methods	Flip charts, flash cards and markers	60

Note: No steps have been written down for this session for reasons recorded below:

(a) In real sense, there is no manual on how PLA methods are applied. It depends on the ability of facilitators of participatory sessions in the actual scene of the planning.
(b) The facilitators are encouraged to improvise, innovate and invent. Hence a blue print is considered inappropriate and hence not provided.
(c) The trainer (who trains) in Micro-Planning is assumed to be a trained PLA practitioner, and would know these steps. An uninitiated trainer cannot impart training on these sessions.

Trainers who wish to have the planning sessions in greater detail are invited to see Chapters 3 and 4 of Amitava Mukherjee: *Participatory Rural Appraisal: Methods & Application in Rural Planning* (Concept Publishing Co: New Delhi) 2004. See also relevant sessions on Micro-level planning in D. Bandyopadhyay, Amitava Mukherjee and Mitali Sen Govai: *Empowering Panchayats: A Handbook for Master Trainers.* (Concept Publishing Co.: New Delhi) 2004.

Session 14 GROUP DYNAMICS

Session Name	MANAGEMENT ORIENTATION : GROUP DYNAMICS AND GROUP BEHAVIOURS*
Duration	250 mins
Venue	Class room
Seating	Sitting on ground in circular form or moving for the game and role play
Session objective	*To widen understanding of participants on group dynamics and develop their skills on appropriate group behaviours.*

Expected Learning Outcomes

- The participants develop an understanding of group dynamics; and
- They acquire the appropriate basic skills on managing group behaviours.

Content/flow and Methodology

Sr. No.	*Session Content*	*Training Methodology*	*Duration*	*Tips for the Trainers*
1.	What is a group and group processes	Large group discussion	30 mins	While briefing "group relate the discussion with their past experiences. • Use simple examples to deliberate meaning of group to the participants.
2.	Participation	• Lecture	30 mins	• Trainer may also use other technique than lecture to deliberate process of participation in panchayats.
3.	Decision making in context to Panchayats	• Case study—who is the killer? • Lecture	45 mins	• Divide the participants into four groups with the help of numbers. • After the group discussion each group must be interviewed separately as to what was their experience in reaching to a decision.

(*Contd.*)

* This session draws substantively on the contribution of Shri Ashok Kumar Singh, Sahbhagi Shikshan Kendra, Lucknow.

Sr. No.	*Session Content*	*Training Methodology*	*Duration*	*Tips for the Trainers*
				• Problem faced by each group must be heard carefully so that assessment of the decision making process may be linked with their experiences by the trainer.
4.	Conflict resolution	Lecture	45 mins	• To organize role play. The trainer should be clear while briefing the roles to the participants.
5.	Communication in group dynamics and group behaviour	Gossip Game/Camel bathing Lecture	45 mins	• Any one of gossip game and "camel bathing game" may be used to demonstrate the process of communication within the group. The procedure of the game must be discussed prior to the game.
6.	Leadership in group dynamics and group behaviour	Educational game (P&T) Lecture	45 mins	• To deliberate on the process of leadership. Educational instrument may be used.
7.	Synthesis of learning	Sharing	10 mins	• Views of all the participants must be sought while synthesizing the learning points.
	Total		250 mins	

METHODOLOGICAL STEPS FOR SESSION 14

1. Introduction

The session aims at orienting the trainees on the group dynamics and developing their skills on group processes. Processes like leadership, communication, decision-making etc. are discussed in the sub-sessions in context to Panchayats.

2. Sub-session 1: What is a group?

In ***Step-2*** the trainer takes the group through a process of learning about the concepts by checking the same against their experience.

2.1. Trainer starts the session by inviting participants view as to what they understand by group? The participants may be probed by asking questions like:

2.2. Ask if a number of people standing on bus station will be called a group? Can number of women standing near well to have water will be called group?

2.3. The trainer may now consolidating the answers of participants the trainer may give his input on following basis.

2.4. Draw the attention of the trainer to the fact that we are all in some way or other, members of group-groups like the family, a club, an organization and so forth.

2.5. Now ask the participants if a group just a collection of people? What distinguishes it from any accidental or incidental gathering of people, from a crowd or mob?

2.6. Based on the responses to the question give the following input: A group has the following characteristics:

- An objective or goal, or a common and shared purpose.
- A framework of boundary in terms of time and space.
- A definable membership which is relatively stable.
- Interaction and interdependence between members.
- A group consciousness or a conscious identification with each other.
- The ability to act together as one unit or organism.

2.7. The trainer may show thus, how a number of individuals standing at a bus stop waiting for the same bus would not qualify to be called a group. But if an accident occurs on the road and these individuals begin to act cooperatively, united by a common concern for the accident victim, they might briefly become a group.

Indicate that a group undergoes through few processes. The processes of the group can be discussed as in the subsequent sub-sessions.

Sub-session 2: Participation

In ***Step-3***, the Trainer now introduces the group processes called "participation".

1. Use Lecture method to:
   - *explain* the process of participation (may draw attention to the kinds of participation) as the issue of participation is an

important process that operates continuously within the group of Panchayat representatives.

- *emphasize* that participation is a fundamental process within a group, because many of the other processes depend upon participations of the various members.
- *indicate* that levels and degrees of participation vary (while some members are active participants—talkative, demanding, volatile, while others are more withdrawn, quiet, passive).
- *point out* that in essence, participation means involvement, concern for the task, direct or indirect contribution to the group goal[21].

3.2. Now discuss the factors which affect members' participation, while a participant writes these upon a flip chart (if none of the participants are literate, the trainer should write them up):

- The **content** of task of the group—it is of interest, importance and relevance.
- The physical atmosphere—is it comfortable physically, socially and psychologically.
- The psychological atmosphere—is it accepting, non-threatening.
- Members personal preoccupation—are there any distracting thoughts their mind?
- The level of interaction and discussions—is adequate information provided for everyone to understand?—is it at a level everyone understands?
- Familiarity between group members—do members know each other from before.

3.3. Invite question and answer session. Ask participants to locate in their experiences the occurrences of these phenomenon.

Sub-session 3: Decision-Making in the Context of Panchayats.

In Step-4, the importance of decision making has to be introduced. To demonstrate the process of decision making within Panchayat, the trainer

21. It may be worth indicating that participation by members is basic to the existence of a group. If members do not participate, the group ceases to exist. But this participation does not mean just physical presence or that everyone speaks. Silent members could be listening very carefully. What needs to be identified and tackled are the members who are "there but not there" those who are indifferent, uninvolved or could not care less. They can potentially damage the group.

can use case study on the decision making (a suggestive case study is attached in the manual as annexure). The case study would help in sharply pointing out the kind of processes that occur in any group engaged in taking decisions.

4.1. Ask the participants to get themselves divided into four groups.

4.2. Ask the four Groups to read the case study. Give sufficient time. If there are barriers to reading the case study the trainer might read the case study to the three should be asked to have a dialogue on the case study and take one decision with consensus. Allow sufficient time.

4.3. Once the discussion the trainer should ask participants to sit in their groups in the plenary, to consolidate their respective discussions. Trainer may like to ask questions like:
   - Could the groups reach to consensus while taking decision.
   - If not what were the reasons?

4.4. Ask the question to each group and record the response either on White/Black Board or Flip Charts. After noting the replies on White/Black Board or the Flip Chart, discuss the reasons why the groups could not reach to a consensus. After the groups have come with their answers, point out that consensus is difficult because different people have different mental set up and come from different background leading to diversity of opinion on a single topic.

4.5. The trainer now uses lecture method to explain different decision making manners within the group. Decision making within a group takes place in one or more of the following manners:
   - The plop
   - Self authorized
   - Pairing
   - Minority group
   - Vote
   - Consensus

Sub-session 4: Conflict Resolution

In ***Step-5,*** the trainer starts the session using lecture method to introduce the concept of conflict resolution. He may relate the content of this session with the previous session on decision making during the lecture.

5.1. Indicate that most groups (for example as group of Gram Panchayat members) find themselves unable to solve problems because they address the problem at a superficial level. After that they find themselves "blocked" because they cannot figure out why the problem occurred and how they can tackle it. Therefore, an effective problem-solving would be to:

- Clearly define the problem: is it what appears on the surface or are there deeper hidden aspects. Use a Problem Tree Analysis for this.[22]
- Try to thoroughly explore and understand the causes behind the problem, which a Problem Tree Analysis helps to do.
- Collect additional information, from elsewhere if necessary, and analyze it to understand the problem further.
- Think of solutions or look for solutions: in this it is useful to stop thinking according to the usual logic and normal sequence, and deliberately think of 'wild ideas' which are apparently not relevant. Creativity and imagination are needed to spot new patterns within the same set of facts. The group should suspend criticism and judgement for a while and should be to generate as many ideas and suggestions as possible. This is called 'brainstorming' in a group, when individuals try lateral thinking.
- Choose the appropriate alternative. There will be some conflict to be resolved there. Collaborative and consensus based resolution is preferable to forcing a choice. Considerable discussion is needed to evaluate the various alternative solutions on the constraints and available resources.
- Implement the solution through a plan, and evaluation how the problem is solved.

Sub-session 5: Communication

In *Step-6,* Trainer starts the session with a game on communication named gossip or camel bathing. Gossip game is given below for reference of the trainer.

22. If the Trainer thinks necessary, he could conduct a mock Problem Tree Analysis.

Training Application	Time Reference: Approximately 5 to 10 minutes. Group size: Unlimited, but best suited for a group of 10 to 25 participants. If the group contains more than 25 participants, subgroups should be formed. Space required: A room that has the potential for flexible seating.
Methodology	1. The trainer asks the group members to form a circular seating arrangement. 2. When the participants are seated, the trainer tells then that they will be playing a familiar game. Gossip. 3. The group leader then explains trainer how the game will be played. The sender must whisper the rumor clearly, but he or she cannot repeat the rumour if the listener has not heard it correctly. 4. The trainer begins the game by whispering one rumour in the ear of the person sitting to his or her right and then another rumour in the ear of the person to his or her left. 5. Both rumours continue around the circle, the last persons to receive them must repeat what they have heard. The original rumours are then read to the entire group.

6.1. After the game starts explaining what was happening. Start by saying that the process which was taking place is called *communication*. Now discuss the definition of communication.

6.2. Stress that communication within a group deals with the spoken and the unspoken, the verbal and the non-verbal, and the explicit and the implied messages that are conveyed and exchanged relating to information and ideas, values and feelings.

6.3. Indicate that to clearly understand the various exchanges while they occur, one has to consider various aspects of communication[23], like direction, mode and reception.

1. *The direction of communication*
    - One-way and two-way communication
    - Communication Networks
    - Communicating 'Upwards' or 'Downwards'
2. *The mode of communication:*
    - Verbal
    - Non-verbal
    - Paralinguistic

6.4. Now discuss some Barriers to effective communication with the participants.

23. The trainer can also draw upon the discussion on the general notes to the trainers.

Personal

(a) Our values, opinions, prejudices and attitudes.

(b) The tendency to see one and only one way of doing things—our way.

(c) The tendency to speak or react before thinking.

(d) Stereotyping people-making quick generalizations.

(e) Words and phrases have specific personalized meaning, we assume the same meanings when they are used by others.

(f) Lack of trust.

Situational

(a) Physical well-being and mood of the individual.

(b) Differences in backgrounds and context between the parties.

(c) Differences in language.

6.6. Emphasize that good communication needs good listening. Discuss the *Guidelines for Effective Listening* as under and while so doing request a participant to write them upon the flip chart:

(i) Concentrate on hearing - we think about 4 times faster than the other person can speak, so our thoughts tend to stray.

(ii) We must listen with an open mind - we often stop listening when we hear some key words - 'red flags' - which touch our personal biases or preferences.

(iii) Pay attention and try to understand what is being said - listen beyond the words, try to understand the feelings, the emotions, what is being implied. Be alert to the various non - verbal messages.

(iv) Do not predict - what the speaker is trying to say - do not jump to conclusions and stop listening, find out for sure whether what you think is true or not.

(v) Do not pretend to have understood - when you have not - clarify your doubts, request the speaker to re-explain, ask relevant questions.

(vi) Do not become defensive and do not argue or interrupt - when the speaker challenges some of our favorite ideas our immediate reaction is to either stop listening or to interrupt and argue.

6.7. Paste the Flip Chart on the Wall and give the participants Flash Cards. Ask them to reflect on the flip chart and make a self - assessment of how good a listener they are individually by giving themselves a score of 2 if they follow the different elements of the Guidelines.

Sub-session 6: Leadership

Step-7. The session aims at imparting knowledge to the participants on leadership skills. Trainer uses game and facilitates a process in which the participants discover their leadership pattern.

7.1. Provide a copy of the exercise to participants. Help out the participants who are unable to read and write.
7.2. Allow the participants to score.
7.3. After scoring of the exercise, trainer uses lecture method to discuss leadership skills emphasizing:
  - Leadership involved focusing the efforts of the people towards a common goal and to enable them to work together as one. In general we designate one individual as the leader. This individual may be chosen from within or appointed from outside. (For example, a pradhan is elected by Gram Sabha).
  - In a small group, the leadership function (unlike the leader) is not static, but is performed by different members of the Group at different times (panchayat members are heads of different committees). Thus one member may provide leadership with respect to achieving the goal of the group (say of while a different individual may be providing leadership to maintain the veracity of the group.
  - It is interesting to note how leadership is assumed, challenged, and changed in the course of a small group's life. The reactions, behaviour and role of the designated leader are also noteworthy.

7.4. The trainer then discusses three leadership styles of roles which a leader needs to play.

  Leadership Styles:
  - The Autocratic Leader
  - The *Lassez-Faire* Leader
  - The Democratic Leader

7.5. Now discuss the three leadership styles of roles which a leader needs to play. Role of a leader are as follows:
  A Leader has to help:
  - Raise the members' awareness and motivation and increase the readiness of members to accept responsibility.
  - Develop group work and group moral.
  - Convince the group that they can effect change.

7.6. Now synthesize the learning points.

- Each participant to list at least one important lesson. The participants should be encouraged talk about the lessons learnt.
- The trainer should write the points on white board or flip chart.
- Club together points which indicate the same or similar lesson learnt.
- Compile one list of lessons learnt.
- If any important lesson learnt is missing, in the opinion of the trainer, she/he should add the missing lesson(s).

Chapter 4

EVALUATION OF TRAINING MODULES

I. Introduction

Keeping in mind the importance of training in capacity building of women members of Panchayats, it is desirable to have a rigorous Evaluation Framework for the training modules for the ready reference of an observer or even the trainer herself/himself. Such a framework has been prepared keeping in mind all causal factors, which would expectedly be impinging upon the training effectiveness[1] of the modules. The validation of the modules has to be made in terms of clearly defined processes and, wherever possible, measurable outcomes. Hence, the evaluation framework suggested is a mix of qualitative comments and numerical grades on a 5-point scale. The observer is expected to hold extensive discussions with the trainers and trainees and give specific suggestions for improvements and replications, wherever possible.

II. Education Schedules

Two Evaluation Schedules have been proposed. Evaluation Schedule I assesses the training module in its entirely and is more detailed. It includes both qualitative and quantitative measures. Evaluation Schedule II is a single numerical sheet common for all sessions. The observer is expected to record detailed session-wise comments separately also.

The ascending 5-point scale for grading each evaluation question is given below:

←――――――――――――――――――――――→

Unsatisfactory   Fair   Good   Very Good   Excellent

Name of the Resource Institute:

Training Module in Use:

Duration of Training:

Venue of Training:

Profile of Trainee Group:

Evaluation Schedule I

An Overall Assessment of the Training Module

Sl. No.	*Focus Areas/Evaluation Questions*	*Training Observer's Qualifying Comments & Suggestions for Improvements/Replications*	*Overall Grade*
1.	Was there a training needs assessment conducted?		
2.	How was the training needs assessment done: review of existing material, interviews, institutional memory, etc.?		
3.	Degree of correlation of training design and content with findings from other sources on which design and content are premised		
4.	Degree of correlation of the training goal and objectives with the felt training needs of the participants.		
5.	Whether the module is State specific and to what degree?		
6.	Is the duration of training appropriate for the State in question?		
7.	Is the mix of classroom and peripatetic training the right one?		

(*Contd.*)

Sl. No.	*Focus Areas/Evaluation Questions*	*Training Observer's Qualifying Comments & Suggestions for Improvements/Replications*	*Overall Grade*
8.	Comment upon the flow and sequencing of the training content. Does the content flow from the "known to unknown drawing upon the knowledge and skill base of the PRI functionaries".		
9.	Comment upon the degree of inclusion in the training content of subject areas and values/perspectives related to desired affirmative actions for the three groups: gender, SCs and STs.		
10.	Comment on the Training Methodology used.		
	1. Whether participatory.		
	2. Variety and mixing of methods[2] and their sequencing.		
	3. Whether choice of training methods matches the training content[3].		
11.	Trainee Learner Status. Assess the average motivation to learn[4] of trainees.		
12.	Training nature and quality of training aids, training literature, etc. that are used.		

Evaluation Schedule II

Please use this schedule to comment and grade the sessions on the given scale of 1-5 for each attribute. Make detailed comments separately for the each session.

Sl. No.	*Evaluation Focus/Question*	*Session Name & No.*									
		1	*2*	*3*	*4*	*5*	*6*	*7*	*8*	*9*	*10*
1.	Relevance of Session subject Area[5]										
2.	Is the Session goal Appropriate?										
3.	Has the Session Goal been achieved?										
4.	Are the Session Objectives appropriate?										
5.	Have Session Objectives been achieved?										
6.	Selection of Venue—is it appropriate?										
7.	Quality of Training Aids used[6].										
8.	Adequacy of session duration.										
9.	How participatory was the training methodology used?										
10.	Skills and knowledge base of the trainer										
11.	Quality of the session pedagogy[7]										
12.	To what extent have the trainees grasped the essence of the main learning points flowing from the session?[8]										
13.	Total										

NOTES

1. Training Effectiveness is defined as the degree of fulfilment of pre-determined training objectives, which are framed based upon the training needs that are identified through a Training Needs Assessment.
2. Record the different training methodologies used like Participatory Learning and Appraisal, case study method, experiential learning, audiovisuals, group work, case work, games, role play etc. and their special effects, if any.
3. Give an overall view of the entire module, since the session-wise choice of training methodology vis-a-vis training content of session will be evaluated separately in Schedule II.

4. Called "Learner Valence", please grade (very high LV = 5) and identify both eager and hesitant/reluctant learners in the course of the training programme and explore and record their profiles explaining very high or very low LV.
5. Assess in discussion with the trainees. The most relevant sessions may be specifically identified, along with the least useful.
6. Record about the nature of the Training Aids used in your separate comment sheet.
7. Assess this in terms of content flow, matching of content and training methodology, degree of participation, whether transfer of knowledge base is from "Known to unknown", trainer attitudes, learner motivation etc.
8. Discuss the learning points with the trainer before the session begins and identify at most 3 points. At the end of the session, do a quick collaborative identification of what the trainees have learnt through the session. Please grade this question depending on whether they have grasped the main learning points and not the number of points.

Chapter 5

CASE STUDIES

I. SOCIAL MOBILISATION

Case 1: Seeds of the Right to Information Movement and Demand for Transparency in Panchayats: The Rajasthan Case

(i) Introduction

The majority of women representatives elected to panchayats are "first timers".

They do not generally have the required information on development programmes implemented by Panchayats. They are further handicapped in many cases by lack of formal education. The institutions of caste and patriarchy have traditionally restricted the participation of women in local politics. Traditionally, women were confined to the four walls of their households, which has over the years affected their access to information on politics, development and projects implemented by Panchayats.

(ii) The Background

In 1990s, the two programmes implemented by Panchayati Raj Institutions (PRIs) all over India were Jawahar Gram Samridhi Yojana (JGSY) (Rural Infrastructure Programme) and Employment Assurance Scheme (EAS) of the Government of India. The purpose of these programmes was to provide wage employment both in lean agricultural seasons in rural areas of India and in case of natural calamities like droughts, floods and earthquakes and additionally create community assets in rural areas. In the allotment of works, the preference was to be given to groups like dalits, adivasis, women and wage labourers living below the poverty line.

(iii) The Problem

In most of the states, rampant corruption amongst Panchayat representatives, officials and contractors made these programmes only partially successful. The Mazdoor Kisan Shakti Sangathan (MKSS), a mass based organisation working for rights of wage labourers, in some Gram Panchayats of Pali and Rajsamand districts in Rajasthan, found 85 per cent of the estimated rural development budget was not spent on development work.[1] The labourers were paid at best Rs. 10 to Rs.14 per day instead of the minimum wages of Rs. 22 per day fixed by the Government of Rajasthan in case of works implemented by Panchayats under the JGSY and EAS[2] programmes. When the labourers demanded their due wages the contractors convinced them that their work was not satisfactory and hence they could only get lower wages.[3] The availability of work was also few. Women were worst affected and they were forced to accept lower wages due to their precarious economic condition and immediate need for cash.[4]

False vouchers and bills were also submitted by Sarpanches and officials to get the sanctions for works done under various development programmes.[5] In many cases the names of dead people were entered in the muster rolls to pay wages.[6] There were other forms of corruption as well. For example in Vijaypura village of Rajsamand district, benami sales shown on paper as public auctions had resulted in the disposal of land on national highway worth over Rs. one crore. The amount remitted to the Panchayats as the auction price for the sale were small amounts of Rs. 500 to Rs.5000.[7] In Devgarh Block of Rajsamand district a group of Anganwadi workers related a story of graft amounting to Rs. 14 lakhs over four years by their lady supervisors.[8] This was from a programme meant for malnourished children with 56 grams of dalia and 8 grams oil per day.[9]

(iv) The Solution

The local labourers were afraid to oppose these powerful contractors, Sarpanches, officials and their henchmen. The MKSS took up their cause. It organised public hearings or "Jan Sunwais", a kind of social audit, to publicly air these irregularities including non-payment of minimum wages. The MKSS mobilised local women who participated in large numbers in these "Jan Sunwais".

The first public hearing took place on 2 December 1994 at Kot Kiran village in Pali district. The hearing revealed half of the names entered in the muster rolls for payment of wages were fictitious and several cases of false bills came to notice.[10] The next public hearing was held at Bhim block in Rajsamand district on 7 December 1994. It was found that M/s. Bhairon Nath and Company had defrauded the block of Rs. 37 lakhs through false billing.[11] The company, which existed only on papers had been checked and cleared by government auditors.

(v) The Outcome

At the "Jan Sunwais", the organisers invited every one to listen and respond. They also invited politicians, administrators, labourers and contractors, if they wished to say to present their case and to defend themselves.

In response to the holding of the "Jan Sunwais" the Gram Sewaks decided to go on strike. They went up to the State Government asserting that their association was answerable only to senior officials and share information with only official audit parties, not with any other organisations like MKSS who were undertaking social audit through the Jan Sunwais. This only helped the movement to expand. The Gram Sewaks refused to part with any information. The denial of such information by the gram sewaks made the people sympathetic to the movement. The MKSS now demanded social audit of all local development expenditure in every Panchayat. They demanded transparency of all information relating to expenditure on development and use of community resources. Thus from a demand for transparency on village development project, the emphasis shifted to national campaign for People's Right to Information (PRI).

In April 1996[12], MKSS workers and large section of villagers of Pali, Rajsamand, Bhilwara and Ajmer, sat for 40 days dharna in front of SDM's office of Beawar in Ajmer to pressurise the Government of Rajasthan to provide information relating to government expenditure on development programmes and pass the "Right to Information Bill". The dharna drew extraordinary support from a wide cross-section of people. People from more than 150 villages of Rajasthan donated foodgrains.[13] The local people of Beawar town contributed Rs. 46,000 to support the movement. The local businessmen provided free vegetables, water, photography and video recording services.[14] The dharna site became an important place, where lawyers, poets, politicians, journalists, trade union leaders, women, social activists, doctors, peasants, workers and ordinary citizen came together to think collectively about what should be done to make the state accountable. MKSS received 400 letters of support from various organizations and individuals.[15] The local, regional, national press placed this issue on their agenda. Widespread press coverage helped spread the message of MKSS, viz., "Right to Information". All the major political parties and trade unions participated in the meetings and supported the movement. Eminent journalists and social activists addressed the meetings and encouraged the MKSS to continue and not give up the fight. The dharna led to the birth of the National Campaign for the People's Right to Information (NCPRI) in July 1997.

(vi) The Transformation

Thus the demand for minimum wages which started in a small backward village of Rajasthan became fight for right to information. The "Right to Information" campaign was an important step towards participatory governance at grassroots level. It was said by some opinion leaders that the struggle was "like second battle for independence". The "Right to Information Campaign" (RTI) attracted more women because it was related with their livelihood issues.

(vii) The Impact

The Ministry of Rural Development, Government of India, also took a firm stand, that if minimum wages were not paid, grants for JRY would be held up.[16] The Government relented and the then Chief Minister of Rajasthan declared on the floor of the State Assembly, on 5 April 1995, that every citizen has the "Right to Information".[17] On payment he/she could demand and receive details of expenditure on development work done out of government funds, over the last five years in the villages. All the related documents could be photocopied and supplied to those who wanted the same, on payment of a small fee. People have a right, the Government of Rajasthan agreed, to receive any information relating to their village/block where development work has been completed under various Government schemes. Subsequently, a "Right to Information Act" was passed incorporating all the aforesaid features.

RTI campaign thus empowered local communities to have access to the information relating to resources available for their development. This right of citizens to secure information relating to expenditure on development programmes helped check the level of corruption in rural development programmes. In a rough estimate, it is reported that RTI campaign contributed significantly in bringing down the levels of corruption in Government programmes worth Rs. 600 crores said to have been spent on drought relief works in Rajasthan in 2001-2002.[18] Now the Sarpanches are more carefull about the development work executed in their Panchayats. People have greater access to government records relating to rural development programmes. The RTI campaign has challenged the undue protection sought by the officials under the garb of official secrecy, and siphon-off public funds, in the name of development.

Social audit has now become a mandatory part of all development and drought relief work. The Government of Rajasthan has also been forced to take action on a few of the prominent cases of corruption in utilization of public fund, unearthed through this exercise. It seems the support of mass based organisation is essential in enhancing the capability of women Panchayat representatives in social mobilisation.

(viii) Some concerns that still remain

Though much has been achieved, the implementation of laws relating to Right to Information has been tardy and poor in Rajasthan. There are no government figures available on how many people have sought information about development programmes of the government and from which office. There are no cases of any formal legal appeals having been filed due to denial of information. For example, when a person in Jaipur district asked for the photocopy of certain documents from a Block office, the concerned authority demanded Rs.10 per copy instead of Rs. 2 fixed by the Government of Rajasthan.[19] And then the Block Office maintained that only documents of the year 2000 are available and that documents pertaining to years 2001-2004 will not be given unless audited by the Department.[20]

Case 2: South Asia Poverty Alleviation Programme in Andhra Pradesh: Social Mobilisation

(i) Introduction

The South Asia Poverty Alleviation Programme (SAPAP) was launched in Andhra Pradesh in January 1995. The programme was supported by United Nations Development Programme (UNDP) and implemented in backward districts of Mahbubnagar, Ananthapur and Kurnool.[21]

(ii) The Background

The focus of the programme was to build institutional capacity to tackle poverty through social mobilization. Thus the programme from its inception focused on social mobilization, skill development and capital formation of the poor at village level.

(iii) The Problem

The villages in these districts were facing frequent droughts and drought-like situation. The majority of the households owned marginal landholding which was not sufficient to sustain their livelihood. Wage employments available in non-farm activities were few and far between. Alcoholism among men was a major social problem in these villages.

(iv) The Solution

Women in these villages were organised through homogenous self-help groups at the hamlet, sub-hamlet and village levels for capital formation. In each district, women constituted nearly 90 per cent of the total membership of self-help groups.[22] The training and skill development programmes for income generating activities, conducting meetings and handling various responsibilities were organised for these self-help groups.

For capital formation the strategy was to encourage small savings and internal lending among members. Funds were provided to self-help groups by creating linkages with government programmes and institutions for providing micro finance.

An institutional linkage was also forged with non-governmental organisations (NGOs) working in the districts. The NGOs were entrusted with the task of social mobilization and capacity building through a network of 22 community coordinators and 121 community volunteers. Each community worker was assigned 5 to 6 habitations.

(v) The Outcome

The programme received support and backing from the Government of Andhra Pradesh. These self-help groups have emerged as a platform for tackling social evils prevailing in rural Andhra Pradesh. These groups have tackled many cases of child marriage, violence against women, child labour, poor condition of widows, liquor consumption and practice of devdasi.[23] These self-help groups help women who are widows, destitutes, deserted, divorced and unmarried women. Many self-help groups have taken legal action for atrocities against dalit women.

(vi) The Impact

The women belonging to self-help groups have participated in Panchayat elections in the State and many of them have won. A Mahila Bank was also formed by one self-help group in Kurnool district. In the process, access to micro credit became the major programme of the self-help groups. The model of social mobilization demonstrated by women self-help groups in the SAPAP was subsequently adopted by the World Bank in its Andhra Pradesh District Poverty Initiatives Project implemented in six districts of Andhra Pradesh.[24] Community investment funds to fund small projects decided by the poor communities themselves have become a major component of the programme. The South Asia Poverty Alleviation Programme based on community mobilization has become a major force on eradication of poverty in Andhra Pradesh.

II. COMMUNITY MOBILIZATION

Case 3: Movement for Community Forest Management: Van Gujjars of Central Himalaya

(i) Introduction

The Van Gujjars are pastoral, nomadic, vegetarian, indigenous Muslim community living in Garhwal region of Uttaranchal and Himachal Pradesh for centuries. They are traditional buffalo herders living in winter in lower Shiwalik hills with their herds of baffaloes and migrating with all their bovine wealth to the higher mountain pastures for summer grazing. The Van Gujjars make a living by selling milk and milk-products. They have evolved a tradition, in both their summer and winter pastures of having separate areas of the forest allotted to each joint family for grazing cattle and living. They have been given forest permits since 1930 which define the areas in the forest within which they can lop trees in order to get fodder for their buffaloes and allow them to graze.[25]

(ii) The Problem

The community of Van Gujjars in Dehradun district, Uttaranchal, was shocked in 1983 when the then Government of Uttar Pradesh (Uttranchal was not formed then) proposed the creation of Rajaji National Park (RNP) in Dehradun carving it from their traditional habitat area.[26] The Van Gujjars' traditional way of life, livelihood and migratory pattern were severely affected and disturbed by the new forest laws governing forest resources and environmental conservation. To wean the Van Gujjars away from th Rajaji National Park, a rehabilitation centre for them was built in Pathari, District of Haridwar, in 1992 by the then Government of Uttar Pradesh.[27] The Van Gujjars refused to move to Pathari. The reluctance of the community to leave their forest habitats, despite intense pressure from the forest authorities, resulted in constant conflict between the community and forest bureaucracy so much so that in 1992 the Van Gujjars were prevented from entering the park area on their return from their summer grounds in the upper Himalayan reaches by the RNP authorities.[28] Their buffaloes were detained outside the park area in Dehradun.

(iii) The Action Taken

The Van Gujjars did not relent. They along with their buffaloes pitched tents outside the park area and demanded that they be allowed to enter RNP, their traditional right. A series of meeting of the Gujjar Panchayat were called. All members of the Van Gujjar community attended these meetings since they affected their traditional right to livelihood and survival, in harmony with forest dwellings. Rural Litigation and Entitlement Kendra (RLEK), an NGO based in Dehradun, supported their struggle The support of RLEK motivated this largely illiterate community to take up their cause at higher levels and gave a radical shape and mass base for the Van Gujjar movement. The Gujjar Panchayat ultimately decided to blockade the Dehradun-Delhi national highway to draw public attention to their plight and indeed it did. The local, national and international media highlighted their problem. NGOs, social activists, lawyers and social scientists supported their cause. Public opinion was overwhelmingly in favour of allowing the Van Gujjars of exercise their right to abode and livelihood inside the RNP. The Government of Uttar Pradesh realized that in this battle against public opinion there could be only one loser: the Government. The Government of U.P. ordered the Rajaji National Park officials to let the Van Gujjars into the protected forest premises temporarily. The forest authorities allowed Van Gujjars to enter the RNP. This, however, did not solve the problem of the Van Gujjars. Though they could enter RNP for many reasons they had to bribe the forest officials to enter the forest.

(iv) The Outcome

The Van Gujjar Panchayat now demanded that they not only be allowed to enter the RNP but that their traditional right on forest resources to be protected and revision of land settlement be mounted to declare 20 per cent of the forest land de-reserved and handed over to village communities comprising Van Gujjars.[29] In order to reinforce their claims over their traditional habitats the community prepared a proposal with the help of RLEK for Community Management of Forests in Protected Areas (CMF-PA) in 1996. The plan proposed to involve Van Gujjars in the day to day management of RNP.

(v) The Impact

The community offered to accept, under the CMF-PA, the responsibility of regenerating the forests protecting its core area and guarding against poaching and timber smuggling.[30] The main objective of the CMF-PA was protecting the eco-system of Shiwaliks, conserving the bio-diversity and protecting the traditional rights of Van Gujjars. The CMF-PA has been formulated in order to increase local control of natural resources to protect them form destruction and decay. But the dispute is far from settled. The fight is on. The CMF-PA has been vehemently opposed by vested interests in the State Forest Department. The Ministry of Telecommunication, Government of India, however, in support of the Van Gujjar community issued two frequencies to RLEK staff and base station for augmenting effective management of forests.[31] The Van Gujjars are quite excited over the ongoing debate on the need to turn RNP into India's community managed park. Only time will tell if this experiment succeeds.

Case 4: Villagers Constructed their Road in Western Orissa

(i) Introduction

The earthen road in drought stricken Sargipali village of Dahita Gram Panchayat in Bargarh district of western Orissa was built by the villagers to connect three far away villages. During the monsoon of 2003, a major portion of the earthen road was washed away. There was a proposal to repair the road by the Government. The villagers of Sargipali wanted to repair the road themselves and earn the money that the government would normally pay to contractors for repairing such a road. In December 2003, the Block Development Officer (BDO) sanctioned Rs.1.42 lakhs to repair the road.[32] Two contractors from Dahita Gram Panchayat area bid for the contracts. The villagers of Sargipali opposed the grant of contractors to the bidders for repairing the road under reference. Sensing trouble, the BDO diverted the money for development work to some other village. The villagers of Sargipalli were aggrieved.

The people of Sargipali called a meeting of the villagers to decide on how to remedy the situation. They decided to fight collectively against the decision of the BDO. The villagers decided to meet the higher officials in the district before taking any precipitative action. To diffuse the situation the District Collector agreed to sanction the money for repairing the road to a self-help group of the neighbouring Dahita village.[33] But the Dahita self-help group was formed by the contractors who had close link with a local political leader and so the needs of the villagers of Sargipali remained unmet. The villagers were even more aggrieved.

(ii) The Problem

The villagers met the District Collector and requested him to cancel the contract of Dahita self-help group and give it to their self-help group. The villagers argued with the District Collector that since the road to be repaired was located in their village, they should be given priority in the sanction of development work. When Sargipali village had ten active self-help groups in 2003, they asked the District Collector why was the contract given to a group in neighbouring village? The villagers decided to repair the road by *shramdan* if money was sanctioned to them by the District Administration, but they will not allow outsiders to carry out the road-repair. The villagers of Sargipali met the BDO and District Magistrate in large numbers and conveyed their decision. In the meanwhile, the Orissa State Legislative Assembly elections were announced on 24 March 2004 and the code of conduct for political parties came in force at that time. Hence no further action was possible. The people had no option but to wait till the election was over. They had to wait for six months.

(iii) The Solution

When the elections were over, the villagers again went to the concerned BDO. The BDO was still adamant to give the contract for repairing the road either to the Dahita self-help group or the work will be done through the line Department. If the repair work was carried out by the Department, the work would have to be done by the Gram Sewak who was also a contractor's henchman. The villagers of Sargipali realised the trick of the BDO in not awarding them the contract for the work. They opposed the new move of the BDO. The BDO did not relent and awarded the contract for repairing the earthen road to the Dahita self-help group. The villagers also were determined to thwart the move of the BDO. When Dahita self-help group started the repair work, the people of Sargipali and neighbouring two villages gathered to protest. The villagers claimed that it is their right to carry out the repair work and that they will not allow cronies of the greedy contractor to usurp their legitimate rights. The protest continued for two days. People lay on the road, making it impossible for the contractors to work. Finally, the contractors had to leave the site, threatening the villagers with dire consequences.

The villagers of Sargipali then met after one month to take a final decision on what should be their next steps. They decided to repair the road immediately by shramdan. The next day at the stroke of dawn about 600 people gathered at the site and began repairing the road.[34] The contractors also assembled but seeing such a huge crowd, they contractors could do nothing. They warned the villagers that since they (the contractors) belonged to the powerful influential group the villagers would waste their efforts and they will not be paid for the execution of the job. The villagers paid no heed to the warning and completed repairing the broken road in three days.

(iv) The Outcome

The first stage of the war was won. Then the battle to get for the rightful dues of the villagers from the Block Office began. The villagers of Sargipali got unexpected support from "Pragatibadi", a prominent Oriya newspaper published from Bhubaneswar highlighting the work done by the village community of Sargipali. The local MLA also visited the village and praised the effort of the villagers. The people demanded they must get paid for the reconstruction of the road. It was their rightful share. They could use the money for other development work in the village. The villagers of Sargipali approached the District Collector for payment of what they considered their due but in vain. The District Collector regretted that since the work of repairing the road had not been sanctioned to them in their name and they do not have any bills, no payment can be affected. The villagers listened calmly and then retorted that if the payment were made to the Dahita self-help group on the basis of some false bills, they will revolt.

(v) The Impact

When the Minister for Agriculture, Government of Orissa, visited Bargarh district, he heard about the incident. He looked into the matter and ordered the District Collector to cancel the old contract awarded to Dahita self-help group and in future to have such work executed only through the village self-help groups. The concerned BDO immediately cancelled the old order. He got the road repair work carried out by the villagers of Sargipali assessed. It was valued at Rs. 38,000 and paid to the Vindhya Vasini self-help group, which had members from village Sargipali.[35] The villagers of Sargipali now have Rs. 33,000 in their kitty plus a work order of Rs.1.04 lakh in the name of their self-help group.[36]

III. CASE STUDIES OF SUCCESSFUL WOMEN PANCHAYAT REPRESENTATIVES

Case 5: Leading By Example: Civic Responsibility in Kosli Gram Panchayat of Haryana

(i) The Background

Kosli Gram Panchayat with a population of 15000 is situated 8 kms from the block headquarters Nahar in Rewari district of Haryana. The Ahirs constitute 80 per cent population of the Panchayat. Smt. Urmila Yadav (56), the Sarpanch of Kosli Gram Panchayat, is serving her third term. In the Panchayat Elections of 2000, she got elected as a Sarpanch from an unreserved seat.

(ii) Problem and Action

The Panchayat suffered sever drinking water problem in 1994.The few existing wells and hand pumps barely catered to the needs of the villagers. Smt. Urmila Yadav mobilised the entire villagers and staged a hunger strike in front of the Sub-Divisional Magistrate office demanding provision of drinking water for the villages.[37] This did not solve the problem. She travelled to the State capital, Chandigarh, to meet the officials in the State Government in the hope that they might take the issue more seriously. She was right! Officials at Chandigarh took up the issue promptly and the village received the required money to build dams, water tanks and water pump houses. Everyone in the Panchayat appreciated the effort of the Sarpanch.

(iii) The Outcome

By improving the drinking water facility in the village, the Panchyat has benefited every household.

The Sarpanch also raised the issue of improper disposal of domestic garbage and waste which caused health and environmental problems. She organised awareness camps to maintain clean surrounding. The Panchayat employed four safai karmacharies and a cart, to carry the domestic waste from the village. The Panchayat bears the cost. The Panchayat approached the State Government through the Zilla Parishad to obtain loans sanctioned under the revenue earning scheme on cent-per-cent subsidy to construct shops near bus stand. With the loan sanctioned, the Panchayat constructed 32 shops and rented them on auction. The rent collected by Gram Panchayat is utilised for the salary of the staff appointed by the Panchayat for the sanitation and other activities of the panchayat.[38]

(v) Other Benefits

Encouraged by the success of their development efforts, the Panchayat has formed anti-dowry and women's empowerment committees, which look after the cases of harassment and atrocities against women. Smt. Urmila Yadav gave Panchayat land to the local telephone exchange and veterinary hospital on rent to increase the resources of the Panchayat.

The Kosli village is a developed model Panchayat in Haryana today mainly due to the dynamic leadership of its woman Sarpanch. There are no major caste and political factions in the Panchayat.

Case 6: All Women Panchayat Kultikiri in West Bengal

(i) The Background

In early 1990s, the National Literacy Mission was launched by the Government of India to achieve full literacy in the country. Like in many States, it was also launched in West Bengal. Kultikiri is a Panchayat in West Bengal, Medinipur district. Women volunteers of Kultikiri (a predominantly tribal Gram Panchayat), were more active and sincere than their male counterparts in the literacy campaign. Women actively campaigned against alcoholism which attracted the attention of local CPI(M) leaders. The "Ganatantrik Mahila Samiti", a mass organisation of the Communist Party of India (Marxist), was responsible for mobilising local women in this sustained movement against alcoholism. The CPI (M), recognising the enthusiam of women in the Panchayat, decided to choose all women candidates to contest Kultikiri Panchayat elections to involve them actively in developmental work. Kultikiri Gram Panchayat elected all its 13 women members in 1993 Panchayat elections.[39] After five years in 1998 Panchayat election, Kultikiri again elected all women to the Gram Panchayat. The Gram Panchayat is situated 55 km away from district headquarters town, Medinipur.

The overall performance of this first all women Panchayat (out of 572 Gram Panchayats in the district in implementing development projects) was adjudged best by Medinipur Zilla Parisad.[40] The Panchayat achieved cent-per-cent literacy in the district. As part of the literacy campaign, women were also taught the harmful effects of using contaminated water and the need to immunise their children. The Panchayat made a significant difference in women's life. By 2003, the Panchayat could achieve cent-per-cent coverage in sanitation as well.

(ii) The Outcome

The attendance of women in Gram Sansad meetings in West Bengal in 2001 was only two per cent whereas it was more than 10 per cent in Kultikiri Gram Panchayat.[41] Though some of the women did not have much political experience, yet all the women members took demonstrative initiative in village development. Being women, they got easy access to the women population in the families of Kultikiri and have been able to build up the consciousness of the villagers regarding education, health and environment. Now the villagers take great interest in the development work. In comparison to the State and the district average, turnout of women in the gram sansad meeting is appreciably high, indicating a positive impact of women leadership on the attitude of village women in terms of participation.

Case 7: Uniting a Divided Community: A Best Practice in Panchayat Leadership

(i) The Background

Ponni Kailasam (40) was elected Sarpanch of Annaikuppam Gram Panchayat in Thiruvarur district of Tamil Nadu. In 1996 Panchayat elections, the post of Sarpanch Annaikupam Panchayat was reserved for women. Only three women came forward to contest the election. Intially, Ponni was reluctanct to contest the election because she had no experience in public life. Her children were too young and had to be taken care of. She also wondered what the elders in the village would think, if she entered politics, which was otherwise considered not a woman's domain.

The villagers persuaded Ponni to contest the election for the post of Sarpanch. Her family members were very supportive, She contested the election and she was elected as Sarpanch. However, Ponni Kailasam had her detractors also. The village was divided on caste and party lines. When she took charge of the panchayat, her task was to convince the members of the Panchayat to think beyond party and caste affiliation, when it comes to the matters of development of the village and unite the village.

(ii) The Work Done

Initially her husband took her to all places where she wanted to go in connection with her Panchayat work as Sarpanch of Annaikuppam Gram Panchayat. Ponni attended all village elders' meetings which are normally held in the night of the first day of the month. She attended training programmes organised by National Institute of Rural Development, Hyderabad; Gandhi Gram Rural Institute, Gandhigram; and State Institute of Rural Development, Chennai. She learnt how to conduct Gram Sabha meetings and how to run the Panchayat administration.

When Ponni took charge as Sarpanch of Annaikuppam gram panchayat the total revenue for the Panchayat from house tax was only Rs. 5000 per annum. She increased the house tax and ensured cent per cent collection. The house tax rate collection in the Gram Panchayat increased to Rs. 18,000 per annum.[42] Ponni called a meeting of all castes and convinced them that if all castes agree to use the same burial ground, then the government grant of a sum of Rs. One lakh for burial ground could be used for the development of the Panchayat.[43] People from all castes accepted her proposal.

She took all the people into confidence and united the village. This shows her ability as a leader to mobilise resources for development work. The Panchayat got one of the best Panchayat award in the state. Ponni again won the second term with highest number of votes in the state.

Case 8: Empowering Women: Kalva Gram Panchayat in Andhra Pradesh

Kalva is a small drought-prone village in Kurnool district of Andhra Pradesh. Most of its people are daily wage earners who work as agricultural labourers or eke out a living as petty vendors. An unlettered woman Sarpanch of the village named Fatima Bi (36) made history in 1998 by winning the United Nations Race Against Poverty Award.

The post of Sarpanch in Kalva Gram Panchayat was reserved for women in 1995. Fatima Bi contested for the post, and she got elected as the Sarpanch of Kalva Gram Panchayat. She was illiterate. Her husband was doing all the Gram Panchayat work on her behalf. One day the District Collector of Kurnool visited the Gram Panchayat and wanted to see the Sarpanch. Fatima's husband met the Collector. The District Collector of Kurnool insisted that he wanted to meet Fatima Bi, the woman Sarpanch of Kalva Panchayat. Fatima came in front of District Collector in veil. She was nervous to meet the Collector, because she had never met any officer. The incidence changed Fatima.

She started taking more interest in Panchayat work. She mobilised women to take active part in the affairs of the Panchayat. The village tank adjacent to the village temple had been choked, and was in disuse for long years. When the women under the leadership of Fatima Bi decided to clean up the tank, the men scoffed at them, saying that they too had tried to clean up the tank earlier but to no avail and had given up, and that the women were wasting their time. When the Fatima Bi entered the tank for cleaning it, it had a magnetic effect: more than 100 women joined her. Within a week, the waterbed of the tank was cleaned up. The tank was made available for irrigation. Now the villagers use irrigation water from the tank, to raise crops of sugarcane, plantations and vegetables.

The efforts of Fatima Bi to execute rural development work in Kalva Gram Panchayat did not stop with cleaning of the tank. She undertook construction of a bidge. The Government sanctioned Rs. two lakhs to have a bridge built in the village. She regularised registration of all documents in Panchayat Office. After Fatima Bi took charge of Kalva Panchayat, a metal road was laid, check dams were built, a new school building constructed and old school building was repaired. Programmes of digging a 5 km irrigation drain and clearing 500 acres of fallow land for paddy collection at a cost of Rs. 2 lakh was also taken up.[44]

Fatima Bi led the women folk to join the Podupu Lakshmi programme (a saving and credit programme) for self-help groups and urged them to save a small amount of money every month. Within a month, 40 self help groups with 300 women members and Rs. 2 lakh savings came up. UNDP was impressed by this achievement and granted Rs.12 lakh as an interest free loan to Kalva Panchayat for development work.[45] The loan granted by UNDP helped many families to start small business to earn a living and improve their living conditions. The enterprising women of Kalva started helping women of neighbouring villages by giving them loan.

UNDP took note of her work on poverty eradication and awarded her Best Sarpanch in South Asia.[46]

Case 9:The Tribal Woman Sarpanch Wages a Lone Battle

Gulbasiya Bai, the tribal woman Sarpanch of Bahiya Tola Gram Panchayat in Sahdol district of Madhya Pradesh, has made the 73rd Constitutional Amendment a reality. The constant encouragement of her family and people in her village made Gulbasiya Bai decide in contesting the election for the post of Sarpanch, Bahiya Tola Gram Panchayat, in the year 1995. She won the election and became Sarpanch of the Gram Panchayat. She again contested for the post of Sarpanch, Bahiya Tola Gram Panchayat, in 2000. She won the election for second consecutive term. In the 2000 Panchayat election, she defeated five candidates. Educated up to only 2nd standard, Gulbasiya Bai has not let her limited education and being a woman inhibit her functioning.

Soon after becoming the Sarpanch of the Gram Panchayat, she began to understand the problems of the village and appreciate the processes of Panchayat functioning. In her first term, on priority basis she got a pond constructed at a cost of Rs. two and half lakh to supply drinking water in one of the villages of the Gram Panchayat. She encountered numerous problems in this venture. Several trips to meet the block officials had to be undertaken but Gulbasiya was certain that she wanted to end the drinking water problem in the village at any cost. And she succeeded.

Then she took the initiative to open an anganwadi centre for the infants of the village.

Gulbasiya Bai personally met officials to get an additional room for middle school constructed. The room was constructed but getting payments proved to be problematic. After several fruitless trips to the block headquarters, she finally approached the local Member of Legislative Assembly (MLA). Gulbasiya presented the problems of the village to the MLA and eventually managed to have a cheque issued to cover the cost of construction of the school building. Gulbasiya got a resolution passed in the Gram Sabha to open a High School in Bayiha Tola. She decided to take the resolution of the Gram Sabha to the State Education Minister. She made several trips to the State capital Bhopal but to no avail. One day she sat at the gate of the MLA's rest house where the Minister for High Schools lived. As soon as the Minister under reference came out of the rest house, she presented the Gram Panchayat resolution to the Minister and approached him for funds. She explained the problem and requested him to issue an order to start a High School in Bahiya Tola Gram Panchayat.[47] The Minister appreciated the efforts of Gulbasiya Bai and the necessity of a high school in the Gram Panchayat, High School was started in 2002.

Once the high-school was set-up, Gulbasiya Bai, fought with the district administration to open a Primary Health Centre in Bahiya Tola Gram Panchayat. After hard toil and relentless follow up with authorities at different levels, a Primary Health Centre was sanctioned. Today her village has a Primary Health Centre. The fair price shop of the Government for distribution of food grain under PDS has also improved during Gulbasiya Bai's regime. Her constant supervision of the government fair price shop deters anyone who tries to commit any irregularities.

Amongst her many contributions to the Gram Panchayat are the following:

1. She is equally serious and committed to sorting out feuds and disputes within households and in the Gram Panchayat in general. The presence of Gulbasiya Bai and other Panches have led to at least a dozen cases being settled purely by their wise counselling.
2. Dissatisfied with the "Below Poverty Line"(BPL) list prepared by the government, she called a special Gram Sabha meeting and with the suggestions and consent of others, a new BPL list was drawn up. The names of the needy families were included.[48]
3. She refused to accept the poor quality of rice supplied for the mid-day meal.

Prior to every Gram Sabha meeting, she informs the whole village about the time and place of the meeting. She goes from door to door inviting people to attend Gram Sabhas.

Case 10: The Blind Sarpanch of Gujarat

Sudha Patel (25) may be the first blind Sarpanch of India. She was elected beating seven contestants. Sudha's father was Sarpanch for 10 years of Changa Gram Panchayat in Anand district of Gujarat. Initially, she was hesitant to contest the election. She was blind, a woman and had not lived much in the village. Immediately after election as Sarpanch, her opponents raised the issue of water scarcity. There was some violence too. Sudha kept her cool, called the police and things were settled.

Sudha initiated several projects like family planning programmes, an open school for workers' children, a public hospital, conference hall and provision of computers in local school. She runs a rehabilitation project for blind and mentally retarded persons. When in Changa, Sudha is in Panchayat Office at 9.30 A.M sharp, accompanied by her rakhi brother. When Sudha took charge, the Panchayat had only Rs.187 in its account. In her five-year term Sudha mobilised Rs. 10 lakh from the State Government for development projects of the Panchayat. All this was possible due to her strong will power and dedication for work.

Case 11: The Struggle for Dignity of a Dalit Sarpanch in Rajasthan

Rajasthan is the first State in India where Panchayati Raj in its earlier incarnation was launched on 2 October 1959. After implementation of the 73rd Amendment to the Constitution of India, Rajasthan was the second State where elections to the Panchayats were held in 1995 under the new dispensation.

In 2000 Panchayat elections, the post of Sarpanch in Badli Gram Panchayat in Ajmer district of Rajasthan was reserved for scheduled caste woman. Smt. Kanchan Devi (55) an illiterate scheduled caste woman contested the election for the post of Sarpanch and won. She was encouraged by her husband to contest the election.

Smt. Kanchan Devi had to face many problems from upper caste people of the Gram Panchayat and officials to work independently, though her husband supported her in all official work.

Smt. Kanchan Devi's family owns six bighas of land, out of which only three bighas were irrigated. The land owned by Kanchan Devi's family was not enough to support the family. Kanchan Devi had to work as a wage labourer to support her family.

Smt. Kanchan Devi initiated new projects like anganwadi centre and drainage system in the Gram Panchayat with the financial support from the State Government. Her opponents, mainly from upper castes, who opposed her candidature for the post of Sarpanch did not allow her to complete the project.

The Panchayat officials also harassed her whenever she visited them in connection with Panchayat work. They passed derogative remarks by calling her caste name. The upper caste people of her panchayat did not allow her to host the national flag at Panchayat headquarter on Independence Day (15 August) 2000. Her opponents from upper castes threatened many ward members of the Panchayat to remove Kanchan Devi from the post of Sarpanch by passing the no-confidence motion against her. Kanchan Devi complained to the higher authorities about the ordeal meted out to her. She had to file a case in the civil court against this discrimination. She had to spend Rs. 40,000 to cover the cost of fighting the case. She mortgaged her family land to get the required money. But Kanchan Devi did not relent.

The Primary School of the Badli Gram Panchayat was running from a dharmashala. Kanchan Devi shifted the Primary School to the newly constructed school building. She converted the dharmashala to a community centre. The community centre was made available on rent for public functions. By giving on rent Kanchan Devi mobilised resources for the Gram Panchayat.

Case 12: Dalit Sarpanch's Fight for Dignity in a Rajasthan Gram Panchayat

The post of Sarpanch in Para Gram Panchayat of Ajmer district in Rajasthan was reserved for scheduled caste (SC) women in 1995. The upper caste members of the Gram Panchayat, who have been controlling the Panchayat, were shocked to lose it to schedule caste woman. To make the best out of the worst, the upper caste members of the Gram Panchayat planned to elect, such a SC woman from Para village who will be under their control.

Smt. Ram Pyari (35), an SC woman educated up to 5th standard from Kali Talai Kheda village, which was part of Para Gram Panchayat, decided to contest for the post of Sarpanch. When the upper caste members came to know about it, they encouraged Ram Pyari's sister-in-law, an illiterate SC woman also to contest. Their plan was to divide the SC votes and defeat Ram Pyari. Because Ram Pyari was educated and assertive, which may not suit the interests of upper castes.

However, Smt. Ram Pyari won the election defeating her rival by a comfortable margin. But the upper caste members of the Gram Panchayat made her life miserable. She found it very difficult to work in a caste ridden Gram Panchayat. Being a woman from dalit background to head the Gram Panchayat was not liked by the upper caste male ward members. The upper caste male ward members abused her in Gram Panchayat meetings. It so happened, one male ward member removed her veil in a panchayat meeting. Removing the veil of a woman in public place is a great insult to the woman in rural Rajasthan.

Smt. Ram Pyari filed the case in the police station. This did not solve the problem. The elected upper caste male members of Kekdi Panchayat Samiti of which Para Gram Panchayat was a part also created problem for her. In many instances, the upper caste members forced her to sign the cheques for drawing money from the Bank, without any verification.

Smt. Ram Pyari realised that it was very difficult to work in the Gram Panchayat opposing the upper caste men. She called a meeting of the respected people of the Gram Panchayat. She requested them to end the conflict. She told the elders that if the conflict in the Gram Panchayat continues, it would be difficult to carry any developmental work. For the interest of the Gram Panchayat they should forget their differences. The village elders intervened. The upper caste male members of the Gram Panchayat were advised to stop creating problem for Smt. Ram Pyari.

Smt. Ram Pyari stopped signing cheques for drawing money without proper verification. The relationship between the Sarpanch and the upper caste Gram Panchayat members improved to the extent that with the help of upper caste male colleagues, Smt. Ram Pyari could construct a Primary School building and renovate the middle school building.

NOTES

1. Aruna Roy *et al.*: "Demanding Accountability", *Seminar*, 449, January 1997, p. 84.
2. "Living with Dignity and Social Justice—Rural Workers Rights to Creative Development, " Mazdoor Kisan Shakti Sangathan, 1993 p. 93.
3. *Ibid.*
4. Madhu and Bharat Dogra: MKSS—Social Change With, Grassroots, June 2002.
5. Nikhil Dey *et al.* "Public Hearing: A Mode for People's Hearing" in *Readings on Right to Information*, Lal Bahadur Shastri National Academy of Administration, Mussoorie.
6. *Ibid.*
7. Aruna Roy, *op. cit.*, p. 83.s
8. *Ibid.*
9. *Ibid.*
10. *Ibid.*
11. *Ibid.*
12. *Ibid.*, p. 84.
13. *Ibid.*
14. *Ibid.*
15. *Ibid.*
16. Madhu and Bharat Dogra *op.cit.*
17. "Peoples Struggle in Rajasthan and the Right to Information: A Document," Mazdoor Kisan Shakti Sanghatan, July 1996.
18. Aruna Roy and Nikhil Dey: "Fighting for the Right to Know in India", *Development Dialogue*, A Journal of International Development Cooperation, Dag Hammarskjold Foundation, Uppsala 2002 p. 85.
19. Geeta Yadav: "Soochana ke Adhikar ki Durdasha", *Panchayati Raj Update*, New Delhi, October 2004.

20. *Ibid.*
21. *Report of the Independent South Asian Commission on Poverty Alleviation*, Kathmandu: SAARC Secretariate, 2003 p. 51.
22. *Ibid.* p. 52.
23. *Ibid.*
24. *Ibid.*
25. *Community Forest Management in Protected Areas*, Rural Litigation And Entitlement Kendra and Natraj Publishers, Dehradun,1997, p.172.
26. *Ibid.* p. 172.
27. *Ibid.*
28. *Ibid.*
29. *Annual Report*, Rural Litigation and Entitlement Kendra, 2002 Dehradun.
30. *Ibid.*
31. *Ibid.*.
32. Rakesh Agarwal: "Villagers outsmart contractors, fix their own road", *Civil Society*, Gurgaon, November 2004.
33. *Ibid.*
34. *Ibid.*
35. *Ibid.*
36. *Ibid.*
37. Parmita Majumdar, "No full stops for Urmila Yadav," *Panchayati Raj Update*, New Delhi, February 2003.
38. *Ibid.*
39. Jaytilak Guha Roy: "Kultikiri: An All-Women Panchayat" in M.C. Gupta and K.N. Kabra (ed): *Public Administration in India*, Gyan Publishing House, New Delhi, 1999, p. 47.
40. *Ibid.* p. 54.
41. *Best Practices in Panchayat Leadership*, Institute of Social Sciences, New Delhi, 2002, p. 65.
42. *Ibid.* p. 77.
43. *Ibid.*
44. Sankuntala Narsimhan: "Tough as steel, soft as silk: Story of a woman Sarpanch of Andhra Pradesh", *Deccan Herald*, December 7, 1997.
45. *Ibid.*
46. Sankuntala Narasimhan: "Women's Role in Gram Sabha", *Kurukshetra*, October 1999, p. 35.
47. Deepak Tiwari, "Gulbasiya Bai wages a lone battle," *Grassroots*, December 2002.
48. *Ibid.*

Appendix-A

GENDER EQUAILTY

I. BACKGROUND IDEAS AND CONCEPTS

Gender Equality as a Goal

The empowerment of women and the promotion of gender equality is one of the eight internationally agreed development goals designed to achieve elimination of poverty.

Millennium Development Goals 3

Goal:
promote gender equality and empower women.
Target;
eliminate gender disparity in primary and secondary education preferably by 2005 and at all levels of education not later than 2015.
Indicators,

- ratio of girls to boys in primary, secondary and tertiary educations.
- ratio of literate females to males of 15-24 year old.
- share of women in wage employment in the non-agricultural sector.
- proportion of seats held by women in national parliament.

Research has shown that education for girls is the single most effective way of reducing poverty. In this context, the elimination of gender disparity in education has been selected as the key target to demonstrate progress towards gender equality/women's empowerment. However, education alone is not enough. Progress towards gender equality in education is dependent on success in tackling inequalities in wider aspects of economic, political, social and cultural life, and this is reflected in the indicators of progress.

A practical guide to gender main streaming. Adopted from Helen Derbyshire: *Gender Manual* (London DFID) 2002.

Gender equality is given such high priority because:

- *Gender is essential to poverty elimination:* There is a growing and compelling body of evidence which shows that women not only bear the brunt of poverty but that women's empowerment is a central precondition for its elimination. Poverty elimination can only be achieved by addressing the disproportionate burden of poverty, lack of access to education and health services, and lack of productive opportunities borne by women.
- *Gender equality is integral to a rights-based approach to development*: Human rights, defined and upheld by the international community, are universal, and based on the equal worth and dignity of all women and men. Internationally agreed human rights include standards of health, education and the right to a secure livelihood, as well as civil, political and legal rights.

Everywhere there are significant ways in which men's and women's responsibilities, opportunities and influence are unequal, although the nature and extent of inequality varies from society to society. Whilst there are instances where men are disadvantage in comparison to women, generally women and girls have fewer opportunities, lower status and less power and influence than men and boys. Millions of women around the world:

- have to work harder than men to secure their livelihoods;
- have less control over income and assets;
- have a smaller share of opportunities for human development;
- are subject to violence and intimidation;
- have a subordinate social position;
- are poorly represented in policy- and decision-making; and
- Gender inequality represents a huge loss of human potential, with cost for men as well as for women.

What does Gender Equality Mean?

Gender equality does not simply or necessarily mean equal numbers of men and women or boys and girls in all activities, nor does it necessarily mean treating men and women or boys and girls exactly the same.

It signifies an aspiration to work towards a society in which neither women nor men suffer from poverty in its many forms, and in which women and men are able to live equally fulfilling lives. It means recognising that men and women often have different needs and priorities, face different constraints, have different aspirations and contribute to development in different ways.

Gender equality and women's empowerment are inextricably linked. Women will only win equality when they are able to act on their own behalf, with a strong voice to ensure their views are heard and taken into account. This means recognising the right of women to define the objectives of development for themselves.

Gender equality and gender equity

There is an important distinction between *equality* of opportunity and *equity* of outcomes:

- *equality of opportunity:* this means that women should have equal rights and entitlements to human, social, economic and cultural development, and an equal voice in civic and political life.
- *equity of outcomes*[1]: this means that the exercise of these rights and entitlements leads to outcomes which are fair and just.

An important message is that gender equality and the empowerment of women is achievable. Great progress has been made in the 20th century. Women enjoy greater freedom and more power than ever before. Progress has been greatest where there has been strong political will; where changes in laws, regulations and policies have been followed through with real action; where resources have been devoted to the explicit goal of reducing gender discrimination. Progress is not dependent on the income level of the society: some development countries outperform much richer countries in the opportunities they afford women.

Another important message is that achieving gender equality is not a one-off goal. Progress can also too easily be eroded. Gender equality needs to be constantly promoted and actively sustained.

Gender Mainstreaming as a Strategy

In 1995, at the Fourth UN International Conference on Women, held in Beijing, "*gender mainstreaming*" was established as the internationally agreed strategy for government and development organisations to promote gender quality. This was in response to consistent lessons that have emerged from at least twenty years of experience of addressing women's

1. This distinction between process and product - rights and outcomes - is very useful. The terms "gender equality" and "gender equity" are often used interchangeably and the difference between them can be lost in translation. The term "equality", when used in realtion to development outcomes, can all too easily carry inappropirate connotations of sameness. Clarity concerning use and meaning is important to guard against this.

needs in development work. To understand what "gender mainstreaming" means and why it is important, it helps to understand the journey that has been travelled to reach this point.

THE "MAINSTREAMING GENDER EQUALITY" APPROACH

The term "gender mainstreaming" came into widespread use with the adoption of the Beijing Platform for Action (PfA) at the 1995 UN International Conference on Women. It represents an attempt by gender advocates to build on the successes of the past and address some of the challenges. It attempts to combine the strengths of the efficiency and empowerment approaches within the context of mainstream development.

Mainstreaming gender equality is a commitment to ensure that women's as well as men's concerns and experiences are integrate to the design, implementation, monitoring and evaluation of all legislation, policies and programmes so that women and men benefit equally and inequality is not perpetuated. The ultimate goal is to achieve gender equality. Gender mainstreaming in integral to all development decisions and interventions; it concerns the staffing, procedures and cultures of development organisations as well as their programmes; and it forms part of the responsibility of all staff.

Gender mainstreaming does not preclude women-only projects. It shifts their focus from women as a target group, to gender equality as a goal. It supports women-only (or men-only) projects designed as strategic interventions to address aspects of gender inequality and promote greater equality.

Emerging Lessons on Mainstreaming Gender in National Policy Frameworks

In the late 1990s and new millennium, the focus of donor-supported development has shifted to a significant degree away from discrete project interventions onto processes concerned with the development and implementation of national policy frameworks for poverty elimination. Evaluation material is beginning to emerge examining experiences of mainstreaming gender in the context of national policy frameworks such as PRSPs (Poverty Reduction Strategy Papers) and SWAPs (Sector Wide Approaches).

Evaluation Findings

National policy frameworks potentially provide the ideal context for gender mainstreaming, concerned as they are with mainstream policy development and effectiveness. They provide a context whereby:

- gender analytical information and sex disaggregated data on men's and women's concerns and experiences can inform national or sector-wide policy and planning processes.
- the importance of gender-aware consultation processes, involving civil society and other stakeholders, is specifically acknowledged.
- national policy commitment to gender equality should be backed up with budgets, effective processes of monitoring, and capacity-building
- the long-term timeframe of PRSPs and SWAPs acknowledges the complex processes of change involved.

However, the potential of national policy frameworks for promoting effective gender mainstreaming is greater than achievements to date. The following problems have been highlighted in all currently available evaluations:

- incorporation of gender issues into PRSPs has, thus far, been minimal. Whilst a few have addressed gender issues in specific sectors (usually health and education) with reasonable depth, the overall coverage is weak and little consistent attention has been paid to gender dimensions of poverty reduction.
- insufficient documentation of gender disparities and gender-disaggregated analysis of poverty is a barrier to recognising and addressing gender issues effectively.
- few PRSPs and I-PRSPs (Interim Poverty Strategy Papers) include specific plans for gender-sensitive consultation processes.
- action to promote gander equality, when included, is too often vague, and not backed with appropriate monitoring indicators
- the donor voice in advocating gender equality goals is inconsistent (to the frustration of partner organisations and staff concerned with equalities issues)
- commitments to gender equality at the national level are subject to "policy evaporation".
- equity outcomes are not achieved unless they are explicity stated and operationalised through well thought out procedures.

II. MAINSTREAMING GENDER IN A NUTSHELL: THE FOUR STEPS

Step 1: Sex Disaggregated Data and Gender Analytical Information

Gender analytical research and sex disaggregated statistical data (about "beneficiary" groups and about management and implementation organisations) is essential to effective gender mainstreaming. Information systems should routinely be disaggregated by sex; gender analysis (an examination of women's as well as men's experiences, needs and priorities) should routinely be part of social and institutional appraisal and monitoring processes; and gender analytical studies should be commissioned to examine particular issues and address information gaps. This information is necessary to identify gender difference and inequality; to make the case for taking gender issues seriously; to design policies and plans that meet women's and men's needs; to monitor the differential impact of policy, project and budget commitment on women and men.

Step 2: Women as well as Influencing the Development Agenda

Women will only win equality when they are able to act on their own behalf, with a strong voice to ensure their views are heard and taken into account.

This means promoting the involvement of women as well as men in decision-making at all levels, and ensuring that men and women committed to the promotion of gender equality are influencing decision-making. "Gender advocates" within government, civil society and donor organisations are most effective when they work in collaboration, identifying and development strategic "entry points" for the promotion of gender equality.

Step 3: Context-specific Action to Promote Gender Equality

Gender mainstreaming is a strategy to promote gender equality and the empowerment of women. Action to promote greater equality of influence, opportunity and benefit should be devised on the basis of context-specific sex disaggregated data and gender analytical information and a clear understanding of women's and men's priorities. Actions need to be explicitly included in policy and project document and frameworks, backed up with staff and budgets, and monitored and reviewed through appropriate indicators of change.

Step 4: Organisational Capacity Building and Change

Gender mainstreaming, as an organisational strategy to promote gender equality, depends on the skills, knowledge and commitment of the staff involved in management and implementation. "Evaporation" of policy commitments to gender equality is widespread. Developing appropriate understanding, commitment and capacity, as well as addressing issue of gender inequality within development organisational change.

Appropriated capacity-buildings activities need to be explicitly included in policy and project documents and frameworks, backed up with staff and budgets, and monitored and reviewed through appropriate indicators of change.

When to Call in Specialist Help

- *Ensuring women's participation:* Poor women, as well as poor men, should always be in a position to speak for themselves. It is essential to create and support opportunities to ensure that this happens. This often means working with female planners, research staff and extension agents, as well as working with representative women's organisations, to enable poor women to express their views in a non-threatening environment and in a way that influences the development agenda.
- *Gender analytical studies:* Good quality gender analytical information is required for policy making, planning and monitoring purposes. Some of this may be available from secondary sources. *Conducting* gender analytical research requires well-developed social and gender analytical skills, and requires appropriately trained and experienced staff or consultants.
- *Promoting gender equality at the community level:* Processes to social change designed to promote greater equality of influences, opportunity and benefit are complex and long term. The challenge of promoting greater equality between women and men should not be underestimated, particularly in contexts of considerable inequality. Specialist skills in participatory negotiated processes of working with community groups are essential and "front line" staff require personal and professional support.
- *Promoting gender equality within organisations:* Processes of organisational change designed to promote equal opportunities within the workplace, and to develop staff understanding of and skills in gender mainstreaming, are also complex and long term. This requires staff with commitment, perseverance and influencing skills, backed up with appropriate resources and support, *Gender training* requires staff or consultants with skills in adult learning and participatory training, in addition to applied and practical understanding of gender analysis and gender mainstreaming.

III. PRACTICAL TOOLS AND GUIDELINES: THE FOUR STEPS ONCE AGAIN

Step 1: Sex Disaggregate Data and Gender Analytical Information

What you Need to Know, and Why

Sex disaggregated data and gender analytical information is fundamental to gender mainstreaming.

Definitions

Sex Disaggregated Data

Sex disaggregated data is quantitative statistical information on difference and inequalities between women and men.

Sex disaggregated data might reveal, for example, quantitative difference between women and men in morbidity and mortality; differences between girls and boys in school attendance, retention and achievement; differences between men and women in access to and repayment of credit; or differences between men and women in voter registration, participation in elections and election to office.

Gender Analystical Information

Gender analytical information is *qualitative* information on gender differences and inequalities.

Gender analysis is about understanding culture, e.g. the patterns and norms of what men and women, boys and girls do and experience in relation to the issue being examined and addressed. Where patterns of gender difference and inequality are revealed in sex disaggregated data, gender analysis is the process of examining why the disparities are there, whether of examining why the disparities are there, whether they are a matter for concern, and how they might be addressed.

What you Need to Know

Beneficiary Groups

The precise sex disaggregate data and gender analytical information needed depends on the sector and context.

There are a number of "gender analytical frameworks" designed to provide guidance on the kinds of questions that are likely to be applicable. Other analytical guidelines, such as the sustainable livelihoods framework, can also be adapted to examine gender issues. However, no set of analytical categories caters to the information needs of every sector and situation. Analytical frameworks can be very helpful but need to be used critical and with care. They should be used to inspire not to restrict thinking.

The most useful starting point in determining information needs is to ask the question:

What do we need to know in order to ensure that policy/project planning/ monitoring addresses the needs of women and men (girls and boys) and benefits both women and men (girls and boys)?

Sector specialists, even those who know little about gender, will able to brainstorm responses to this question and come up with an initial "gender analytical framework" of their own. This is a good point to refer to existing analytical frameworks i.e. do they include categories of enquiry that would be useful in your working context, but which you haven't considered?

This manual includes an outline gender analytical framework to assist this process to brainstorming. See outline gender analytical framework: beneficiaries. For sector-specific guidelines, see the GEM website.

Development Policy-making, Management and Implementation Agencies

In recent years research has drawn attention to the ways in which development agencies reflect in their structure, procedures and organisational culture gender inequalities found wider society. Evaluations have also consistently drawn attention to the "evaporation" of policy commitment to gender equality as a result of inadequate procedures in management and implementation agencies, and lack of commitment, understanding and skills amongst development functionaries.

The effective management and implementation of initiative to promote gender equality enshrined in planning and policy documents requires action *to develop staff commitment, understanding and skills and to promote greater gender equality within development organisations* themselves. The design of appropriate capacity-building activities requires analysis of development organisation at the planning stage.

The manual includes an outline gender analytical framework to assist this process to analysis. See outline gender analytical framework: development organisations.

When and Where you Collect Information and Data

- it is important to draw on *existing sex* disaggregated data and gender analytical information.
- attention should be focused on ensuring that *all data collection systems* (existing and newly created and including national, local, sectorial and organisational systems) are routinely disaggregated by sex.
- *gender analysis* should be part and parcel of the routine processes of policy and project appraisal and monitoring. Gender analysis of beneficiary groups should be integral to social appraisal and monitoring processes, and gender analysis of development organisations integral to *institutional* appraisal and monitoring processes.
- *new gender analytical studies* should be conducted or commissioned to address information gaps or to update existing information.

Use of Gender Analytical Information and Sex Disaggregated Data

The collection of gender analytical information and sex disaggregated data is not an end in itself. It is required for certain specific tasks. These are:

- *Making the case for taking gender issues seriously:* Advocates seeking to promote attention to gender equality need relevant, up-to-date, context-specific information on gender difference and inequalities and men's and women's different priorities and needs. Advocating gender equality on the basis of assertion and rhetoric is of limited effectiveness. Sex disaggregated data is particularly powerful for advocacy purposes, producing clear statistical evidence of gender difference and inequality.
- *Policy and project planning and review:* Context-specific gender analytical information and sex disaggregated data is necessary to:
  - ensure that women's as well as men's experience and priorities inform the development agenda.
  - devise appropriate actions to promote greater equality of influence, opportunity and benefit for women and men in beneficiary groups.
  - devise appropriate actions to develop staff commitment, understanding and skills in development organisations.
  - monitor the differential impact of policy and project commitment on women and men and review activities accordingly.

Category of Enquiry	**Issues to consider**
◆ Role and responsibilities ◆ where (location/pattern of mobility) ◆ when (daily and seasonable pattern)?	◆ *productive role* (paid work, self-employment, and subsistence production) ◆ *reproductive roles (domestic work, childcare and care of the sick and elderly)* ◆ *community participation/self-help (voluntary work for the benefit of the community as a whole)* ◆ *community politics (representation/ decision-making on behalf of the community as a whole)*
Assets ◆ what livelihood assets/ opportunities do men and women have access do? ◆ what constraints do they face?	◆ *human asset (e.g.* health services, education, knowledge and skills) ◆ *natural assets* (e.g. land, labour) ◆ *social assets* (e.g social networks) ◆ *physical assets* (transport, communications) ◆ *financial assets* (capital/income, credit)
Power and decision-making ◆ what decision-making do men and/or women participate in? ◆ what decision-making do men/women usually control (able to make decision)? ◆ what constraints do they face?	◆ *household level* (e.g. decision over household expenditure) ◆ *community level* (e.g. decisions on the management of resources and services) ◆ *local government level* ◆ *national government level*
Needs, priorities and perspectives ◆ what are women's and men's needs and priorities? ◆ what perspectives do they have on appropriate and sustainable ways of addressing their needs?	◆ *"practical"* gender needs (needs arising in the context of the *existing gender roles/assets)* ◆ "strategic" gender needs (i.e. requiring changes to existing gender roles/assets to create greater equality of influence,

(*Contd.*)

	opportunity and benefit e.g. increasing women's access to decision-making. ◆ perspective on improved services and delivery systems such as prioritised services; choice of technology; location, type and cost of services; systems of operation, management and maintenance etc.

Outline gender analytical framework: development organisations

The following is a general analytical framework, to assist gender analysis of development organisations.

Questions and areas of enquiry should be adapted as appropriated for the purpose of advocacy, policy/project planning or monitoring and evaluation.

Category of Enquiry **1. WORK PROGRAMME**	**Issues to consider**
Policy and action plans ◆ gender policies ◆ attention to gender in all policies	*Gender policies* ◆ is there a gender policy? When was it developed, who was involved in formulation? ◆ is it based on context-specific gender analytical information and sex disaggregated data? ◆ implementation and monitoring procedures? All policies ◆ are gender issues included in other policies? To what extent? Are the gender aspects based context-specific gender analytical information and sex disaggregated data? ◆ implementation and monitoring procedures? ◆ impact of mainstream policy (sector restructuring; introduction of user fees) on women and men.

(*Contd.*)

Category of Enquiry	Issues to consider
Policy influencing	◆ what is the attitude of senior management staff to gender issues? Who does the management consult with (internally and externally) about gender issues? ◆ who are the formal and informal opinion leaders? Do they take gender issues seriously? ◆ which external organisations and people have an influences on the organisation? Do they take gender issues seriously? ◆ What are the decision-making bodies? What role do women and men play in decision-making?
Human resources ◆ gender focal staff ◆ all staff	◆ is there a designated gender unit/staff member? Since when? structure/mandate/resources? What do they do? How effectively? Perceptions of gender focal staff/perceptions of staff in the rest of the organisation? All staff ◆ responsibility for gender equality issues? Training? Knowledge and skills? Attitude to gender? ◆ is sensitivity to gender issues included in job descriptions/assessed at interview/monitored at appraisals?
Financial resources ◆ gender equality initiatives "on the ground" ◆ staff capacity-building initiatives	Gender equality initiatives "on the ground" and staff capacity-building ◆ funding for what activities, to what effect? ◆ funding for what activities, to what effect?

(Contd.)

Category of Enquiry	Issues to consider
System, procedures and tools	◆ is attention to gender issues included in routine systems and procedures (information systems; appraisal, planning and monitoring procedures? ◆ have staff been issued with guidelines/information/tools on gender mainstreaming?
2. WORKING CULTURE	
Staffing statistics	◆ numbers of men and women at each level in the organisation, and according to role/sector. ◆ interview/recruitment/promotion/training and career development sex disaggregated statistics
	◆ wages, i.e. sex disaggregated statistics
Men's and women's practical needs	◆ does the organisation create a safe and practical environment for women and men (consideration issues like transport arrangements, working hours, travel commitments, toilets, childcare responsibilities)
Organisational culture	◆ how does information flow in the organisation i.e. formally and informally? To what extent are women/men included in communication networks? ◆ what are the main shared valus of the organisation? Do these relate in any way (explicitly or potentialy) to gender equality? ◆ is decision-making centralised or decentralised? To what extent do individual staff have "room for manoeuvere"? ◆ what is the attitude towards male/female staff? ◆ incidence/perceptions of sexual harassment?

(*Contd.*)

Category of Enquiring	Issues to consider
Staff perceptions	◆ male and femal staff perceptionsl of "gender" issues at work
Policy and action	◆ does the organisation have an equal opportunities policy or equivalent directive? What does this policy cover? How has it been implemented and promoted? To what extent does it affect practice within the organisation?

Gender Budgets

"Gender budgets" or "women's budgets"[2] are analyses of government budgets to establish the differential impact of revenue raising or expenditure on women and men and on different groups of women and men. They are designed to inform public policy debate, and as such are a particularly important lobbying tool in the context of national policy frameworks.

Budgets are the most important government economic policy instruments. They reflect the spending choices a government has made to achieve social and economic objectives in the context of specified revenue raising activities and predicted revenue. In order to identify the differential impact of budget expenditures on women and men, these categories of expenditure are important:

- expenditure specifically targeted to groups of women or men to meet prioritised needs,
- expenditure specifically targeted to promote equal opportunities for women and men, and
- general or mainstream budget expenditure making goods and services available to the whole community.

Typically 99 per cent of expenditure falls into the latter category and in this context, a budget can appear to be gender-neutral instrument of policy. Sex disaggregated data and gender analytical information is needed to expose the differential gender impact of mainstream budget expenditure commitments.

---

2. In the evolution of this process, the initial focus was on auditing government budgets for impact on women and girls. More recently, gender has been used as the category of analysis, and the term "gender budgets" is more often used.

Participants in gender budgeting exercises can include government, parliamentarians or civil society organisations, or a combination of these. A gender budget may cover expenditure and/or revenue, and may focus on selected sectors or all sectors. They might examine past budgets, past actual expenditure, estimate current budget allocations or future budget as projected in medium term expenditure frameworks. They are conducted and used by governments to report on what they have done to meet women's needs and promote gender equality. More commonly, they are conducted by civil society group and provide information for parliamentarians and civil society group to use in lobbying for greater gender equality.

A number of gender budgeting tools and approaches have been developed. Choice depends on the availability of data, the expertise of personnel, and the link between national budgets and national policy, as well as practical constraints of time and access to computers and software.

Gender budget tools

Gender-aware policy appraisal: this is the most common approach. It begins with the assumption that budget reflects policy. Analysis involves scrutinising the explicit and implicit gender implications of national and suctorial policies, examining the ways in which priorities and choices are likely to reduce or increase gender inequality.

Gender-disaggregated beneficiary assessments: this is a more participatory approach to policy analysis i.e. asking actual or potential beneficiaries the extent to which government policies/programmes match their own priorities.

Gender-disaggregated public expenditure incidence analysis: this compares public expenditure for a given programme with data from household surveys to reveal the distribution of expenditure between women/men, boys/girls.

Gender-disaggregated tax incidence analysis: this examines the relationship between national budget and the way time is used in households. In particular, it draws attention to the ways in which the time spent by women in unpaid work in accounted for in policy analysis.

Gender-aware medium term economic policy framework: these are attempts to incorporate gender into the economic models on which medium term economic frameworks are based.

Gender-aware budget statement: this is an exercise in government accountability which may use any of the above tools. It requires a high degree of commitment and co-ordination throughout the public sector

(*Contd.*)

(*Contd.*)

as ministries and departments undertake and publicise an assessment of the gender impact of their line budgets.

Adapted from Diane Elson (1997) "Tools for gender integration into macro-economic policy" in Link into Gender and Development, 2, Summer, p.13, cited in Budlender, D and Sharp, R (1998) "How to do a gender-sensitive budget analysis: contemporary research and practice", Commonwealth Secretariat and AusAid.

Step 2: Influencing the development agenda

In order to ensure the women's as well as men's needs, priorities and constraints are recognised and addressed and influence the development agenda, all processes of policy development and project design should involve:

- participatory consultation with women as well as men in the beneficiary groups.
- women as well as men in decision-making at all levels.
- gender equality advocates (men as well as women) devising ways of opening up spaces to ensure women's active involvement in consultation and decision-making.

This means finding ways to ensure that:

- women's groups are actively involved in consultation and decision-making processes.
- the range of women's views and needs is adequately represented. Different women (and men have different needs on the basis of class, ethnicity, age and family composition, and other factors. Urban, middle class women do not necessarily accurately represent the view and priorities of poor, rural women.
- the usual process of stakeholder analysis (drawing up a table of stakeholders; assessing the importance of each stakeholders and their relative power and influence; and identifying risks and assumptions that will affect project design) include:
  - women and men as separate stakeholder groups,
  - where appropirate, different stakeholder groups amongst women (and men),
  - clarity regarding stakeholder groups which include *both* women and men,
  - consultancy teams, working groups, management teams and implementation teams include women and men,

- gender equality advocates (in government, civil society and donor organisations work in collaboration, thinking collectively and strategically about advocacy strategies.

Women in Decision-making: Community Level Issue to Address

Traditionally, women are often excluded from decision-making at the community level. A number of factors combine to bring this about. These include traditional attitudes concerning the role and status of women, and also aspects of women's own work burden, knowledge, skills and confidence. Poor women's confidence can be undermined by less exposure than poor men to that world outside their immediate home, and by limited language and literacy skills. Even when steps have been taken to include women in community level decision-making, too often women have been token representative on community committees with a passive role and few real responsibilites. Problems for women can be compounded during negotiations with local authorities. Community based groups may have been able to achieve considerable levels of women's participation, but decision-making power may lie at higher levels of the local administration, where women are not so well represented. Community efforts are often frustrated by bureaucratic delays or unwilling staff at the local/municipal government level, and women community representatives can be particularly vulnerable because of their generally lower social status.

Increasing Women's Involvement in Community Decision-Making Gender Analysis

Before taking action to involve women in community level decision-making, it is important to be fully aware of existing gender roles, structures and attitudes in relation to decision-making at the community level.

Planning to promote women's involvement in community level decision-making should be devised on the basis of a clear understanding of existing gender roles, and on the basis of male and female community members' perspectives and priorities.

On this basis

- appropriate ways of strengthening women's involvement in decision-making need to be specified in planning documents, included in implementation staff TORs (terms of reference) and supported with necessary funding.

- criteria for monitoring and evaluation of women's participation must also be established. Indicators of effectiveness should include qualitative as well as quantitative aspects of participation.

Activities to promote women's involvement

- Practical measures to promote women's involvement in decision-making include the following:

Community consultation processes

- practical measures are needed to ensure that project information reaches women, that they are able to attend meetings and that meetings provide a forum in which they can actively participate.
- women themselves will often have insights on the best way to work around male dominated power structures.
- open discussion involving men and women may facilitate women's participation but specific measures may also be needed to overcome the defence or muting of women's views in front of men.
- particularly in large communities, it may be necessary to follow up large meetings with,smaller planning groups, including key women representatives, where women's roles, responsibilities, priorities and constraints can be elaborated in more detail.
- given the limitation on poor women's time, considerable outreach work and flexibility is required about when and where to meet. One approach has been to arrange meetings in situ at, for example, water supply sites or clinics.
- working with existing women's NGOs or community organisations is a way to involve women directly. However, such organisations tend to be monopolised by more affluent women with more free time, and may exclude poorer sections of the community.
- women's organisations are not necessarily "gender-sensitive", in the same that they may have limited understanding of ideas concerning gender mainstreaming and gender equality. It may be useful to take steps to strengthen the gender sensitivity of CBOs and networks.

Activities to gain the support of men

- early consultation with men, particularly community leaders, and attempts to promote positive attitudes towards women's active participation, are important. Where women are involved in separate activities or training, the potential advantages should be explained, and/or complementary or parallel activities organised for men.

- men's negative attitudes to women's increased involvement have often shifted once the benefits to the community, households and women themselves have been demonstrated.

Promoting women's active role in community level decision-making

- women's involvement in selecting candidates is likely to result in a higher and more dynamic level of women's participation.
- the quality of women's participation in committees, as well as the quantity, needs to be improved. For women who are unused to assuming positions of authority, considerable groundwork may be needed to develop the self-confidence and assertiveness skills necessary for dealing with village authorities. Women representatives may need special training, in leadership skills, confidence building and communication. Similar building and communication. Similar training should be offered to men to avoid alienation.

Links with local authorities

- local women's needs are often addressed most effectively by building gender-sensitive partnerships between community representatives and local authorities. This involves:
- supporting and training community representatives to negotiate effectively for gender-sensitive services.
- training staff in municipal authorities to increase their understanding of gender issues, needs and rights, as well as their responsibility for delivering gender-aware responses.
- developing activities to increase information to marginalised groups, including women, about the services and resources they can expert, e.g. service charters setting out standards of provision.

Working in Network and Coalitions

Networking is fundamental to effective gender mainstreaming. It is professionally ineffective and personally undermining for organisations and individuals seeking to promote gender equality and women's empowerment to work alone. It the context of developing national policy frameworks, it is essential for gender advocates within government and donor organisations to work collaboratively with each other and civil society groups.

Tips for Network Effectiveness

Great expectation can accompany the establishment of networks, only to find that membership trails off, little is achieved and members cease to meet. To maximise effectiveness, networks need to pay attention to the following:

- *clear thought to membership:* this involves thinking through what each member will contribute, and what they will gain, as well as factors concerning the overall coherence and viability of the group.
- *well thought out need and goal:* it is important for members to reach agreement on a clear purpose and goal. This is motivating and gives a general direction to the group.
- *good leadership:* networks work most effectively when members feel actively involved and responsible. The leader should have a strong commitment to the network goal, respect for the members and a facilitative, inclusive style.
- *good communication with members:* this includes regular meetings, the agenda circulated in advance, and minutes circulated afterwards.
- *effective and efficient meetings:* meetings should give a sense of progress towards the goal. Provide an opportunity for members' views to be heard and to reach consensus on decisions.
- *clear, realistic and agreed action plan:* actions need to be agreed bearing in mind members' resources, time availability, opportunities, skills, knowledge and influence.
- *concrete results:* achievement is highly motivating. Modest expectations, accompanied by tangible progress, are more motivation than ambitious goals with no clear strategy for bringing about tangible change.

Advocacy and Lobbying

Gender Advocates

Persuading those in position of power and authority to take gender equality and women's empowerment seriously is key to making progress. This is the role of "gender advocate" with government, civil society and donor organisations. Gender advocates can be men and women, and individuals or organisations. They may understand this responsibility as part of their designated role, or purely on the basis of their own motivation and choice.

Gender advocates requires patience, persistence and commitment. They need the ability to think strategically and to take advantage of unexpected opportunities. They need to be able to recover from setbacks, be willing to compromise and recognise the significance of modes, gains and breakthroughs. Promoting gender equality and the empowerment of women is a long-term, complex and difficult task.

Gender advocates face different opportunities and constraints in different contexts.

Government Based Advocates

In many cases, advocates operating within government ministries are highly constrained in their room for manoeuvre. Razavi (98) description of gender advocates describes their situation well: "supplicants trying to persuade those not convinced of the intrinsic value of gender equality, in terms least likely to generate resistance, that gender issues need to become a priority".

Civil Society Based Advocates

Civil society based gender advocates are often freer to express their views than those working within government. However, their degree of influence and leverage over government decision-making will depend on a number of factors:

- the extent to which women's empowerment and gender equality is accepted as a desirable goal by the government and in wider society.
- the government's history of addressing women/gender issues.
- the government's degree of dependence on civil society support (e.g. need for voter support to remain in power).
- government decision-making ideology and procedures.
- the existence and capacity of internal gender advocates fighting for a similar agenda.

Donor Based Advocates

The majority of donor organisations have a stated commitment to the promotion of gender equality (a notable success for gender advocacy). The problem lies in translation this commitment into action. In the context of donor-funded *projects*, the range of stakeholders involved in planning and design is comparatively small and the donor organisation is often in a powerful position to influence the planning agenda. As a consequence, *if* attention to gender equality is important to the donor, and the staff involved in planning have the appropriate knowledge and skills, then measures to promote gender equality are likely to be included in the project design. The most appropriate role for gender advocates in this context is to develop appropriate gender mainstreaming knowledge and skills amongst planning staff.

In contract, the development of national policy *frameworks* is a complex process of negotiation involving multiple government, donor and non-government stakeholders. Individual staff and organisations, including donors, have limited power on their own to influence the agenda. This provides a very different context for donor based gender advocates to promote attention to gender equality. It is essential for gender advocates from donor organisations, ministries, parliament and civil society groups to work in conjunction in identifying strategic entry points for the promotion of gender equality. It is unsustainable, in appropirate and unnecessary for donors to promote an agenda of gender equality single-handedly. Donor based advocates should:

- promote, as far as possible, co-ordination between donors on gender equality issues.
- ensure that staff from different sectors are aware of, and speak in favour of, gender equality policy commitments.
- seek out and support (with funding, training and consultancy support) gender advocates within partner ministries. Development assistance can play a very important legitimating role, supporting the advocacy work of gender staff.
- support civil society advocacy organisations.
- participate in gender networks and agree joint strategies.

Advocacy Strategies

Effective advocacy (for individuals or organisations, government, civil society or donor advocates) involves:

- identifying appropriate "entry points". These could be:
  - international, national, sectorial or organisational policy commitment to gender equality.
  - new research findings, or analyses of sex disaggregated data.
  - the support of key individuals in powerful positions.

  - specific events (electronics, international conferences, local conferences, issues in the headlines).
  - new initiatives.
  - reviews of existing initiatives.
  - research funding.
  - funding for training.
- developing strategic alliance and recognising the need for compromise.
- developing a well argued case for taking gender issues seriously, drawing on appropriate sex disaggregated data and gender analytical information.
- moulding arguments into a share that fits the goals, culture and procedures of the targeted organisation or process.
- using a language that is bold and appealing to policy makers and practitioners, quite different from the complexity of academic gender analysis.
- making clear, well thought and realistic suggestions for change. In constrained circumstances, suggestions for change may have to be confined to least worst scenarios and damage control, rather than to a more ambitious concerns with the promotion of gender equality.
- anticipating opposing arguments and developing reasonable responses.
- recognising the importance of small incremental steps towards the long-term goal of gender equality.
- revisiting strategies to take account of what has been achieved and learned as well as to access new opportunities and changing circumstances.
- recognising that gains made towards the long-term objective of gender equality cannot be taken for granted.

In individual meetings, remember to: be brief, be clear, be accurate, be persuasive, be timely, be persistent and be grateful!

Linking Gender Equality and Poverty Elimination

Gender advocates need to win allies and press their claims successfully against rival claimants. In an unsupportive context, the most effective course of action is to demonstrate positive spin-offs from gender mainstreaming, in terms that are compatible with the overall policy environment.

The current international policy focus on poverty elimination provides a relevant and conducive context for gender mainstreaming. There is a growing and compelling body of evidence which shows that women not only bear the brunt of poverty but that women's empowerment is a central precondition for its elimination. The undoubted links between the elimination of poverty and the promotion of gender equality opens up considerable space for attention issues in all aspects of mainstream policy-making and planning.

In making links between poverty and gender equality, it is important not to impel that gender inequality is caused by poverty, or that measures to address poverty will automatically address gender inequality. Progress on gender equality is dependent on political will not on the income level of the society. Some developing countries outperform much rich countries in the opportunities they afford women.

Step 3: Action to Promote Gender Equality

What does Gender Equality Mean?

Gender mainstreaming is a strategy to promote the goal of gender equality and the empowerment of women.

Gender equality does not simply or necessarily mean equal numbers of men and women or boys and girls in all activities, nor doe it necessarily mean treating men and women or boys and girls exactly the same.

It signifies an aspiration to work towards a society in which neither women nor men suffer from poverty in its many forms, and in which women and men are able to live equally fulfilling lives. It means recognising that men and women often have different needs and priorities, face different constraints, have different aspirations and contribute to development in different ways. It means recognising the right of women to define the objectives of development for themselves.

Outline Gender Equality Action Framework

Choice of action to promote gender equality should be made on the basis of clear gender analytical information and sex disaggregated data, and on the basis of women's own priorities and concerns. It is wholly inappropriate for development organisations to devise actions to promote gender equality and women's empowerment without having gone through these two steps.

This outline gender equality action framework is designed to assist in planning discussions. In all sectors and contexts, possible action to promote gender equality broadly falls into the listed categories. Agreed actions to promote gender equality should be included in policy and planning documents, and backed up with staffing, resources and indicators of change.

Type of Action	Issues to consider
ORGANISATION LEVEL	
Information systems and research	◆ collating and commissioning targeted gender analytical research ◆ establishing sex disaggregated information systems.
Building the capacity of staff in management, policy-making and implementation agencies	◆ developing staff gender-related skills, knowledge and commitment through e.g. training workshops, consultancy support, provision of guidelines
Promoting gender equality in policy-making, management and implementation agencies	◆ development of procedures to promote equality in recruitment and career development
Solidarity and networking	◆ activities to link together individuals and groups working for gender equality.
BENEFICIARY LEVEL	
Addressing women's and men's practical needs	◆ recognising and addressing practical needs/problems identified by and particular to either women and men e.g. developing domestic labour saving devices for women
Promoting equality of access and benefit	◆ promoting greater gender equality in relation to resources, services, opportunities and benefits e.g. increasing women's access to previously male dominated employment opportunities.
Increasing equality in decision- making	◆ promoting women's and men's equal participation in community level decision-making institutions and in community representation
Addressing the ideology of gender	◆ working with beneficiary groups to reflect on gender norms, traditions and values e.g. participatory community workshops on HIV/AIDS. ◆ addressing inappropriate gender stereotypes e.g. reviewing school text books for in appropriate gender stereotyping

When and if to Include Gender

Policy and project documentation, which is typically substantial, is important for planning, discussion and approval purpose. However, subsequent management, budgeting and review processes focus on the logical framework summary. Therefore:

- if gender issues are relevant to the policy or project, *explicit references are required in the logical framework.* Inclusion in social and institutional annexes or in social and institutional appraisal sections of the policy/project documents is not sufficient.
- if the policy/project is concerned with making an impact on poor people's lives, it is hard to imagine circumstances where gender would not be relevant in some way.

How and Where to Include Gender

The extent to which gender issues are included in logical frameworks depends on the motivation, influence and knowledge of the people involved in drawing them up. In many situations, staff with the motivation to include gender equality issues lack the influence to put this into practice. In this situation, it is important to bear in mind that almost any mention of gender/ women in the logical framework is better than nothing, and advocacy activities should be geared to this end. This ensures that at least some attention is paid to gender issues in process of management, resource allocation, and monitoring, and it opens the door to increasing attention to gender issues in review processes.

However, where staff are in a position to address gender issues more systematically in the logical framework, it is useful to bear the following points in mind:

Target Groups

- It should always be clear from the logical framework *who the policy/ project is targeting:*
  - this should be clear from the use of sex disaggregated indicators.
  - it should be clear which activities and outputs are targeted to women, which to men and which to both.
  - replacing general terms such as "the poor" or "poor farmers" with, where appropriate, "poor men and women" and "poor male and female farmers" makes women as well as men clearly visible and avoids misunderstanding.

Purpose and Goal

The promotion of gender equality (benefit for women as well as men) should be as aspect of the *purpose and goal* of all development policies/projects concerned with impacting on people's lives. This should be reflected in indicators and, where possible, also in the wording of the purposes/goal statement. See "gender-sensitive indicators".

If benefits to men and women are part of the goal and purpose, specific *activities/outputs* will be required to bring this about and need to be included in the logical framework.

Output

It may be useful to have one output specifically concerned with targeted activities for women. However, it is important not to ghettoise women's activities within one output with a very small claim on resources and no influence on the rest of the policy/project. *Targeted outputs of this kind should complement activities to mainstream gender throughout the policy/project.* Benefits for women as well as men should be considered as an aspect of each output.

It is principally important to include gender in output indicators and associated activities. See "gender-sensitive indicators".

Activities

The promotion of benefits for women as well as men requires targeted activities, back up with human and financial resources. Resources allocation is directly linked to the activity line of a logical framework. See "outline activity framework"

Gender-sensitive Indicators
What are they designed to measure?

Gender-sensitive indicators allow measurement of benefit to women and men. Depending on the policy/project, this might include:

- the impact/effectiveness of activities targeted to address women's or men's practical gender needs i.e. new skills, knowledge, resources, opportunity or services in the context of their existing gender roles.
- the impact/effectiveness of activities designed to increased gender equality of opportunity, influence or benefit. e.g. targeted

action to increase women's role in decision-making; opening up new opportunities for women/men in non-traditional skill areas.

- the impact/effectiveness of activities designed to develop gender awareness and skills amongst policy-making, management and implementaiton staff.
- the impact/effectiveness of activities to promote greater gender equality within the staffing and organisational culture of development organisation e.g. the impact of affirmative action polices.

There is no standard or agreed-upon method for measuring women's empowerment. Aspects of empowerment can be reflected in numbers (such as an increase in numbers of women in positions of power), but above all, empowerment concerns women's perceptions of their own lives and experiences. To measure qualitative aspects of empowerment, it is important that it is clearly defined. Most definitions stress two main areas:

- a personal change in consciousness involving a movement towards control, self-confidence and the right to make decisions and determine choices.
- organisation aimed at social and political change.

The greater the degree of existing gender inequality, the more subtle change are likely to be. It is important in this context for indicators to recognise the significance of modest gains and breakthroughs.

How do they Measure?

Gender-sensitive indicators need to capture quantitative and qualitative aspects of change.

Quantitative Indicators

Quantitative indicators refer to the numbers and percentages of women and men or organisations involved in or affected by any particular group or activity. Quantitative indicators draw on the sex disaggregated data systems and records that have been examined during processes of policy or project planning. The availability of quantitative baseline data means that indicators usually include some element of target setting. For example:

- women form at least 33 per cent of water committee members by the end of year 2.

- at least 50 per cent network members developed a gender policy by the end of year 3.
- equality in girls and boys access to primary education by 2005.
- 25 per cent increase in number of female police officers by 2005, from a baseline of x per cent.

Monitoring information should be available through routine data systems and records.

Qualitative indicators

Qualitative information refers to perceptions and experiences. Qualitative information is vitally important. It is not enough to know that women are participating in an activity: the quality of their participation and experience, whether in community level meetings, primary school classes or uses of public services, is all-important.

Qualitative indicators (as well as quantitative indicators relating to visible change at the community level) should be developed in conjunction with beneficiary groups. In project documents it is qualitative indictors to be developed with beneficiary groups in first six months of the project". This creates the space to develop indicators in conjunction with beneficiary groups once they have fully understood the nature of the project. (What changes would they like to see? What will the change look like? How can it be measured?) This process should take place using qualitative methods such as focus group discussions and informal interviews.

It is only possible to set target for qualitative change if baseline data is available. This requires baseline surveys: it is highly unlikely that appropriate baseline data will be available from secondary sources. Where baseline data is available on experience and perceptions, targets for qualitative change can be set.

For example:

- at least 50 per cent of women participating in water committees report active involvement in management and decision-making by the end of Year 2 (from a baseline of 10 per cent at the start of the project)
- at least 70 per cent of women respond positively to evaluation of police handling of their case in targeted police stations by the end of Year 3 (from a baseline of 5 per cent average at the start of the project).

Where baseline data is not available, or is not easily aggregated into numbers and percentages, it is necessary to resort to general statement of improvement. For example:

- significant improvement in staff knowledge, skills and attitudes on mainstreaming gender equally in participating organisation by the end of year 3 (where each organisation starts with markedly different levels).
- significant increase in quantity and improvement in quality of media reporting or gender violence.

Information on qualitative indicators should be collected through evaluation surveys. Depending on the indicators, these might be questionnaire surveys reviewing perceptions and experiences of agreed indicators, or participatory methods such as focus group discussions and case studies.

Policy Information Makers (PIMs) maker on removal of gender discrimination checklist

To achieve a significant score for "removal of gender discriminaiton", project should meet the following criteria: PIMs maker on removal of gender discrimination checklist

- equality between women and men in explicity promoted in activity documentation (i.e. the project explicitly aims to promote benefit for women as well as men).
- gender analysis has been carried out either separately or as an integral part of standard procedures (i.e. gender analystical information should be included, at least, in th social annex and the social appraisal section of the project memorandum).
- gender analysis has been incorporated into activity design such that the activity meets a number (at least 4) of the following criteria:
  - gender-sensitive strategics and implementation plans are incorporated and reflected in the activity budget.
  - specific means have been designed to help overcome identified barriers to women's full participation in the activity.
  - specific means have been included to help ensure equitable control by women and men over activity output.
  - gender-sensitive indicators including impact indicator, have been or will be developed for monitoring and evaluation.
  - gender skills are used in design and will be used in monitoring and evaluation.
  - gender-sensitive consultation is carried out at all levels and stages (i.e women as well as men have participated in project design and will continue to be involved in implementation and management).

Categorising Policy Frameworks

Marking is currently done on the basis of project frameworks. Given the weak link between the donor project framework and the focus and development of partner government policy frameworks, it is not yet clear how the internal marking system will apply to PRSPs and SWAPs.

Step 4: Organisational Capacity Building/Change

Policy evaporation: What is policy evaporation?

Since the early 1990s, many governments, donor organisations and NGOs have taken equality in their work. Receatedly and consistently, evaluaitons of gender mainstreaming have found that policy commitments to gender equality "evaporate" in planning and implementation processes, with the result that impact on women's and men's lives is very limited. The following finding are typical:

- there is a lack of reliable systems and procedurs in place; for example, attention to gender equality is not systematic in policy-making, planning, implementation and evaluation.
- high level commitment made by government are often not reflected in sectoral polices.
- there is a general lack of understanding on what mainstreaming entrails.
- there remains a tendency to view women as a sector, and not address gender equality in standard processes of sectoral analysis and planning.
- gender equality is not systematically included in the TORs of stff and consultants.
- gender-awareness amongst staff is not necessarily easily translated in policy and planning initiatives: there is a need for tools.
- mainstreaming gendr equality is often reduced to a women's component in projects that has a very small claim on resources.
- concern for gender equality can be seen as imposed by donor agencies, leading to lip service from partner agencies.

What does it happen?

The extent to which gender equality policy commitments will be formulated and then effectively implemented depends on the understanding, skills and commitment of staff in policy-making, planning and implementation roles.

Most development organisations in the north and south have not yet built significant staff capacity in gender mainstreaming. As a result, only a small minority of staff have the level of understanding, skill and commitment to act effectively and consistently in line with gender equality policy commitment. For more staff, whilst sympathetic to the issues, lack confidence, understanding or skills. There is additionally a proportion of staff in development organisations in the north and south hostile to the notion of gender equality. Staff responsible for promoting attention to gender issues are frequently under-resourced. Too often, they lack the time, resources, skills and positioning to undertake their role effectively.

Implications

It is unrealistic to expect that commitments to the promotion of gender equality, expressed in policy and planning documents, will be effectively implemented without significant resources being devoted to developing staff commitment, understanding and skills. This is a long-term process of organisational change with political and technical dimensions.

Organisational Capacity Building Framework

Activities to develop staff understanding and skill in gender mainstreaming should be developed on the basis of a clear understanding of existing levels of knowledge. This assessment should be part of the process of institutional appraisal. See outline gender analytical framework: development organisation.

Staff with designated responsibility for mainstreaming gender and building staff capacity will almost always be necessary. Their "entry points" to capacity-building and opportunities to promote attention to gender will vary in different organisations and plans should allow them a degree of flexibility.

Capacity-building initiatives should be included in policy documents and project plans, backed up with staffing and resources, and measured with appropriate indicators of change.

Type of Action	Issues to consider
Gender focal staff	
(with responsibility for spearheading, supporting and sustaining gender mainstreaming in the organisation as a whole) Financial resources	◆ clear and agreed TORs ◆ training in gender mainstreaming and advocacy ◆ professional support i.e. back-stopping consultancy, network Budget allocation for: ◆ staff capacity-building activities ◆ gender equality initiatives
Capacity building strategies ◆ gender policy and action plan ◆ staff gender training ◆ internal and extenal networks ◆ internal and external networks ◆ development of checklist and guidelines ◆ commissioning gender research ◆ developing sex-disaggregated information systems ◆ including gender issues in staff TORs/interviews/appraisals ◆ monitoring and reviewing policy commitments	Note: Appropriate strategies will vary in diffent organisations and contexts. It is important for planning to allow focal staff the flexibility to take advantage o opportunities, set realistic goals and recognise that setback will occur.
Political will/management support **Equal opportunities**	In all contexts, political will and management support are crucial. Gender staff need to think strategically about ways of promoting sustaining and capitalising on this. Attention needs to be paid to gender within the structure, culture and staffing of development organisation as well as in their policies, programmes and procedures.

Appendix-B

SOCIAL CAPITAL[1]

Social Capital

In addition to removing social barriers, effective efforts to reduce poverty require complementary initiatives to build up and extend the social institutions of the poor. Social institutions refer to the kinship systems. Local organizations and networks of the poor can be usefully discussed as different forms or dimensions of social capital.

Kinds of Social Capital: Bonding, bridging and linking social capital

Distinguishing among different dimensions of social capital within and between communities is useful for understanding the problems faced by poor people.

- **Bonding Social Capital:** The strong ties connecting family members, neighbours, close friends and business associates can be called bonding social capital. These ties connect people who share similar demographic characteristics.
- **Bridging Social Capital:** The weak ties connecting individuals from different ethnic and occupational backgrounds can be referred to as bridging social capital. Bridging social capital implies horizontal connections to people with broadly comparable economic status and political power.
- **Linking Social Capital:** A third dimension linking social capital consists of the vertical ties between poor people and people in positions of influence in formal organizations (banks, agricultural extension offices, the police). This dimension captures a vitally important additional feature of life in poor communities: that their members are usually excluded—by overt discrimination or lack

1. Adopted from World Bank: *World Development Report 2000* (Washington: The World Bank) 2000.

of resources—from the places where major decisions relating to their welfare are made.

Research on the roles of different types of social networks in poor communities confirms their importance. An analysis of poor village in rural North India, for example, shows that social groups (*bonding social capital*) play an important role in protecting the basic needs of poor people and mediating against risk. In contrast, the more extensive leveraged network of the non-poor (*linking social capital*) are used for strategic advantage, such as procuring better jobs and higher wages and seizing new economic opportunities (in some cases by directly mobilizing to secure a disproportionate share of public resources and services).

Strikingly similar results emerge from work on the relationship between enterprise performance and the structure of business networks in Africa. Poor entrepreneurs operating small local firms in traditional industries form "solidarity networks," sharing personal information about members' conduct and intentions in order to reduce risk and uncertainty. In contrast, larger regional firms form "innovation networks" which share knowledge about technology and global markets in order to increase productivity profits and market share. Studies of agricultural traders in Madagascar show that social relationships are more important to traders than input prices. Close relationships with other traders are used to lower the transaction costs of exchange while ties to creditors and others who can help out during times of financial hardship are vital sources of security and insurance. In Bolivia, Burkina Faso and Indonesia, field surveys attempting to measure household social capital have found a positive association with household consumptions, asset accumulation and access to credit.

Researchers and practitioners have long recognized that the bonding and bridging social capital in local organizations is necessary but insufficient for long-term development. In Kenya, a participatory poverty assessment found more than 200,000 community groups in rural areas, but most were unconnected to outside resources and unable to help poor people rise out of poverty. The creation of linking social capital is essential, and external support has often been important in its emergence. External support—from NGOs and religious organizations for example—(*bridging social capital*) can help create social capital that increases the voice and economic opportunities of poor people. This support is most effective when it is sustained over time, emphasizes capacity building, and is based on a sensitive understanding of the local conditions and relationship of trust and partnership.

How does social capital affect development?

There are at least four views on the relationship between social capital and development. The Narrowest holds social capital to be the social skills of individuals—one's propensity for cooperative behaviour, conflict resolution, tolerance, and the like.

A more expansive meso view associates social capital with families and local community associations and the underlying norms (trust, reciprocity) that facilitate coordination and cooperation for mutual benefit. This view highlights the positive aspects of social capital for members of these associations but remains largely silent on the possibility that social capital may not impart benefits to society at large and that group membership itself may entail significant costs.

A more nuanced meso view of social capital recognizes that group membership can have both positive and negative effects (Coleman, 1990; Burt 1992; Massey and Espinoza, 1997). This approach broadens the concept of social capital to include association in which relationships among members may be hierarchical and power sharing unequal. These forms of associations and networks address a wider range of objectives: some of them serve only the private interests of members, which others are motivated by a commitment to serve broader public objectives. This view emphasizes that groups, in addition to providing benefits to members, can make significant non-economic claims on them.

A macro view of social capital focuses on the social and political environment that shapes social structures and enables norms to develop. This environment includes formalized institutional relationships and structures, such as government, political regime, rule of law, the court system, and civil and political liberties. Institutions have an important effect on the rate and pattern of economic development (North, 1990; Fukuyama, 1995; Olson, 1982).

Some experts maintain that social capital recognizes that micro, meso and macro institutions coexist and have the potential to complement one another. Macro institutions can provide an enabling environment in which micro institutions help sustain regional and national institutions by giving them a measure of stability and legitimacy and by holding them accountable for their action.

While the mechanisms by which social capital operate are generally well understood there is less consensus on whether they qualify as social capital as "capital" (in many cases norms and institutions) have the durability and lasting effects associated with capital. Some argue, however, that the sacrifice of a present for a future benefit, typical of traditional forms of capital, is not present in social network to the extent that these networks are built for reasons other than their economic value to participants. Even so, social networks and organizations are clearly key assets in the portfolio of resources drawn on by

(*Contd.*)

(*Contd.*)

poor people to manage risk, who advance their interests through such organizations as country clubs and professional associations, but their relative importance in greater for poor people.

Social capital has its dark side however. For example of networks are isolated, parochial, or working at cross-purposes to society's collective interests (gangs, drug cartels), the social capital within them serves perverse rather than productive purposes, undermining development. Organized crime syndicates, such as those in Latin America and Russia, generate large negative externalities for the rest of society-lost lives, wasted resources, pervasive uncertainty (Rose, 1999). And in India, for example, obligations to family members and pressures to fulfil community expectations lead many young girls to drop out of school.

This approach characterizes the work of Myrada, an Indian NGO delivering micro finance services. Myrada acts as a medium-term intermediary between poor people and commercial banks. Its initial task is to mobilize the bonding social capital within village communities to form credit management groups and then over time to form regional federations made up of representatives from each credit group (thereby enhancing each group's bridging social capital). From the outset credit management groups hold accounts with commercial banks, progressively gaining the confidence and skills they need to participate independently in formal institutions (linking social capital). After even years of training and hard-won experience, group members are able to manage these accounts—and even arrange for annual external audits—without the involvement of Myrada staff, who move on to start the process afresh.

Mobilizing and Creating Social Capital in Development Projects

Development programmes have relied on local groups of project beneficiaries or local associations to improve the success of development projects for more than two decades. What is new is the umbrella label social capital to refer to the underlying social force or energy.

In Bangladesh Grameen Bank relies on groups of poor women to implement programmes, and the Bangladesh Rural Advancement Committee on groups of village workers with little or on land. In Pakistan, the Aga Khan Rural Support Programme gives assistance to village organizations to supplement their self-help efforts. The Kenya Tea Development Authority worked with grower committees to promote production, obtaining a one-third share of the country's tea exports within 15 years. The 6-S movement in nine West African countries organized peasant federations in more than 2,000

(*Contd.*)

(*Contd.*)

communities to help farmers overcome the hardships of the dry season. The Centre for Social and Economic Development in Bolivia has supported more than 250 peasant organizations that promote programmes in agriculture, live- stock, forestry, artisan production, and community infrastructure.

Local groups have also been used frequently in irrigation, water supply, and sanitation programmes. The Orangi Pilot Project in Pakistan provided low-cost self-help sewerage facilities and other services to poor settlement and helped autonomous local institutions implement projects. In Cote d'lvoire rural water supply improved significantly when responsibility for maintenance was shifted from the national water distribution company to community water group. Breakdown rates were reduced from 50 per cent to 11 per cent, while costs fell nearly 70 per cent. These results were sustained, however, only in villages in which well-functioning community organizations existed and demand for water was high.

In many cases, challenging existing norms and practices increases the social capital of previously excluded groups while decreasing the power of local elites, helping reduce obstacles to poverty reduction, development programmes such as women's micro finance in Bangladesh change the social relationships in a village indeed, their success depends on it. Breaking the grip of moneylenders, overcoming the resistance of certain religious leaders, and giving women more decision making power within their household all require a fundamental realignment of traditional social relationship. Many development programmes are inherently political, and powerful vested interests can be expected to mobilize against reforms that seek to erode their position in the name of poor people. Development researchers, policymakers, and practitioners must recognize these tensions and respond appropriately.

Many aspects of social norms and practices also help generate and perpetuate poverty. Discriminatory practices associated with gender, ethnicity, race, religion, or social status result in the social, political and economic exclusion of people. This creates barriers to upward mobility, constraining people's ability to participate in economic opportunities and to benefit from and contribute to economic growth. It also constrains their effective participation in political processes and civil action to ensure that state institutions are accountable to citizens and responsive to their needs.

Appendix-C

CRITICAL STEPS IN SOCIAL MOBILISATION[1]

1. **Efficiency and creativity of the poor—the starting point:** Self-initiatives of the poor form the essence of a process of participatory development, where the poor operate as conscious subjects of change. They reflect on their life-situations, and take decisions to bring about changes to improve their social and economic status. The underlying assumption which now has a material basis is that the poor are creative as well as efficient. They are capable of taking self-initiatives for their development, but social processes have often operated to deny opportunities for the practical expression of people's creativity. A meaningful development process must lead to a liberation of the creative initiatives of the poor.*
2. **From objects to subjects:** Conventional top-down models for development, explicitly or implicitly treat the poor as objects of change and the relation between the intervener and the poor often takes the form of a subject acting upon an object. It is assumed in these top-down welfare models that the poor have no knowledge-base or that their knowledge is irrelevant-unscientific, and the poor have to be told and instructed as to what they should do or they are merely waiting for some charity. The outcome is a paternalistic and delivery approach—that is, an attempt to bring development to the poor through deliveries of knowledge and resources from outside. It is also often a way of tranquillizing the poor. Fundamental to the initiation of a process of participatory development** is the break up of this dichotomy of subject and object and the transformation of

---

1. Extracted from *Readings on Pro-Poor Planning through Social Mobilization, South Asia Vol. 1, The Strategic Option for Poverty Eradication*, edited by Ponna Wignaraja & Susil Sirivardana, published by Vikas Publishing House Pvt. Ltd., New Delhi. *We thank Dr. Ponna Wignaraja for granting us permission to use this material.*

* Thus releasing the creative initiatives of the poor is the first step in the process of social mobilization.

** Read "social mobilization".

the relation into one between two knowing subjects resulting in a creative tension between two knowledge streams, namely, poor people's experiential knowledge and the formal knowledge introduced from outside. It is a dialogical process of creating social change. This is also the essence of participation.*

3. **Conscientisation and awareness raising:** Poor people can be expected first to investigate and analyze their reality. Then they undertake self-initiatives for change when they become conscientised, that is to say, when they become critically aware of their life-situation (the reality of life) to begin to perceive self-possibilities for changing that reality. Hence, the first step in the generation of a process of participatory development is to assist the poor to critically reflect upon, analyze and understand the socio-economic reality in which they live. Reality has to be posed to the poor as a problem to be investigated and as a challenge to transform. The reality that the majority of the urban and rural poor face is poverty and underdevelopment in particular, low level of production, income and consumption and the inability even to retain a part of the surplus they generate. Hence, the problematisation of the reality must lead to an investigation and analysis of the totality of life in poverty and under-development.** The assumption here is that there is considerable potential for the poor to improve their lives which remain underutilized. Such potential for development should form the focus of problematisation and subsequent analysis by the people.
4. **Exploration of self-possibilities for actions:** When the poor carry out such investigations and analysis, they also begin to perceive self-possibilities to deal with the factors in their poverty, hence to change the reality. Alternative possibilities of action will be explored and the feasibility for such actions will be examined using the poor people's own knowledge and experiences and drawing from the knowledge available from outside. Resources, requirements and constraints for each action will be carefully studied. This is a process of the poor doing their own planning at the local level.***

---

* Thus eliciting the knowledge of the poor people and recognizing the same as important is the second step in the process of social mobilization. It may be noted by the trainer that the knowledge that poor people themselves have in often called 'tacit knowledge' and the knowledge which outsiders bring to the process is called 'explicit knowledge'.

** The investigation and analysis of their own problems by the people themselves is the third step in the process of social mobilization.

*** Planning by the people for their own upliftment is the fourth step in the process of social mobilization.

5. **Organizational consciousness:** In order to initiate actions, the poor need to organize themselves in a manner (as decided by them) that best suits their purposes. They may decide to build new organizations of their choice or use existing organizations over which they have effective control. The important point here is the availability of organizational mechanisms and support systems in which the poor have confidence, over which they have control, and which they can use for their actions. Poor women would need to build separate organizations initially, to take care of the double burden, of being women and poor, and then link into the general organizations of the poor.*
6. **Initiation of action:** The poor tend to make a beginning with those actions which they can undertake with their own resources and which they feel could be implemented with success. They tend to start with fairly simple actions. The resources required for such actions are mobilized within the community itself, through collective actions to generate funds. The success of these initial actions gives them some experience in self-initiatives and also enhances their confidence in their abilities to bring about changes in their life-situations. They then embark upon more actions and go into larger and more sophisticated actions which involve claiming and using resources from outside. When they reach this stage, they begin to make claims and bargain for resources available from the social system so that their own resource base is strengthened and supplemented, thereby improving their capacity to initiate more actions. There is, then, an interaction between the poor groups and the socio-economic system with the poor making claims, bargaining for improvement in their access to social resources, while at the same time mobilizing their own resources to further the development process. As a result of this assertion, the socio-economic system will now begin to respond to the needs and requirements of the poor and to serve their interests better.**
7. **Sensitive support system:** This is where a sensitive support system is required. As it permits the poor to expand their base and multiplies the process. The support system can be an NGO, the government, a bank or a donor agency. At present, they are "delivering inputs" to the poor. But these resources are often diverted to the rich. This is where reorientation and sensitization of the support system comes to be another critical element in social mobilization.***

---

* Organizing the poor is the fifth step in social mobilization.

** Action by the poor is the sixth step in social mobilization.

*** This reorientation and sensitization of the support system is the seventh step in social mobilization.

8. **From action to reflection:** Reflection on actions, that is to review and evaluate the ongoing actions as a regular practice, is undertaken by the poor groups themselves and constitutes an important element in a participatory development process. Reflection enhances the knowledge and understanding of the poor and helps improve the quality of their actions. Participatory monitoring permits self-corrective actions to be taken while the problems are small. Participatory monitoring is a critical part of participatory development and cannot be separated from the total process of social mobilization and participatory development.*
9. **Capacitation of the people:** As the people's self-development process unfolds, people will begin to improve their capacities to conceive development ideas, plan, implement and manage development actions. A wide range of opportunities will be created for the practical expression and development of talents and skills that lie dormant among the poor. Leaders, intellectuals, animators, managers, etc. will emerge from the action process reducing over a time the dependence on outside catalysts. The poor will tend to become increasingly self-reliant in their thinking and action and begin to develop autonomous capacities for action.** The women's movement has raised poor women's consciousness and now the gender and equity issues have to be responded to not only at the philosophical level but also through concrete development actions undertaken collectively by poor women's groups.
10. **Diversification and multiplication of actions:** Initially, the organizations of the poor will naturally tend to start with the problems and issues of immediate concern to them and which they can tackle with confidence. With increasing conscientisation and experience gathered in action planning, they will tend to diversify their actions to include other aspects of their socio-economic lives. Self-initiatives are **educational** experiences which expand people's horizons. New problems, issues and needs will be identified for investigation, analysis and initiation of actions. The success of one action creates the possibility of undertaking another, setting in motion a flow of successive actions. Furthermore, the process tends to multiply from one group to another and from one village to another. Successful actions of one group demonstrate to others in a village the possibilities of self-development. Moreover, after a

---

* Participatory monitoring is the eighth step in social mobilization. There is a growing literature on the subject on which the trainer can bank.

** This is the ninth step.

point, people's groups tend to develop an urge to expand the process among others, for they begin to realize that is it only when several groups join hands and begin to act together that they will have the strength and the bargaining power to tackle larger issues of common concern to them. The logical outcome of this process is an empowerment of the poor, the development of their capacity of self-development and the emergence of the poor as a counter-power within the socio-economic system capable of asserting their rights and claims to improve their lives. As the sensitivity of the support system increases, the total social mobilization process becomes complete.

Appendix-D

ROLE OF THE CATALYST/ ANIMATOR/FACILITATOR[1]

As has been mentioned, a process of participatory development rarely emerges as a spontaneous phenomenon. The poor need to be stimulated and sensitively assisted to initiate such processes. In order to undertake self-initiatives for change, the poor need to understand the socio-economic reality in which they live, perceive self-possibilities for bringing about changes in that reality, develop the capacities to translate the possibilities into concrete actions and to manage the actions. This is not a matter of 'skills' training in the narrow sense of technical skills or a manipulative process in the name of 'participation'. All categories of the poor need to develop their intellectual skills (to investigate, reflect upon, analyze and understand) as well as their practical skills (to organize, implement and manage actions). This defines the role of the "outsiders" whether they be called catalysts, change agents, animators or facilitators, namely, to assist the poor to bring out and acquire the intellectual and practical knowledge needed for their self-initiated development process. The role of the outsiders may be conceived as consisting of two main elements, namely, animation and facilitation.

1. Animation

It is a process of assisting the poor to develop their intellectual capacity to investigate the reality of their life-situations, analyze the relevant issues, and understand the factors creating poverty and deprivation and through such understanding to perceive self-possibilities for change. They are animated when they understand the reality and perceive possibilities for changing that reality. The outcome of animation is conscientisation and awareness creation. Animation is the outcome of a specific mode of

---

1. Extracted from *Readings on Pro-Poor Planning through Social Mobilization, South Asia Vol. 1, The Strategic Option for Poverty Eradication*, edited by Ponna Wignaraja & Susil Sirivardana, published by Vikas Publishing House Pvt. Ltd., New Delhi. *We thank Dr. Ponna Wignaraja for granting us permission to use this material.*

interaction between the outsiders and the poor. These persons are called catalysts, animators or facilitators. They can be outsiders to the particular location or persons thrown up from within the local process. The essence of this interaction mode is the evolution of subject-to-subject relation between the two parties (replacing the conventional subject-to-subject relation). The poor have a knowledge-base rooted in experience, practice and living with nature and society. This knowledge has its own validity and rationality. On the other hand, outsiders bring with them knowledge derived from formal education. These are two different knowledge streams each having its own scientific basis. The delivery approach to development seeks to transfer formal knowledge to the poor and disregard the poor's own knowledge as unscientific or irrelevant. It is a subject to object relation. On the other hand, a participatory approach seeks to achieve an interaction between the two knowledge streams creating a mutual learning process. It is an interaction between the two worlds, capable of systematizing the knowledge of the poor, creating new knowledge and generating seeds of change. Animation seeks to break the dichotomy between subject and object and to evolve, as far as possible, a relation between two equals.

Such an interaction mode requires the adoption of a dialogical approach and even these steps cannot be taught or applied mechanically. Teaching instruction and transfer of skills will be replaced by discussion, dialogue, stimulation of self-reflection and analysis, and sharing of experience and knowledge. The starting point for this process should be an attempt to initiate a dialogue with the people on the reality of their life-situations. The reality that people face (poverty, underdevelopment and deprivation) should be posed to the people as a problem for their investigation, as a challenge for them to respond. By raising key questions such as why do we have low incomes? Why is our production low? Why do we buy our needs at high prices and sell our products cheap? Can we not find new kinds of work in the informal sector? What access do we have to different kinds of resources? Why do we eat certain kinds of food? The catalyst/animator has to stimulate/provoke the people to come out with ideas, issues and factors that they perceive as barriers in improving their livelihood. Dialogue with the perceptions of issues pertaining to their life-situations.

Dialogues enable the poor to systematize their own experiences. This is also an investigation into their reality and research. Besides, the interaction with the animator enables them to improve their knowledge base by absorbing the relevant formal knowledge brought in by the animator. The outcome is a synthesis of their own and formal knowledge. From such problematisation, analysis and the knowledge creation that follows, they will begin to perceive self-possibilities for change which form the basis for their actions to change the reality. Hence, actions are rooted in the investigations and analysis carried out by the people themselves assisted by the animator. This approach may be contrasted to the normal run of development projects where the professionals and the poor are at best involved in the implementation phase of the projects.

2. Facilitation

Animation is a necessary but not necessarily a sufficient condition to enable the poor to undertake and manage development actions to transform their realities. There are a host of factors which operate to keep the poor passive rather than active. Given their bahaviour patterns (often non-innovative and non-experimental in nature) and lack of experience in undertaking self-initiatives for change, it will take time before they begin to develop the confidence in their abilities to bring about changes. Hence, an external input in the form of facilitation is often required to assist the poor to initiate actions for changing their conditions. Animation by breaking mental barriers begins to show possibilities for change. Facilitation is an attempt at assisting the poor to overcome practical barriers to action. The catalyst/ animator with his/her formal education, wider knowledge of socio-economic contexts, and links with the governmental machinery and service delivery personnel should be able to assist the people to cope with their practical problems. Such facilitation can take several forms such as:

(a) Assisting them to acquire basic management and, where necessary, technical skills, building on their own knowledge.
(b) Assisting them to develop contacts with formal service agencies, institutions and bureaucracies relevant to their action programmes and to develop skills and knowledge required to deal and negotiate with them.
(c) Assisting them to improve their access to material resources, such as credit available within the socio-economic system.
(d) Assisting them to translate their developmental ideas into concrete activities and programmes and to work out the implementation plans (a kind of consultancy role).
(e) Facilitation can also result in the reorientation and sensitization of the support system, as a result of the ensuing dialogue, apart from the more formal re-training of the support system staff.

3. Progressive Redundancy (Self Liquidation)

An important characteristic of the animation and facilitation roles should be its transitional character, that is, its progressive redundancy over time as the poor develop their own capacities to initiate, undertake and manage their development. The catalyst/animator's interaction with the poor must lead to capacity build-up among the people, and a crucial test of an animator's success must ultimately be his/her ability to render his/her role redundant over time within a given community or village so that she/he is released to start similar work in another village. Self-liquidation (the ability of an animator to phase out from a given village) becomes important in two respects:

(a) To ensure that the poor become self-reliant, that they develop the capacity to manage their actions without critical dependence on outsiders; and
(b) To ensure multiplication of the participatory development process such that the animator is released to move into other villages to start similar work.

Appendix-E

PARTICIPATORY MONITORING AND EVALUATION PROCESSES[1]

Irrespective of whether they emerge spontaneously or the activities start with a particular entry point, their evolution must be seen as a self-generating process where each stage is built on the collective experience of the previous stage. This is how the process is made sustainable. Thus, this collective experience needs to be continuously assessed and corrective actions taken systematically while the problems are still small and manageable. This is the task of monitoring and evaluation.

Conventional evaluation requires an outside evaluator who, in a sense, exercises control over the process. But in a situation of participatory development, internal evaluation provides the necessary control and reinforces the capacity for self-management. The internal motivational objective is to raise the understanding of the experience by the poor through collective assessment, improved articulation, problem solving and commitment to the task they have set for themselves. They also learn from their total experience and derive a political resolve towards group action for overcoming difficulties and achieving their objectives. Individually, they cannot go very far, given the magnitude of the problems they face. This is also what is meant by empowerment.

Participatory monitoring and evaluation information on activities rests with the people. They, on their own initiative, seek help and assistance from the administrative power. The organizational structure does not lay down any 'duties' for the functionaries except for responding to the needs of the poor when they get articulated. The decision-making, therefore, rests in the immediate vicinity of the 'information'.

The specific criteria to be used for participatory evaluation cannot be laid down in a prescriptive manner. However, a set of criteria, derived from the experiences on the ground which though not all quantifiable, measurable and observable, is indicated visually in the form of a sociogram for monitoring the total social mobilization process for poverty alleviation.

---

1. Extracted from *Readings on Pro-Poor Planning through Social Mobilization, South Asia Vol. 1, The Strategic Option for Poverty Eradication*, edited by Ponna Wignaraja & Susil Sirivardana, published by Vikas Publishing House Pvt. Ltd., New Delhi. *We thank Dr. Ponna Wignaraja for granting us permission to use this material.*

The criteria in the sociogram are all interrelated and mutually reinforcing. However, they deserve to be presented separately not only for their own sake but also more importantly, because they contribute to each other's growth and thereby to the total process. If one element in the process is not moving forward, it can easily be identified and strengthened. The three major planks that deepen social consciousness and lead to the empowerment of the poor are attitudinal change, the capacity for self-management and the economic and social base of the poor. It is axiomatic that the economic base of the poor has to be improved over a period of time through a dual process of savings investment and asset creation and the emancipation of the poor from economic and social bondage, to enable them not only to be more productive and keep the surpluses in their own hands. The establishment of a self-reliant activity base will mutually reinforce the process of promoting positive attitudinal values. Conscious attempts to diagnose, assess and mutually stimulate such values will bring them to the fore and will contribute to turning them into a driving force for further action, contributing to a deepening expansion of the process itself. Ultimately, the process as a whole, which starts with the release of the creativity of the poor, has to be judged by the increase in their social consciousness, empowerment and self-respect.

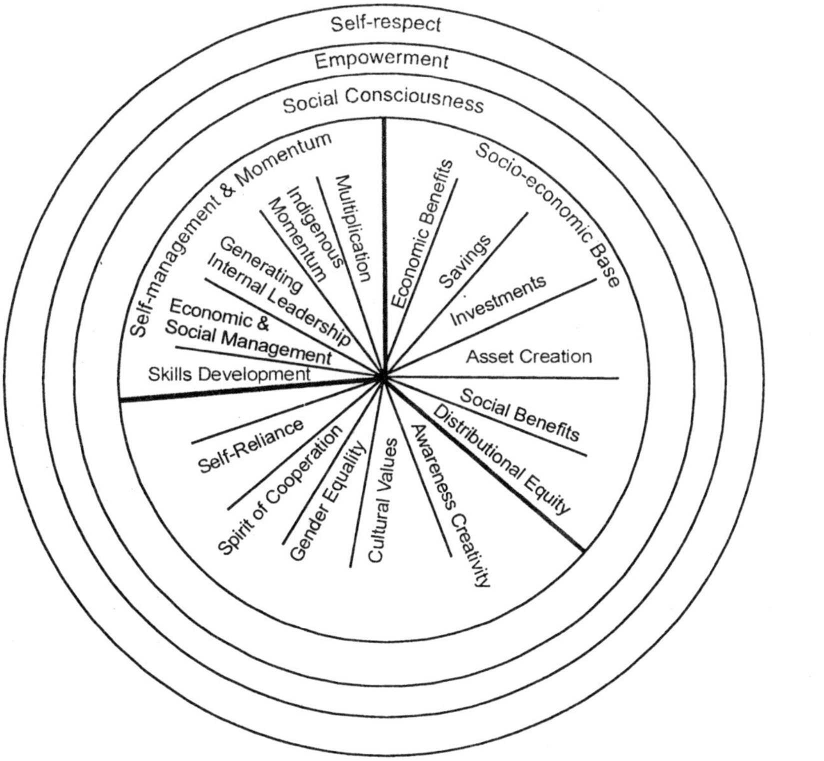

Appendix-F

STAGES OF NETWORK/GROUP

Once the meaning of group/network is discussed, participants move on to the stages of group formation. Following are the group/network stages discussed in the training. These are:

1. Forming
2. Storming
3. Norming
4. Performing
5. Adjourning

The detailed characteristics of these stages are as follows:

1. Forming

- This stage is characterized by dependency and they look to group leader for guidance.
- Here individuals are placed in a group.
- Each individual strives to make an impression within the group to establish a personal identity.
- Participation is limited.
- Individuals begin to look at the task and its purpose.
- The group is essentially evolving ground rules.
- Serious topics and feeling are avoided, as group wants to touch safe topics.

2. Storming

- This stage is characterized by intra-group competition, conflict and lack of purpose.
- Conflicts arise over leadership, structure, power and authority.
- Fear of exposure or fear of failure of task can polarize the team into sub-group.
- Individuals can become hostile towards each other, and express their individuality pursuing or revealing personal agendas.

- If successfully handled and the team moves to a problem-solving mentality, this leads the group to a more meaningful and desirable next stage.

3. Norming

- This stage is characterized by development of group cohesion and overcoming of tensions; group norms and practices are established.
- Members begin to know and identify with one another.
- Group members accept and acknowledge each other's achievements and contributions.
- Members start sharing feelings and ideas and giving feedback.

4. Performing

- This state is characterized by interdependency in both personal relations as well as in task functions.
- Members take on roles to achieve collective activities, as they have now learnt to work together.
- Roles become flexible and functional.
- Group energy is channeled into identified tasks, goal congruence enhanced.
- The group is now a team and is most productive.

Trainer's note: Every group does not reach this stage.

5. Adjourning

- This stage is characterized by termination of the project.
- This is a planned disengagement stage that has opportunity for recognition of performance.
- Members can say personal good byes.
- This provides staging ground for next project/activity.

The trainer should also inform the participants how to deal with difficult persons operating at each stage. A list of difficult persons is as under:

(a) An aggressor, who attacks everyone's ideas and is aggressive?
(b) A positive personality—someone who is task oriented?
(c) A dominator—a Mr. Know All?
(d) A shy and retiring person?

(e) A rejector?
(f) A bored and thick-skinned person?
(g) A trapper?
(h) A person with limited vocabulary?
(i) A procrastinator?
(j) An integrator?
(k) A destructor?
(l) A disinterested participant or person?

Index

POSTERS

Poster No. 2

Minor Irrigation, Water Management and Watershed Development

सिंचाई, जल प्रबंधन एवं जलागम विकास

This poster is a part of the printed book *Empowering Women Panchayat Members: Handbook for Master Trainers Using Participatory Approach* by D. Bandyopadhyay and Amitava Mukherjee published by Concept Publishing Company, New Delhi-110 059 for Rajiv Gandhi Foundation, New Delhi.

Poster No. 1

Agriculture and Agriculture Extension

कृषि एवं कृषि विस्तार

This poster is a part of the printed book *Empowering Women Panchayat Members: Handbook for Master Trainers (Using Participatory Approach)* by D. Bandyopadhyay and Amitava Mukherjee published by Concept Publishing Company, New Delhi-110 059 for Rajiv Gandhi Foundation, New Delhi.

Poster No. 2

Minor Irrigation, Water Management and Watershed Development

सिंचाई, जल प्रबंधन एवं जलागम विकास

This poster is a part of the printed book *Empowering Women Panchayat Members: Handbook for Master Trainers (Using Participatory Approach)* by D. Bandyopadhyay and Amitava Mukherjee published by Concept Publishing Company, New Delhi-110 059 for Rajiv Gandhi Foundation, New Delhi.

Poster No. 3

Animal Husbandry, Dairy and Poultry

पशुपालन, दुग्ध परियोजना एवं मुर्गीपालन

This poster is a part of the printed book *Empowering Women Panchayat Members: Handbook for Master Trainers (Using Participatory Approach)* by D. Bandyopadhyay and Amitava Mukherjee published by Concept Publishing Company, New Delhi-110 059 for Rajiv Gandhi Foundation, New Delhi.

Poster No. 4

Fisheries

मत्स्य पालन

This poster is a part of the printed book *Empowering Women Panchayat Members: Handbook for Master Trainers (Using Participatory Approach)* by D. Bandyopadhyay and Amitava Mukherjee published by Concept Publishing Company, New Delhi-110 059 for Rajiv Gandhi Foundation, New Delhi.

Poster No. 5

Social Forestry and Farm Forestry

सामाजिक वन एवं कृषि वन प्रबंधन

This poster is a part of the printed book *Empowering Women Panchayat Members: Handbook for Master Trainers (Using Participatory Approach)* by D. Bandyopadhyay and Amitava Mukherjee published by Concept Publishing Company, New Delhi-110 059 for Rajiv Gandhi Foundation, New Delhi.

Poster No. 6

Minor Forest Produce

वन उत्पाद

This poster is a part of the printed book *Empowering Women Panchayat Members: Handbook for Master Trainers (Using Participatory Approach)* by D. Bandyopadhyay and Amitava Mukherjee published by Concept Publishing Company, New Delhi-110 059 for Rajiv Gandhi Foundation, New Delhi.

Poster No. 7

Small Scale Industries and Food Processing Industries

लघु उद्योग एवं खाद्य प्रसंस्करण

This poster is a part of the printed book *Empowering Women Panchayat Members: Handbook for Master Trainers (Using Participatory Approach)* by D. Bandyopadhyay and Amitava Mukherjee published by Concept Publishing Company, New Delhi-110 059 for Rajiv Gandhi Foundation, New Delhi.

Poster No. 8

Khadi, Village and Cottage Industries

खादी, ग्राम एवं कुटीर उद्योग

This poster is a part of the printed book *Empowering Women Panchayat Members: Handbook for Master Trainers (Using Participatory Approach)* by D. Bandyopadhyay and Amitava Mukherjee published by Concept Publishing Company, New Delhi-110 059 for Rajiv Gandhi Foundation, New Delhi.

Poster No. 9

Rural Housing

ग्रामीण आवास

This poster is a part of the printed book *Empowering Women Panchayat Members: Handbook for Master Trainers (Using Participatory Approach)* by D. Bandyopadhyay and Amitava Mukherjee published by Concept Publishing Company, New Delhi-110 059 for Rajiv Gandhi Foundation, New Delhi.

Poster No. 10

Drinking Water

पेय जल

This poster is a part of the printed book *Empowering Women Panchayat Members: Handbook for Master Trainers (Using Participatory Approach)* by D. Bandyopadhyay and Amitava Mukherjee published by Concept Publishing Company, New Delhi-110 059 for Rajiv Gandhi Foundation, New Delhi.

Poster No. 11

Fuel and Fodder

ईंधन एवं चारा

This poster is a part of the printed book *Empowering Women Panchayat Members: Handbook for Master Trainers (Using Participatory Approach)* by D. Bandyopadhyay and Amitava Mukherjee published by Concept Publishing Company, New Delhi-110 059 for Rajiv Gandhi Foundation, New Delhi.

Poster No. 12

Means of Transportation and Electrification

यातायात के साधन एवं विद्युतीकरण

This poster is a part of the printed book *Empowering Women Panchayat Members: Handbook for Master Trainers (Using Participatory Approach)* by D. Bandyopadhyay and Amitava Mukherjee published by Concept Publishing Company, New Delhi-110 059 for Rajiv Gandhi Foundation, New Delhi.

Poster No. 13

Education

शिक्षा

This poster is a part of the printed book *Empowering Women Panchayat Members: Handbook for Master Trainers (Using Participatory Approach)* by D. Bandyopadhyay and Amitava Mukherjee published by Concept Publishing Company, New Delhi-110 059 for Rajiv Gandhi Foundation, New Delhi.

Poster No. 14

Libraries and Cultural Activities

पुस्तकालय एवं सांस्कृतिक क्रियाकलाप

This poster is a part of the printed book *Empowering Women Panchayat Members: Handbook for Master Trainers (Using Participatory Approach)* by D. Bandyopadhyay and Amitava Mukherjee published by Concept Publishing Company, New Delhi-110 059 for Rajiv Gandhi Foundation, New Delhi.

Poster No. 15

Markets and Fairs

बाजार एवं मेला

This poster is a part of the printed book *Empowering Women Panchayat Members: Handbook for Master Trainers (Using Participatory Approach)* by D. Bandyopadhyay and Amitava Mukherjee published by Concept Publishing Company, New Delhi-110 059 for Rajiv Gandhi Foundation, New Delhi.

Poster No. 16

Health Services

स्वास्थ्य सेवायें

This poster is a part of the printed book *Empowering Women Panchayat Members: Handbook for Master Trainers (Using Participatory Approach)* by D. Bandyopadhyay and Amitava Mukherjee published by Concept Publishing Company, New Delhi-110 059 for Rajiv Gandhi Foundation, New Delhi.

Poster No. 17

Welfare of Handicaps

विकलांगों का उत्थान

This poster is a part of the printed book *Empowering Women Panchayat Members: Handbook for Master Trainers (Using Participatory Approach)* by D. Bandyopadhyay and Amitava Mukherjee published by Concept Publishing Company, New Delhi-110 059 for Rajiv Gandhi Foundation, New Delhi.

Poster No. 18

Welfare of Weaker Sections

कमजोर वर्गों का उत्थान

This poster is a part of the printed book *Empowering Women Panchayat Members: Handbook for Master Trainers (Using Participatory Approach)* by D. Bandyopadhyay and Amitava Mukherjee published by Concept Publishing Company, New Delhi-110 059 for Rajiv Gandhi Foundation, New Delhi.

Poster No. 19

Public Distribution System

सार्वजनिक वितरण प्रणाली

This poster is a part of the printed book *Empowering Women Panchayat Members: Handbook for Master Trainers (Using Participatory Approach)* by D. Bandyopadhyay and Amitava Mukherjee published by Concept Publishing Company, New Delhi-110 059 for Rajiv Gandhi Foundation, New Delhi.

Poster No. 20

Maintenance of Community Assets

सामूहिक सम्पत्तियों की देखभाल

This poster is a part of the printed book *Empowering Women Panchayat Members: Handbook for Master Trainers (Using Participatory Approach)* by D. Bandyopadhyay and Amitava Mukherjee published by Concept Publishing Company, New Delhi-110 059 for Rajiv Gandhi Foundation, New Delhi.